...The Dream Continues

RVing

ALASKA

AND

CANADA

Sharlene "Charlie" Minshall

Gypsy Press

Photography by author. Author photograph page 203 by Gary Clark.
Photograph printing by LightningSource.

I

Taylor Highway, AK

Atlin Mountain, Atlin, BC

...The Dream Continues

RVING

ALASKA

and CANADA

Sharlene "Charlie" Minshall

Edited by
Janet L. Wadlington

Gypsy
Press

Published by Gypsy Press
150 Rainbow Drive, #5024
Livingston, Texas 77399-1050
U. S. A.

Copyright © 1997 and 2002 by Sharlene Minshall
First Printing   1997
Second Printing   2001
Third Printing   2002, completely revised
Printed in the United States of America
Library of Congress Catalog Card Number: 97-93847
ISBN 0-9643970-4-8

NON-FICTION TITLES

by

Sharlene "Charlie" Minshall

RVing Adventures with the Silver Gypsy

RVing Alaska and Canada

Full-Time RVing
How to Make it Happen

RVing North America
Silver, Single, and Solo

Freedom Unlimited:
The Fun and Facts of Fulltime RVing
Co-author, Bill Farlow

In Pursuit of a Dream

Order Form and More Information
(Back of book)

About the Author

1996

Sharlene "Charlie" Minshall began writing monthly columns and free-lance articles about her RV lifestyle in 1986. They range from the "How-to" to the "Why-not." She delves into the nitty-gritty humor of real RV problems like using the telephone, computer intricacies, and loss of memory. She touches on the serious, the silly, and the sad side of life. A Florida reader says her columns are more like "essays."

While continuing as a columnist, she still contributes other freelance writing, and in addition to *RVing Alaska and Canada,* has authored these RV-related books:

Full-Time RVing: How to Make it Happen
RVing North America: Silver, Single, and Solo
In Pursuit of a Dream and
Freedom Unlimited:
The Fun and Facts of Fulltime RVing (co-authored)

The author gives Life on Wheels seminars on the RV lifestyle. She tells positive, humorous, and very personal tales of the joys and woes of life on the road as a silver, single, solo gypsy, or as she puts it...

To clarify, I do not stand before you as an expert on anything. You ask then, "Why are you here?" It is more because I am not an expert, but I did it anyway. I'd like to share my eleven years of full-time RVing experiences and the lessons I've learned (or not).

In that time, I have traveled 180,000 miles by RV, and countless miles by car, four-wheel machine, airplane, helicopter, paraglider, ultra-light, train, bus, dunebuggy, motorcycle, bicycle, raft, canoe, kayak, ferry, mule, horse, cross-country skis, and water skis. Let's see, what have I forgotten...oh...

These boots were made for walkin', and walkin' they have done,
I've traveled not with expertise, but boy have I had fun!

As of the 2002 revising of "RVing Alaska and Canada," and almost sixteen full-timing years, the author has increased total travel to about 260,000 miles. The Sprinter's odometer hovers at the 215,000 mark and he is still going strong. Charlie acquired the deed to an Escapee Rainbow Park North Ranch RV lot near Congress, Arizona, in 2001. To it she added a 1988 40' Royales International fifth wheel for stretching out a bit during the winter months.

Add "dog-mushing," jet-boating, and tundra-buggying to the transportation means, and another book to the list in 2001, "RVing Adventures with the Silver Gypsy."

Dedication

I dedicate this book
To
The Lord,
who keeps me on, out, and in,
On the road, out of trouble, and in touch with good people
To
My brothers and sisters
Ted and Mary Stilwell
Dick and Vivian Stilwell
Leo and Pat Stilwell
Dean and Dorothy Stilwell
Note 2002: As always when time marches on, we lose treasured influences in our lives. My brother, Ted, died in 1997, and my sister-in-law, Dorothy, in 1998.
To
Rebecca
MBG (My Beautiful Granddaughter - 2002) who at thirteen towers above me
To
Will Norvelle
MHG (My Handsome Grandson - 2002) who at four continues to warm my heart
To
My supportive and special sons-in-law
Bill Wadlington and Tom Norvelle
To
My treasured daughters
Janet Louise and Tracey Anne
To
Old "Gold" Friends and New "Silver" Friends
who have touched my life and my heart somewhere, somehow,
and made this lifestyle an adventure to remember forever.

Acknowledgments

Special thanks
To
Camilla Bowman, Tracey Norvelle, Jane Parker, and Duane and Marilyn VanderWater for their "time-under-pressure" reading of *RVing Alaska!* It was tremendously helpful to have different points of view. *Thanks to Jan Adams at North Ranch for a last over-all 2002 perusal.*

I can always count on constructive criticism and loving encouragement from daughter, Tracey. Via telephone, E-mail, and Priority Mail from Virginia to Washington, she held my hand as I progressed through two books. Thanks, Love; you're the greatest. *She sent me blooming daffodils to keep my spirits up during this revision.*

Daughter, Janet, was so much more than an editor. As a computer consultant, she often rescued my sanity after I had lost 298 pages of a 192-page book, to what I feared most, oblivion. She was the calm and the hugs in the midst of my mental storms. She was my joy and laughter when all systems were go. Thanks, Honey; I couldn't have done it without you. *Major thanks for an entirely new 2002 front cover.*

In 2002, I continue to have the wonderful support and encouragement from my daughters and their families, not just in writing books, but in feeling their blessings on my bumper as I travel North America and beyond. Without the Lord as my Shepherd and the kids as my encouragement, I couldn't do what I do or go where I go.

CONTENTS

Chapter		Page

Introduction... 1

Maps 3... 3

1   Preparation 5

2   More Preparation 18

3   Beautiful British Columbia.. 31

4   Prince George to Whitehorse 41

5   Golden Circle Loop and on to Fairbanks 53

6   The Spell of the Yukon 61

7   Flying with the Eagle-ites.. 72

8   The Mighty Yukon River 79

9   Chicken Tracks to Anchorage 96

10   Down on the Kenai 107

11   The Bear Facts 119

12   The Hope of My Universe... 137

13   "Build a Road and She will Come"................................. 147

14   The Fair and the Fireweed 158

15   Doing the Dempster... 172

16   Headin' Home Alone #1.. 182

17   Headin' Home Alone #2.. 188

18   Parting Thoughts 200

Glossary

Resources

Miller's Landing, Seward, AK

Igloo, Kotzebue, AK

Introduction
It charms me! It excites me!
It overwhelms me!
I love it!
ALASKA!

You might say I'm a fan of William H. Seward, Secretary of State to Presidents Lincoln and Johnson. He arranged for the purchase of Alaska from Russia. "Seward's Icebox," as many Americans called it in 1867, was purchased for $7,200,000. We paid a whopping two cents an acre for this amazing land of 100,000 glaciers and over 40 mountain ranges.

Alaska was declared the 49th United State in 1959; and in the process, it became not only our largest, but also our northernmost, westernmost, and easternmost state. Honest! The Aleutian Chain extends into the Eastern Hemisphere.

It isn't just Alaska that thrills me. It is the getting there as well. The route across Canada is equally as beautiful. Crossing the border and knowing I'm on the way to our Great Frontier, gives me goosebumps.

It has been my privilege to visit Alaska four times. Each trip I have returned to favorite haunts, discovered different places, met delightful people, and experienced new adventures. The 1996 trip was to be my farewell to Alaska. I was certain I would get the North completely out of my system. Ha! The longer I stayed, the longer I wanted to stay and I couldn't resist going back again five years later.

I originally wrote this book in 1997, after my third trip. In 2002, I added 28 more pages of pictures, comments, information, and adventure from the 2001 trip. To make it less confusing, additions and comments are *italicized* or the year is under the title to denote the time period.

Please use the Glossary in the back to understand unfamiliar terms. Maps #1 and #2 will clue you in to the whereabouts of cities and routes.

Sometimes I wonder at the audacity that allows me to feel so comfortable traveling alone. I suspect it's just plain blind faith in the good Lord, that He will look after those of us who are as dumb as rocks about mechanics.

I've learned enough over almost 16 years of full-time RVing, to know a macerator from a Michelin, but not much more. I rather envy my four brothers who grew up taking things apart (probably without permission), and putting them back together again. In the process, they learned how things worked or why they didn't. Perhaps someday I'll solve the puzzle. What was I doing while they were getting down, getting greasy, and piecing engines together? All those who know me well, will vouch for the fact I wasn't studying the culinary arts. Maybe I was gardening.

Because I drive the motorhome almost every day, I'm very aware of what it sounds like and feels like, as it bounces down the highways and byways. When it doesn't sound "right," it is my first inkling of a problem. I fix it or have it fixed. The Sprinter's odometer turned over 200,000 miles on BC Route #97 in 2001. Since I have replaced most everything bit by bit, I had intended to have a whole new motorhome by the turn of the century, but that didn't happen. The last trip I was towed three times. None of this had anything to do with the gasoline engine by the way. It is purring along just great, thank you.

But back to Alaska, I'll base mileage from the Washington border. It is roughly 2,500 miles from Seattle, Washington to Anchorage, Alaska. Give or take a few miles to see everything, you could easily add 8,000-10,000 miles to your odometer. If at all possible, plan this trip for no less than three months. If you love it, you won't regret it. If you hate it (I can't imagine), you can always leave early.

My purpose in writing this book is not to pass myself off as an expert. I'm an every day Jill who loves Canada and Alaska and I've told you the good and the bad and the straight of it. The book is meant to give you not only an insight into RVing it, but to extend your possibilities into canoeing, flying, mushing, and playing with the grizzlies.

Trips to Alaska in 1987 and 1992 are extensively covered in *In Pursuit of a Dream* and *RVing North America: Silver, Single, and Solo*. I have mentioned some of those places or activities but did not go into them as comprehensively as in the original books.

If you aren't contemplating a trip to Alaska, please settle back with a cool drink, and we'll go for an armchair adventure you won't forget. Actually, it might be more apropos to get a hot drink, we're leavin' for glacier country.

If you're driving a RV, the ideas, suggestions, and comments are to make your RV trip smoother and more fun. The added personal experiences are to encourage you to visit our 49th state before it changes any more than it already has. I hope before another year goes by, you'll be

RVing ALASKA and CANADA
and loving it!

God Bless!

"Charlie"

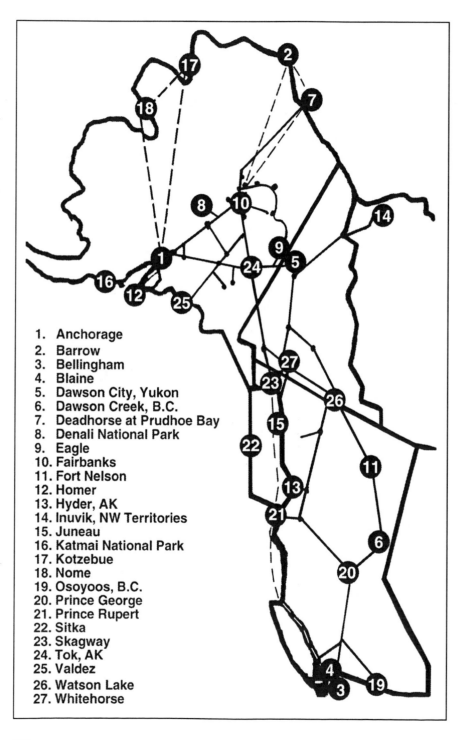

1. Anchorage
2. Barrow
3. Bellingham
4. Blaine
5. Dawson City, Yukon
6. Dawson Creek, B.C.
7. Deadhorse at Prudhoe Bay
8. Denali National Park
9. Eagle
10. Fairbanks
11. Fort Nelson
12. Homer
13. Hyder, AK
14. Inuvik, NW Territories
15. Juneau
16. Katmai National Park
17. Kotzebue
18. Nome
19. Osoyoos, B.C.
20. Prince George
21. Prince Rupert
22. Sitka
23. Skagway
24. Tok, AK
25. Valdez
26. Watson Lake
27. Whitehorse

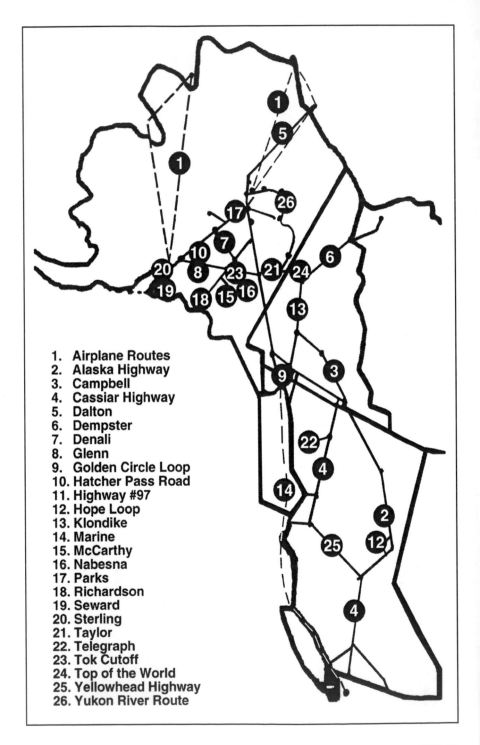

1. Airplane Routes
2. Alaska Highway
3. Campbell
4. Cassiar Highway
5. Dalton
6. Dempster
7. Denali
8. Glenn
9. Golden Circle Loop
10. Hatcher Pass Road
11. Highway #97
12. Hope Loop
13. Klondike
14. Marine
15. McCarthy
16. Nabesna
17. Parks
18. Richardson
19. Seward
20. Sterling
21. Taylor
22. Telegraph
23. Tok Cutoff
24. Top of the World
25. Yellowhead Highway
26. Yukon River Route

1996
I drove up in the April snows
When the frozen lakes and streams were beginning to melt
Spring and summer arrived in
A dazzling array of wild flowers
Autumn was yellow, orange, bright red...and glorious
The Sprinter pushed snow through
The mountain pass returning from Inuvik in late September
I knew then, I had come full circle
And I definitely did not have the far North out of my system

Preparation

Hi!

My first trip to Alaska in 1987 was in the back of a pickup truck! Honest, it was better than it sounds. Dick and Mary Carr were preparing an itinerary for their caravan company and took me along to take pictures and write a brochure. They stayed in the travel trailer they were pulling, and I lived under their truck cap. I was grateful for a taste of Alaska. In 1992 and 1996, I drove my Sprinter motorhome up and discovered I still didn't have Alaska out of my system. I wrote the first edition of this book in 1997, and then much to my surprise, I went back for an extended trip in 2001. Obviously I should never say it is my last trip!

I felt this book would help RVers be less overwhelmed. Many of these things you should do before you leave your driveway on your way to anywhere. As you read further, you will realize I didn't necessarily follow my own advice at all times, and I did have a few problems, but that's par for this Silver Gypsy's course. Let's begin.

How do YOU feel?

We will discuss extensively the health of the chassis and the RV, but they are both secondary concerns to your personal health. There are doctors, clinics and hospitals; but remember, the distances between towns are often great. Locations listed on the map are occasionally just that, listed. In the lower 48 when a place is on the map, it might have some substance. In North Country, it could be a store or gas station, or it might be closed for life, because it's historical...and you'll be hysterical.

If you have existing health problems, check with your doctor. Plan to stay in campgrounds or towns. Take prescriptions, insurance papers, and medical cards with you (Are they good in Canada? Check with your insurance company). As with any trip that takes you many miles from home territory, give thought to insurance for emergency medical care. If you become ill, you might have to be flown to a major city (or another country), for special care.

It's scary being sick, but if you're "Goin' in the brambles where the rabbits wouldn't go," it can be terrifying. There are few things I fear in solo RVing. Getting sick is one of them. It is frightening. It hasn't happened often and it won't stop me, but it is frightening. Do you have any physical limitations? Think ahead and ask questions before going on tours. With serious considerations out of the way, let's get on to the fun.

What should I do ahead of time?

GET THE MILEPOST MAGAZINE!

The most important advice I can give you is to buy the Milepost Magazine. Don't leave home without it. New ones come to the bookstores in April. It is a guide filled with priceless information, milepost by milepost, throughout Canada and Alaska. Truth is, the Milepost is all you need, but then again, this book is more fun. They can give you information, but

I have walked the walk, canoed the canoe, mushed the dogs, and driven the miles.

Even if you are using a Milepost that is a year old, it will give you most of what you need to know. Businesses open and close quickly; information can't always make the latest issue. While I consider the Milepost to be the greatest all-time guide, not everyone advertises in it. More facilities and services are available than what you will find in the Milepost pages. One more thing about the Milepost, study it before you go. It can be confusing, but it will all become clear as you become familiar with it.

When I stop for the night, I like to go through the Milepost and get an idea what I'm going to see the next day. I check ahead for services. Where can I find a telephone, gasoline, propane, car wash, fresh water, dump station, campground, groceries, pizza fix, or whatever else I need.

For hiking, biking, exploring beyond the main highways, or taking cruises, I recommend buying the Alaska Atlas and Gazetteer. Everything is topographically mapped. Even though the cruise companies include small maps, the topo maps give details of all the nooks and crannies for your notes or photographs. A necessity if you are really traveling into the boonies offroad, is the Alaska Wilderness Guide. This and the Milepost are both published by Vernon Publications.

I am not one for nitty-gritty trip planning years in advance, but an Alaska trip requires thinking ahead. Yes, there are stores and mechanics and supplies, but the distances are great and the prices are high.

Get Maps and information!

The best overall map of Canada and Alaska will come with the Milepost magazine; however, I like individual large maps. I don't find Atlas maps as detailed as I like. They are great for a quick overall perusal.

Send for maps and information from each Province, Territory, and Alaska. They will send good maps and let you in on activities and whatever is unique in their area. Trip routing and material are usually available from RV organizations, Family Motor Coach Association, Escapees, Good Sam, Coast to Coast, etc. Computer buffs can do an Internet search and get another ton of information.

I use a highlighter pen to mark where I'm going or where I've been. (Sometimes I use a different color for each direction because most of the time, I don't know whether I'm coming or going.)

The fun of going to Alaska is the anticipation. Pour over maps and brochures, go to slide shows or lectures, watch TV programs, read books (please), and talk to people who have been there. They can tell you whether the Moose Dropping Festival at Talkeenta, Alaska, or the International Gold Show at Dawson City, Yukon, are farces or fun. But, be careful, it is their opinion.

I can't count the number of times I would have missed something I really enjoyed because someone else didn't like it. We all have different ideas of fun. Check it out yourself if you have a real interest. If you are going somewhere specific, request material from the Chamber of Commerce of a nearby town.

Keep in mind because of weight restrictions, everything you take into a RV should have a dual purpose. A map is a stupendous conversation starter. Open a map on a picnic table or carry one to the recreation hall or laundry. You will soon have numerous RVers draped over your shoulder. They'll point to where they have been or where they want to go and give you advice about which route to take whether or not they have ever been there. (Great Uncle Herbert was there 10 years ago and the road was lousy.) If a map doesn't clue you in to your destination, and it doesn't work initiating a conversation, use it as a fire starter.

Visit all the information booths, centers, and kiosks. Free information and maps are invaluable. Maps are often kept behind the desk and you have to ask for them. If not during the trip, it is nice to have maps for identifying slides or pinpoint something in your log when you return.

Information centers are also super places to meet other RVers and exchange road conditions and other information. But again, it is their opinion. Take it with a grain of salt. Mix it with your own knowledge, information and desire, then toss out what you don't want to hear, like my taking the road to McCarthy. Two out of three told me the road was nearly impassable. I chose to believe the one who said, "It isn't so bad if you're careful." It was the worst washboard gravel road I ever traveled, but then again, I would have missed a fantastic experience if I hadn't followed my own desire.

Keep material organized. Keep it handy. I've never done this in my life, but it's a great idea.

When should I go?

The average tourist goes mid-June to mid-August because the attractions are open, and generally the weather is at its best then. I like going in April to watch the ice-clogged streams and lake ice melt and see the mountains in snow. It's great for slides. You will very likely drive or sit in snow for a few days if you go early or stay late. I figured if anybody keeps their roads clear, those in the North Country would have the equipment for it. They live with snow. I like experiencing the seasons.

During the traveling season, thousands of RVers drive around the loop and down the Kenai, staying on the main highways. Because I have gone up for longer periods of time, when everything gets clogged with RVs, I find a nice streamside campsite or do some backroad exploring. The sheer number of RVs, of course, is a good case for towing a tag with you. You can get around better and quicker, and find parking.

How long should I stay?

As long as possible! It is a lengthy journey. Give it time. Don't try to do it in less than six weeks. Yes, it is possible; but personally, I like to see where I am traveling, talk to people, and get a feel for the communities. It's fun to take side trips or flights to places and cultures I couldn't see anywhere else. Possibilities are limited only by your imagination, and in some cases, your wallet.

If you enjoy scenery, you will be thrilled with the whole trip. If, God forbid, you should get up there and not like it, you can always head for home earlier than you planned. You might even get hooked, like me, and go back for longer periods of time each trip. I think three months is the least amount of time anyone should take for the entire trip. If you are someone who sees Europe in a weekend, three days will work.

Where will I stay?

The choice to drive up early and return late, means I boondock (dry camp) a lot. The Milepost will tell you where the campgrounds are, fees, and usually when they open and close. Most campgrounds do not open until mid-June and they close by September. However, there are many places to park. Private parks are definitely not open until the main season. Public parks are sometimes open for parking but have no facilities.

I choose a wide spot next to a lake or stream for overnighting. There are many rest areas, official and unofficial. If you are stuck without a campground and you are apprehensive about doing this, ask if you can spend the night in a business parking lot or near an information center. Be sure you are not on private property or obstructing anyone or anything. It all comes down to using good old common sense.

It is against my religion to make reservations except at a really busy tourist site during high season (Denali - Anchorage - Fairbanks), then reservations are probably best. Parks fill up by late afternoon. Don't expect to always find fancy parks. You are in North Country. Both Canada and Alaska have some very nice parks but many are forged out of the countryside. Even if they have the amenities, they are not fancy by any means. If you must have electric, sewer, and water, I suggest good planning.

My favorite campsites are near water, trees, and nature in the recreation areas.

My rules for boondocking outside designated camping areas

- If it is posted, don't stay
- Don't block anything
- Don't knowingly park on private property (without permission)
- Be unobtrusive
- Don't dump anything or leave a mess

- Leave it better than you found it
- If it is a public area (Rest area -- Wal-Mart, etc.), stay only one night.
- Get there after 7 p.m., leave early
- Keep a quiet, low profile

Do not go to northern Canada and Alaska expecting major RV resort facilities like you find in Arizona, Texas, California, or Florida. Relax, enjoy what the North is all about. I go there because I love the scenery, and away from Anchorage and Fairbanks, the slower pace. That doesn't mean drive your RV on a busy main highway going 35 miles an hour, gawking at the scenery. It means stop in the pullouts, or stop early in the day, or stay a couple of days in one spot. Don't rush it.

Someone wrote to me asking if they would have problems getting into campgrounds with a 37' rig. If your RV is ultra big, check site sizes in the Milepost or campground directories. Some campgrounds and/or gravel roads cannot accommodate, and are not advised, for large vehicles. I don't think you will have any problems if you are on the main roads. There are size restrictions in some recreational parks.

What should I take to wear?

The weather varies even during July and August. Elevations and the time of day make a big difference in your personal comfort. Take cool and warm clothes and dress in layers. Take good walking (or hiking) shoes, warm socks, boots, rainwear, and a windbreaker. I wore hiking boots almost the entire time. They looked horrendous by about the third month, but that was when they were really getting comfortable.

Break your shoes in before you need them!

I broke in my leather hiking boots by putting them on, lacing them up, and getting them soaked. I wore them until they were completely dry and conformed to my foot. I got rid of them when they fell apart.

It wouldn't hurt to have some dress-up or semi dress-up clothes, depending on your choice of activities. Casual dress goes almost anywhere. I did take off my hiking boots to go to church, but I wouldn't have been the only one with hiking boots on if I had chosen to wear them.

What other "Stuff" should I take?

You know what you and your spouse (or your family) need to keep plugging along (or perhaps unplugging). These are only suggestions of what you might take. Your list will depend on your individual needs and the type of activities you will be involved in.

Ace bandages

Antacids

Antibiotics

Anti-diarrhea medicine

Antihistamines

Aspirin, or whatever you use for a painkiller. Certainly, if you have a favorite brand, take it with you.

Band-Aids

Dressings

Extra pair of glasses (and a copy of your prescription + Repair kit) (In not following my own advice, I had to buy an emergency pair in an Anchorage Wal-Mart 2001.)

Eye drops

Hydrogen Peroxide

Insect repellent

Laxatives

Liquid antiseptic

Medicine for motion sickness

Mosquito netting (if you are really bugged by bugs)

Pepto Bismol

Prescription for allergies

Sleeping remedies (A mask to keep out all that daylight!

Sunscreen

Tick repellent

If you are already a RVer, you probably have everything you'll need in your medicine chest. I carry only a few basics plus Alka Seltzer for sewer tank headaches (Yes, it works to put a couple of packets into the sewer tanks to clean off the indicator light corrosion).

Repellent

Take plenty of mosquito repellent. No one believes me when I say I use repellent only two or three times a summer. Bugs are worse in some areas than others and in some seasons more than others. One of the worst places was at the Fairbanks Chena River Recreation Area. They were so thick their landings and take-offs kept me awake at night.

Mosquitoes and I generally don't get along and I didn't look forward to bugs of any kind, but I spent plenty of time outside and wasn't bothered that much. Take the repellent. Everybody is different, and you'll probably need it. Some of the hints from the National Park Service are:

- **Don't wear perfume or other scented products.**
- **Wear light colors or pastels. Bright, patterned, or dark clothing attracts insects.**
- **In grassy, brushy, or wooded areas, wear tightly woven fabric.**
- **Tuck your pant legs in your socks and your long-sleeved shirt into your pants.**

- Wear a hat.
- Check yourself for ticks after every outing.
- Only female mosquitoes draw blood. If you see one wearing a skirt, smack her before she gets ya.

Alaska has black flies and "no-see-ums," as well as mosquitoes. You no see um the no-see-ums, but if you suddenly start dancing "The Chicken" when you ain't in Chicken, you'll know you found 'em. Wearing long sleeves and long pants with cuffs tight to your body helps. I was also not bugged by black flies and no-see-ums.

I've come to the conclusion since I didn't have a problem with bugs, maybe I'm not sweet enough, but then who'd believe that? It could be propaganda to keep the tourists in the lower 48. Those Alaskans are sneaky. They tell everybody Alaska has two seasons, mosquitoes and no mosquitoes.

Logs

I keep a log for mileage, repairs, and gasoline, plus costs and receipts, and another for activities, places, weather, and thoughts. It is fun to read after you get home. You'll be surprised how often you refer to it for clarification (or to win an argument). One thing about traveling solo, I win _most_ of my arguments.

Photography

If you're into photography, take lots of film. It is easier to find print film than slide film unless you're in a bigger city, and it is expensive.

- **Take telephoto lens. This will allow you to get good animal shots without getting too close**
- **Frame photos with trees, branches, flowers, people**
- **Flash photos do not work for distances**
- **Include people or rocks or trees for perspective**
- **A tripod is helpful for low-light shots**
- **In the foreground, capture sand, footprints, a brick wall**
- **Take a couple of disposable panoramic cameras**
- **Landscapes are best taken early morning/late afternoon**
- **Use a gray or cloudy day for dramatic or moody pictures**
- **ASA 100 is a good all-purpose film.**
- **Higher speed ASA 200 or 400 for animals in low light**

Companions

This is a good time to mention companions. Should you choose to take someone with you in your rig, or caravan with one or several rigs, remember it is a long trip. Are you super good friends who can be honest with each other? Do you like to travel long days or stop by 2 or 3 in the afternoon to relax and enjoy your surroundings? Is your dawn's early light at 5 a.m. or 11 a.m.? Be sure you are compatible.

If you would enjoy their company but you don't want to wait at every turn, consider meeting them at a pre-designated area by evening. That way you can all enjoy the trip and keep your sanity (providing you had some before you left).

Fellow caravaners or companions or commercial caravans are the greatest if you are the least bit apprehensive about driving <u>anywhere</u> on your own.

Now, let's get more serious here.

What is the condition of your RV?

How good or how old are your fire extinguishers? Notice, I said extin-guishers, as in plural. You should have one for your tag, as well as how-ever many you need inside for the size of your RV. An extinguisher in an outside hold should be considered a necessity.

Check out your water heater, furnace, and refrigerator. Heat feels great on some of those cool Alaska mornings and evenings. How is your water pump working? How old are your house batteries? (Do they have enough water in them? (I have a tendency to forget the poor things be-cause they are under the bed pedestal and hard for me to reach.) Do you have battery corrosion preventative? Do you have repair material for a leaky roof?

<u>Begin your journey with a vehicle that is in good condition.</u>

Your immediate enjoyment, and fond memories of this fabulous trip (or any other), will be enhanced a hundred-fold if you

BEGIN YOUR JOURNEY WITH A VEHICLE THAT IS IN GOOD CONDITION!

Notice I repeated that because it is important!

What should I take?

Many RVers are driving to Alaska these days; consequently, towns have increased in size. RV repair facilities and parts stores have prolifer-ated. Still, distances are great and it is wise to have some items for your specific RV.

Take extra engine and transmission oil; power-steering and brake fluids; gasoline and oil filters; air cleaner; headlights; and a variety of belts (air-conditioning, alternator, fan) and hoses, (radiator, heat and A/C) with you. Whatever is on the vehicle should be new, or nearly new, be-fore you drive a mile down the road (A good idea no matter where you are going). If you can't replace parts yourself, you might find someone who can replace them, easier than you can find the needed parts.

Take two spare tires if possible. If you are traveling April or before, or September and later, be prepared to do some driving in snow. Use all-weather tires or tires with good tread and traction devices. Are they prop-erly inflated? It will make a difference in your gas mileage. Do have an ice scraper or a shovel, some sand? Do you have a tire pressure gauge? Even better, do you know how to use it?

Don't forget the little guy you are towing behind you. Are you packing a few extra parts and a <u>GOOD</u> tire for him (Not one of those *puny* things that hides under the mat)

Windshield wipers should be in excellent condition. Take extras, along with extra windshield cleaner. Check fuel and water pumps. How is the exhaust system? How are your brakes? Is your cooling system OK? How about in-house, outhouse, and hazard lights? Does your cruise control work properly? With the great distances, you'll want your cruise. Make sure the radio works. In some areas you can tune in for road, park, or travel conditions. How old is your engine battery? Do you have jumper cables? Don't forget the flashlight (spare batteries), jumper cable, nylon rope, come-along, and tow cable. Of course I didn't have half this stuff but don't tell anybody!

Everybody wants to know the answer to the all-important question,

"How are the roads?"

Don't let stories of the Alaska Highway scare you to death. Have you driven our Interstates down here? What do you do when you hit a stretch of bad highway?

If you have the sense God gave you, you slow down and take it easy until the road improves.

That is precisely what you do when you hit questionable highways in Canada and Alaska.

Yes, the Alaska Highway is completely paved, as are the Richardson, Tok, Parks, Glenn, Seward, etc., but all have at least occasional stages of "heavedom." Except for the road from Tok to Glennallen, which has been mostly bad any time I've driven it, the other roads have bad <u>sections</u>.

Narrower, winding gravel roads, such as the Cassiar and Top of the World in Canada, and Taylor Highway in Alaska, are being widened, paved, and/or chip-sealed. Curves are being straightened and shoulders added. You'd better get up there before they ruin the whole place!

Frost heaves will be a seasonal problem until such time as the powers that be can overrule nature, and that ain't likely to happen.

Rough spots in both countries are marked with flashers, flags, or signs. Trust me; when you see a marker of any kind, there is a reason -- <u>pay attention</u>!

Also, if you travel really **early** in the spring, road crews will not have had time to repair the roads. Roads improve as the season progresses.

Phone numbers for road and mountain pass conditions, are listed in the Milepost; however, I found most of them had been disconnected between information gathering and magazine printing. Look in the phone book or newspaper when you are in town or ask someone. People in the North live by the weather. They know where to check weather conditions. Definitely do this if you are traveling early or late. Even better, get a hand-held, battery-powered, weather radio. Mine has been invaluable.

As with the traditional frost heaves, also cut your speed with bad weather conditions. Ice, snow, mud, and rain make road surfaces potential skating rinks. Gusts or wind devils hitting the broad surface of a RV can throw you. Northern Canada and Alaska have mostly two-lane roads. Travel slower during bad weather conditions. Unhappy campers may gather behind you. Use pullouts to let people by. If possible, stay off the road during bad weather, or at least during the busiest times of the day.

Now,

What about the rumors I hear concerning broken axles, springs, etc.?

What about them? Certainly you can have a flat tire or break down under any circumstances, no matter how well prepared you were when you started, or how good a condition everything was in when you crossed the border. But, if you are very aware of conditions (watching those flagged bad sections), and your speed is reasonable, you probably won't have problems. If you are in such a hurry, why go?

To me it is not the flagged sections that are the worst. I hate the "swells." These are generally not marked because they are not a "break" in the pavement. Watch the road ahead of you. If the white stripe at the side starts doing the dipsy doodle, that is your first clue to slow down, and quickly. If these are driven at just a trifle of an angle, it is possible to get past them without a problem (after slowing down). If you do hit one head on and at full speed, you will get a teeth-rattling jolt as your front end connects with the returning pavement.

Watch business driveways. They are often extremely steep for drainage purposes and definitely not RV friendly. Especially if you are towing, but even if you're not, either find another entrance, another business, or drive up or down at an angle to keep from bumping or dragging.

Please remember, speed is directly relational to anguished springs, broken axles, chipped windshields, and creative alignment.

Anyone can have problems no matter how carefully they drive. But...the biggest gripers are blustery hot dog RV drivers who forgot a long time ago what "vacation" or "leisurely trip," means. They stop late. They start early. In between, they drive like a bat out of a very hot place. They aren't getting anything out of the trip, wouldn't dream of going back, can't see what anybody sees in the place (probably because they missed the whole thing), and will be dag-nabbed sure whoever is with them, isn't going to enjoy any of it either.

I've run into people like that. Their description of the trip always made me wonder which Alaska they visited. It never resembles any of my trips, even over the same route.

In 2001, I talked with a couple in Hope. His comment when I asked if they were having a good time, "Yeah, but I'd never come back again." His tone made me wonder. I discovered they had forgone traveling to Dawson City and Chicken because they heard Top of the World and Taylor Highways were rough. O.K. I can understand that. They went through Fairbanks. I asked if they visited Alaskaland, the Chena River boat trip or the University of Alaska museum. No, they hadn't stopped. Nor did they stop at Ester's Malamute Saloon. Denali National Park was too busy. How they happened to drive off the beaten path to get to Hope, I'll never know. If I hadn't experienced any more of Alaska than that, I wouldn't want to go back either!"

What happens if I do break down?

Communications

Do you have a CB? Channels 9 and 11 are monitored for emergencies on most of the Alaska Highway system. Most truckers use channel 19. A cellular phone? Are you carrying flares or flags? How about a big sign for the window that screams for "HELP?"

NOTE: In 2001, my electrical system completely shut down between Delta Junction and Tok heading south. I was able to wrestle the Sprinter off the road before it stopped. By the time I checked all possibilities and discovered I couldn't do anything to improve the situation, it was dark. No traffic at night on the Alaska Highway the end of August and no working CB anyway. I went to bed.

In the middle of the night I remembered I had a cell phone with me, even though I was no longer signed up with a service. I knew I could, but had never tried to use the cell phone sans service, as an emergency communcation. The inverter still worked so I plugged in the phone. Within a half-hour, it miraculously showed bars. I called 911 and was transferred twice before I reached someone who called a tow truck that came about three hours later.

The reason I stopped the cell phone service was that it was costing me a fortune. In places I chose to travel, it seldom worked. However, services are improving and in an emergency, it is a great idea to have one. I was fortunate to be in a place where it worked that time.

For crying tears in a bucket, if you have major problems, don't let it ruin your trip. Plan in a little extra moola, or a little leeway on your credit card, or last but not least, a rich relative you can call in case something big goes wrong.

First of all, spend less than a $100 and get a towing service that will pick up anywhere without an extra fee (covering both RV and tag), and transport you to a good repair facility. If you don't carry towing insurance anywhere else, carry it when you travel Alaska and Canada (Does it cover you in Canada?). The fees for any long-distance towing bill will take care of a year of towing insurance cost.

Worst case scenario

You are returning from Heaven only knows where and you break down. Unless you are traveling unusually early or late in the season, other cars or RVs will be on the road. Use the CB or cell phone to call your RV tow service or a repair facility in the next town. If all else fails, flag a car/truck/RV down and ask them to make a call for you.

If you are truly apprehensive about going somewhere off the beaten path, call a friend or relative and tell them when you are leaving and when you will be back, or leave word with the RCMP, a ranger, or the police. Stick precisely to that schedule. If you don't call them or return within a specified amount of time, presumably someone will look for you.

OK, what if the repair facility or wrecker can't possibly get to you before tomorrow (because of distances or time). Are you off the road? Did you set flares? Once you are off the road as far as you can get and you've put out the flares or you've driven to a pullout, relax, you are fortunate, you are already at home.

**All the poor earthbound souls zooming by in cars
can't go to the refrigerator,
mound a bowl with non-fat frozen yogurt
plus non-fat chocolate syrup,
or sprinkle it with 25% less fat, dry-roasted peanuts.
You can.
Relax. Watch the marmots sleep or the flowers grow.
I told you to take at least three months.**

Don't yell at your mate. Chances are they didn't have a thing to do with the problem. Even if they did, be magnanimous, try not to notice.

It is written on the road somewhere in big black letters, that RVs only have major breakdowns on weekends. After you are in town and you find you will be there a couple of days in the repair shop, don't do something really boring, like being bored. Look at it as an adventure. Walk (You've heard of that mode of transportation haven't you?) around town, visit the information center or a museum or have a cup of espresso in the cafe where the locals hang out. Pick up a hometown newspaper. Find out what's happening in that community. Go to church. Go to a movie. Go to a garage sale or flea market. Church, garage sales, and flea markets usually only happen on weekends. This scenario, of course, is another reason for pulling a tag.

Before you know it, your RV will be fixed, the bill will be paid, and you will be on your way. You might as well have an adventure as a frustration. I do all this, honest. Of course, first I cry in frustration, stomp my feet in anger, pray for forgiveness, and ask for help with the problem, then I relax and go from there. Life is good.

A piece of advice

If you have had major repairs and it is at all possible, drive in the area for a couple of days to see if everything is working as it should. More than once I have traveled 500 miles only to find the fix has gone awry. After driving that distance, I paid to have the problem fixed somewhere else rather than return. The same is true if you have repairs before your trip. Drive your rig a few weeks before starting the trip to Alaska. You can't always detect problems ahead of time but this gives you a fighting chance.

I asked to have my brakes and fluid checked. After the brakes went out on the Alaska Highway's Suicide Hill, I went back to the job list. I found that the fluid was checked but not the actual brakes. That was clearly my fault because I didn't spot it. There is a definite advantage to "Making a list and checking it twice" with the mechanic. Brakes are obviously a major concern.

Wow! My brain is on overload (It doesn't take much). Continue to the next chapter for more Alaska/Canada suggestions. In the meantime,

Remember

*1) You do not **have** to get off the main highway to see the beauty and excitement of Canada and Alaska.*

2) Be aware, listen, carry the essentials with you. Make sure you, and your entire vehicle, are in good working order.

3) Use common sense when it comes to your health, RV, dealing with people, and driving the roads.

4) Instead of griping because it's more expensive or the roads aren't perfect or it "isn't like in the lower 48," thank God it isn't. Appreciate the scenery, the people, and the different cultures. Relax! Enjoy!

Pick up a booklet in an information center called, "Help Along the Way" which lists Emergency Medical Services for Alaska Travelers. It has a lot of helpful information in it.

...More Preparation

TLC (Tender Loving Care)

I have gotten into the habit of doing a "walk-a-bout" around the RV and tag almost every time I stop. It stretches my legs and tells me if everything looks OK. I have discovered more than one dead dual (tire) I didn't know about. Thump your tires several times a day if you're driving a lot of miles. Check your engine oil every day. Watch your mileage. This is not the time to neglect having your oil and filter changed. Check the transmission oil, the brake fluid, and the air filter. If you travel the gravel, take the air filter out occasionally and tunk the dust out of it or change it.

Travel with your lights on, it may not help you see, but you will be more easily seen.

Bathing your baby

Even when you are traveling paved roads, you will have some dusty, dirty, road construction. If you are driving gravel roads during dry weather, expect dust. If it rains, expect mud, maybe to the point of roads being impassable. Calcium chloride is sometimes used for dust control. Wash it off as soon as possible. RV washes are listed in the Milepost or advertised on highway signs. Pressure washes are sometimes offered at campgrounds for a fee. Some stations offer pressure washes for a fill-up of fuel. They work great. Don't aim it directly into vented doors leading to the refrigerator or water heater. Occasionally you may see a portable unit set up. For $1 a foot (at that time), let somebody else do the work.

How should I protect my vehicle?

I have named the elaborate rock guard on the Sprinter's front, *Overkill*. It would have been perfect 20 years ago, but it is no longer needed to the extent it was then. Most people limit their guards to protecting the headlights and grill. I have driven all the major gravel roads. If you share them with trucks, you are more apt to get chips. I have *Overkill* and I still got a chip (in Mexico). It flew right over the rock guard. You can never be fully protected.

In 2001, I napped briefly in a rest area on the Kenai Peninsula. Fifty miles down the road, I stopped to take a picture. When I got out, I saw this note written on a napkin and stuffed into the side door handle, "We love your Alaska book. We are 'on the road' all the time now. No, your front protector is not overkill." It was signed "Terry & Michael Sroufe." Much later, I curiously looked in my Escapee directory and sure enough, there they were. I dropped them a note and received an e-mail in return.

It will help protect your trailer or tag to have a full-length guard on the back of your RV or truck. Most shields I see are plastic covers or screens made of PVC pipe and wire mesh or hardware cloth. Just for pulling, fasten carpeting over the complete front of your tag. You might also consider protection over the cabover window for a truck camper or Class C motorhome.

Safety Devices

Propane sensors, smoke alarms, and flat-tire detectors are great safety devices. Tire alarms should be on both RV and tag. They let you know when a tire has blown or gone flat. A flat dual tire or a towed vehicle flat tire is a fire waiting to happen. I know. I check my tires often and I've found some heavy-duty blue smoke a couple of times because I didn't realize a dual had met its demise.

Should I take my tow vehicle?

I have never pulled a tow vehicle to Alaska. Many people have a tow vehicle because they set up in campgrounds, then drive the tow everywhere. It is a good idea. Because I instinctively knew I would explore washboard, bumpy roads to out-of-the-way places where I needed good clearance, I left the tow in the lower 48 *(And in 2002 I still haven't replaced the one that died in 1998 – one of these days)*. I like having the Sprinter with me. I always have its convenience and safety and I can choose to stay a day or a week. It is a matter of personal choice.

Where can I...
Dump sewage--Fill with water--Get propane

The Milepost magazine and visitor centers have this information. Think ahead about dumping and filling needs. Running out of propane is only a problem if it is the middle of the night, 40 miles beyond nowhere. It is available in most towns. Watch your gauges.

Some towns, such as Dawson City, Homer, Sitka, have free public water and dump stations. Fuel stations advertise them. Some are free; others charge a fee. Fuel stations usually offer the service free if you get a fill-up. If you are there during the season, it isn't a problem.

If you are off-season, the facilities may not be available because of the weather. Give yourself leeway. The Fred Meyer store in Soldotna is kind enough to have overnight RV parking and a free dump station and water. (Please buy something if you take advantage of their amenities.)

Visitor centers are only open from mid June through August but people are friendly (if you're friendly). All you need to do is open your mouth and ask. If the first person can't answer your question, they'll likely point you to someone who can. If you're always lost, like me, this is important.

How do I get there?

People with limited time fly into Anchorage, rent a RV, and make "The loop," seeing the main attractions. This is OK, but they miss the beauty and excitement of Canada, and a whole lot of Alaska. Those who do not want to drive their big rigs or subject a new or ultra-large RV to trip rigors, fly in and rent or buy a truck and camper to make the trip. RVing by ferry is a great way to travel. If possible, drive one way and ferry the other. Should you decide to use the Alaska State Ferry system,

Make your reservations 5-6 months in advance!

The Alaska Marine Highway ferries are available between Prince Rupert, BC, and Skagway, Alaska, or between Bellingham, Washington, and Skagway, Alaska. Alaska State Ferries departing from Bellingham do not stop in Canada. BC Ferries provide service throughout BC's coast. Previously I had only ferried between Skagway and Haines. *In 2001, I returned via the ferry system. I'll tell you about that later.*

Driving to Alaska is a long way,
but don't let the distances intimidate you,
they are just roads!

Roads must be driven mile by mile with a smile, just like anywhere else. Check the map from the Washington border through Canada and to and through Alaska. There are two distinct loops. One loop begins at Prince George on #97 to Dawson Creek and then follows the Alaska Highway, eventually coming back along the Cassiar and following the Yellowhead Highway to Prince George. The other major loop is from Tok, Alaska, to Fairbanks, Anchorage, and back to Tok. I've made a list of places where you might make decisions.

Possible routes and decisions

Roads might be gravel, chip-sealed, or paved, as well as narrow, two-lane, or four-lane (seldom).

Decision time: Prince George, British Columbia, Canada
North on Hwy #97 to the Alaska Hwy at Dawson Creek **or**
Alternate: West along Yellowhead Hwy to the Cassiar Hwy (Route 37) (Mostly chipsealed) and north to junction with Alaska Hwy near Watson Lake.
Possibility: Hwy #97 north, turning on #29 along Peace River, Hudson's Hope, connecting with Alaska Hwy north of Dawson Creek.

Decision time: Watson Lake
West to Whitehorse and Skagway
Alternate: to Dawson City via the Campbell (Gravel) and Klondike Hwys.

Decision time: Whitehorse
Alaska Hwy to Tok

Alternate: North to Dawson City via Klondike Loop (Hwy #2 - paved), ferry, Top of the World and Taylor Hwy (Gravel) to Tok. **Possibility:** Side trip to Eagle (Gravel).

Alternate: Klondike Hwy to Skagway, ferry, Haines Hwy to Haines Junction connecting with Alaska Hwy.

Decision time: Dawson City
Cross Yukon River to Top of the World Hwy, Taylor Hwy, Tok
Possibility: Dempster Hwy (Gravel) north to Inuvik, NW Territories (Must return same way)

Tok: Whether you choose to leave Tok on the Alaska Hwy or Glenn Hwy, either direction will eventually take you around the Alaska loop (with alternate side trips) and return you to Tok. My personal preference is Fairbanks first because I spend more time in the Kenai area.

Decision time: Tok
Alaska Hwy to Delta Junction (Official end of the Alaska Hwy) and continue to **Fairbanks** via Richardson Hwy
Glenn Hwy (Glenn cutoff) to **Glennallen** then Anchorage

Decision time: Glennallen
Continue Glenn Highway to Palmer/Anchorage
Possibility: Richardson Hwy to Valdez (Must return or ferry). (Side trip to Chitina, McCarthy, Kennicott (Gravel) (Return same way).

Decision time: Fairbanks
Parks Hwy to Denali Nat'l Pk/ Anchorage
Possibility: Dalton Hwy (Gravel) to Prudhoe Bay along Trans-Alaska Pipeline (Must return same way)

Decision time: Palmer:
Parks Hwy to Denali Nat'l Park and Fairbanks and back to Tok
Possibility: Glenn Hwy to Anchorage and Kenai Peninsula

Kenai Peninsula:
Anchorage: Seward Highway to Hope/and or Seward
          Sterling Highway to Homer Spit (Return to Anchorage)
Decision Time: Anchorage
To Fairbanks/Tok
To Glenallan/Tok

Now we've completed the "loop" one direction or the other and we are back at Tok. If you came up the Alaska Highway, now is decision time to go to Dawson City via Taylor and Top of the World (Gravel) or continue south on the Alaska Highway until just before Watson Lake.

Decision Time: Junction 37 - Continue Alaska Highway south

Alternate: Cassiar Highway south to Yellowhead Highway

Decision Time: Turn to Stewart/Hyder at Meziadin Jct.
(Must return same way)

Decision time: Yellowhead Highway
West to Prince Rupert (and ferries)
East to Prince George and home (Depending on where home is)

Decision time: North of Cache Creek on Hwy #97
Continue on #67 and cross the border at Sumas, WA.
Alternate: #99 west to Vancouver (15% grades) and cross border at
Blaine, Washington

Pets

Are you going to take Little Lulu along? Again, I'm not saying this to scare you, but you are heading for the North Country where wild animals are "King." Any animal, but especially little dogs and cats, are vulnerable to eagles, bears, wolves, and coyotes. Don't let them roam outside. Keep them on a leash and stay with them. Don't leave them outside on a leash by themselves. Keep an eye on your pets.

Properly tag and license your pet. This will help if it does get lost. Does your pet get motion sickness? You should stop often to stretch your own legs, and it is good for your pet, too.

If pets are taken aboard the ferry system, they must stay in the RV. You are allowed feeding and exercising times three times a day.

"Lions and tigers and bears, Oh My!"
(Well, maybe not lions and tigers)

The North Country is bear country. There are three kinds, but you are most likely to see black or brown bears (hopefully, from a distance).

They are wild!
They are dangerous!
Their presence is not to be taken lightly!
They do not like surprises!

I don't say that to scare you so much as to make you cautious. Bears are majestic and exciting. They are curious and intelligent. They will usually avoid people. If you are hiking, make your presence known with singing, speaking loudly, or using bear bells (Of course humorous Alaskans and Canadians refer to bear bells as "Dinner Bells!"). If possible, travel in a group. **Never get between a baby and its mother**. There may be more than one baby. They frequently have multiple births.

If you are in a vehicle and you see any animal by the side of the road, take its picture from inside. Do not get out of your vehicle. Do not send your children or spouse (unless his insurance is paid up) to stand by the bear for a picture (If you think that is obvious advice -- I have seen people make some really stupid moves to get a picture).

Do not give them food.
"A fed bear is a dead bear"

Do not be guilty of helping them become dependent on human food (or even food not so human, like mine).

Now, God forbid you should ever come nose-to-nose with a bear. Nose to nose is unlikely since black bears are five feet in length (150 - 250 pounds), and brown bears are seven to nine feet in length (400 - 600 pounds). You can imagine how tall that makes them when they are standing on their hind legs...as in **v e r y t a l l**!

Chances are quite good you never will, but as you will read later in this book, there is always a possibility. What do we teach our children about possibilities? Know what to do, **just in case**.

Do not scream and run!
You cannot outrun a bear
If you start running, it will chase you
Because it <u>thinks you are dinner</u>
Do not climb a tree
Black bears can easily climb trees
Grizzlies can shake you out of them
As in all emergencies
(and this is classified as an emergency)
Remain calm.

Let the bear know you are human by speaking in a normal voice. Wave your arms to help it identify you. If it cannot tell what you are, it may come closer or stand on its hind legs to get a better look or smell. A standing bear is usually curious, not threatening. Back away slowly. If the bear follows, stop and hold your ground. (By then, I would faint and definitely be holding my ground!)

Continue waving your arms and talking. If it gets too close, raise your voice and be more aggressive (Yeah, right!). Bang pots and pans; use any type of noisemaker. Never imitate bear sounds or make a high-pitched squeal. (Scream in bass?)

Now we get down to the nitty gritty.

If a <u>BROWN</u> bear
(grizzly -- the one with the hump behind its head),
attacks you,
fall to the ground and play dead. (As if I'd be playing!)

Lie flat on your stomach or curl up in a fetal position with your hands behind your neck. Usually (that word is used a lot), a brown bear will break off its attack once it feels you are no longer a threat. Remain motionless for as long as possible. If you move, a brown bear may return and renew its attack, and you must again play dead.

**If you are attacked by a <u>BLACK</u> bear,
fight back vigorously.**

Don't think I am not serious because my asides are cavalier. I can do that because I am safe behind my computer, inside my cozy home on wheels. Once a woman became quite upset with me because I was RVing alone through the wilderness and thus, hiking alone. She became quite indignant and said, "Just what would you do if you were confronted with a bear?" I answered her in one extremely truthful word, "Defecate!"

My biggest fear is that with my advanced CRS (Can't Remember Sugar), I would forget which color of bear I should fight, and for which I should curl up and pretend to be dead. I think the second would be an unpicked choice and I wouldn't be pretending!

Living in a RV doesn't mean you can be a careless camper. Never leave anything outside anywhere (even in a campground) that has even the smell of food on it. Bears often shred coolers and have been known to annihilate cars to get into the trunks. I have seen relatively few bears packing can openers so you are reasonably safe in the confines of your tin can on wheels. *I'll tell you later about an experience in 2001 that made me question the last statement.*

Moose

Moose are also dangerous. Moose cause more injuries in Alaska each year than bears. An Alaska moose is the world's largest member of the deer family, tipping the scales at up to one-half ton, and standing over seven feet tall at the shoulder. As with all animals, they are extremely protective of their young. Do not get between them.

As I said somewhere in the book, if you share the path with a moose, you are the one that needs written permission to proceed. They sometimes attack vehicles. Don't do anything to try to intimidate them.

**As always, remember that <u>we are the visitors</u>.
This is their land.
Look, laugh, photograph, but leave alone.**

There, now that you are completely discombobulated, let's continue. Just remember that I am the world's biggest wimp, so if I can make four trips to Alaska and manage, you can, too (Of course my hair is already silver). Animal information and how to cope with them, is available at all information places.

Miscellaneous Tips

• If you aren't happy with where you are parking and you have no

choice, leave a light on, play a radio talk show, leave drapes closed.
- Always be aware of your surroundings.
- Never display your money in public. You never know who's watching.
- If you don't have a deadbolt lock on your RV, put one on.
- Do not leave anything valuable within sight from a window.
- If you sleep with the window open, wedge a bar in the track, leaving the opening small. Sleep with your head at the opposite end. (I've only done this a couple of times but it makes sense to me.)
- If you use an ATM machine, find one that is inside a business or in a well-lit area. Hide Your PIN number as you enter it into the ATM. Be exceptionally aware of your surroundings. Do this in the daylight.
- Park with your RV door toward the business you are going into.
- Lock your RV when you are refueling, especially if you are alone.
- Shut off all propane before you refuel or fill with propane.
- Never open your door until you know who's there. Look through the window. If you still don't know who it is, talk through the window.
- Extra rolls of paper towels are great for stuffing in places to eradicate rattles or protect something fragile.
- Have the correct key ready as you reach your RV or tag.
- Lock the doors once you are inside.

Expenses

<u>1996</u>

Mileage WA border to border – 9,612 miles (149 days)	
Gasoline:	$2,243
Major Maintenance & Supplies: (tire & brake,Misc)	$1,967
Camping fees:	$ 238
Annual Alaska State Pk. camping sticker:	$ 100
Propane/sewer:	$ 215

<u>2001</u>

Mileage WA border to border – 8,418 miles (128 days)	
Gasoline:	$2,169
Major Maintenance & Supplies (Tires,starter,Misc)	$2,126
Camping fees:	$472
Annual AK St. Pk. camping sticker no longer available	
Propane/sewer:	$161
Groceries/Dining ($8.92/day)	$1,143

Consider many things when looking at my costs. My maintenance and supply costs are higher because I rely on others to fix problems. The Sprinter is a senior citizen with no discounts. I stayed in 4 BLM, 7 State, 3 USFS, 11 City, 23 private, 2 Canadian campgrounds for a total of 50 nights. I boondocked 78 nights. Campground fees were higher and the AK camping sticker is no longer available to out-of-staters. Sometimes I used campgrounds for e-mail hook-ups, other times because of location.

I ate out a lot (about half the grocery/dining amount) because I had company or wanted company. I ferried home so gasoline was less (and probably maintenance as well!). For my 27' (measured 28') Sprinter, the ferry cost was $1,974 with two one-week stops from Skagway, AK, to

Bellingham, WA, a 16-day trip with no cabin.

Choices

• Food/restaurants	• Do you want a little bill or a big bill -- eat in or eat out? Top-o-the-Mark Vs Grizzly's Cafe
• Entertainment	• Two hour, l/2 day, all day, two day excursions; night life in Anchorage; photo journey; flight
• Admission fees/tours	• Free museum, hike, scenery, floorshow, day cruise, flightseeing?
• Parking/Ferries	• Big blue canoe ride or drive; small ferries are free (Across Yukon/Mackenzie/Peel) All-day parking or tour and park in their lot
• Laundry	• If possible, do it in larger towns.
• Film/processing	• You could wait until you get back but if you're there long, you may want to see what you have, and ID them. Do in a bigger city.
• Souvenirs	• Will these excite you as much when you get home and start dusting them? Do you really want your granddaughter to have a fur bikini or your grandson, an Ulu knife?
• Campgrounds	• BLM/NPS/USFS/state/private/boondocking
• Misc. expenses	• Postage/telephone/newspapers

Most expenses, with the exception of fuel and maintenance, are subject to the choices you make.

Crossing borders

They ask different questions each time I cross the border. This time, the border guard asked if I had firearms, fruit, plant materials, and what route I was taking north.

I have heard a lot of grumbling about crossing the border into Canada. On one occasion, the guard asked me the same questions over and over. He didn't seem to believe my solo traveling or my destination point. I haven't figured out yet why he was so suspicious. He had someone come to check the inside of the Sprinter, but she only gave it a cursory glance as she walked through, and asked, "What is he looking for?" I figured if they didn't know, I didn't know.

Don't get smart with them or kid around. They have a job to do, and they usually do it without smiles or a hint of personality. As innocent as we might be of breaking the rules, they often deal with the seamier side of humanity. *Since the tragic events of September 11, 2001, we can expect more questions and expanded inspections.*

Credit cards and cash

Bigger businesses throughout Canada and Alaska now accept major credit cards. The thing I appreciate about using credit cards, is that you receive the Canadian exchange rate for the day you are making the purchase, and you are not subject to a business giving you only 15% or 20% of a 30+% exchange rate.

Carry Canadian and US cash with you. Again, most places accept credit cards, but some villages are just plain too small. Exchange your money at a national bank after you cross the border. *In 2001 in Eagle, Alaska, I was low on cash but they had no qualms about taking out-of-state checks. They didn't even look at my ID. Very few small places have banks or ATM machines.*

Laws

You must cross the borders when they are open, and some of them are not open 24 hours. Watch your timing. It is illegal to cross without going through customs.

Remember that purchases legally made in one country, may be illegal in the other. Check the legalities of handcrafted items such as ivory, seal products, feathers, whalebone, fur, etc., before buying them.

Going into Canada

Passports are not required for United States Citizens to enter Canada or return to US.
Proof of citizenship must be carried:
Birth or baptismal certificate with photo; ID such as driver's license.
Proof of residence may be required.
Minors: In addition to above, must have notarized letter of consent by both parents and/or guardians.

Medicine

Properly identify any medicine containing narcotics or habit-forming drugs (in original container), and carry the prescription or doctor's statement as proof that you are using them under a doctor's direction.

Exemptions
Keep your sales receipts

United States: If you have been in Canada 48 hours or more, you may have $400 US duty-free exemption (Every 30 days). There are limitations on alcohol and tobacco.

Canada: You are allowed necessary personal effects, duty free. You may have, duty-free, certain amounts of alcoholic beverages and tobacco. You are allowed fuel to a normal tank capacity of the vehicle. (Fuel is sold by the litre: 1 US gallon = 3.78 litres.)

Gifts

Canada: Gifts may be imported by visitors, duty and tax-free, provided the value of each gift doesn't exceed $60 (Canadian) and gifts do not consist of tobacco products, alcoholic beverages or advertising material.

Sporting goods and equipment

Canada: Visitors may take the usual personal sporting goods and equipment, i.e., boats, motors, camping equipment, cameras, TVs, etc., into Canada by declaring them on entry.

In RVs, we have TVs, VCRs, computers, etc. It wouldn't hurt to list everything, especially large items such as boats, motors, golf equipment, etc., along with the approximate values, or have the receipts.

Pets

Canadians: Dogs and cats over the age of three months, need a health certificate signed by a licensed veterinarian that clearly describes the animal, and declares the animal has been vaccinated against rabies within the past 36 months. The animal must be healthy, under control, and on a leash at the time of entry.

Americans: Rabies vaccination certificate issued within six months.

Seat belts

Required for all passengers in Alaska, Canadian Provinces, or Territories. Child restraint laws vary according to age or weight. Check it out.

Taxes

Alaska: No statewide tax. Cities and boroughs may levy a sales tax up to 6%, plus special taxes on goods and services.

British Columbia: Provincial sales tax is 7%. Also, room and lodge taxes.

Northwest Territories: No territorial sales tax.

Yukon Territory: No territorial tax.

Firearms

Canada: All firearms must be declared when you enter Canada. If undeclared firearms are found, they will be seized, and possibly criminal charges filed. This may include seizure of the vehicle in which they are carried.

Visitors are prohibited from transporting handguns through customs, unless specificially authorized by the Bureau of Alcohol, Tobacco, and Firearms. Other firearms are allowed if they have legitimate sporting or recreational use. All types of firearms must be transported unloaded. They must be kept out of sight and locked up.

Firearms fall into three categories, non-restricted, restricted, and prohibited weapons. The list of rules and regulations for firearms is as long as your long gun. I am not going to list them here. If you have weapons of any kind, or have questions, send for the booklet through Revenue Canada.

In addition, they will not allow mace, pepper spray, or stun guns. The long list of no-nos in this category also requires that you get the booklet if you intend to carry such things. It would take me four years to list them, and I don't even know what some of them are (or want to!).

The Milepost has comprehensive information on border rules, and information is also available on the Internet.

Plants / fruits / vegetables

Some fresh fruits and vegetables commonly grown in Canada may be taken away from you. I had to throw a lovely new bag of potatoes into Canada's trash bin. Think twice before you stock up previous to crossing the border. House plants (rolling houses, too), supposedly do not need to be declared.

Vehicles

Registration is a must, or a contract if it is rented. Non-Resident Inter-Provincial Motor Vehicle Liability Insurance Card from your insurance company. (It is proof of financial responsibility.)
Trip accident policy recommended.

A British Columbia regulation change in April 1997, increases the weight threshold of vehicles being towed by motorhomes, to 4,400 pounds. This means that coordinated brake control and an emergency breakaway device may only be required if the laden gross weight of the towed vehicle is 4,400 pounds or greater. However, the new regulation adds a requirement that any towed motor vehicle weighing 40% or more of the motorhome's gross vehicle weight rating must be equipped with coordinated brakes and an emergency breakaway device.

GST tax

This 7% Goods and Services Tax is applied to most items and services in western Canada. Non-Canadians may apply for this GST rebate on some items.

You qualify for the 7% tax refund if:

You are not a resident of Canada
Have your original receipts (Credit card slips are not acceptable)
Your total refund claim is a minimum of Canadian $14 for each tax you are claiming. For eligible goods, each individual receipt has to show a minimum of Canadian $3.50 for each tax you're claiming. You can apply for cash refund up to a maximum of $500 Canadian.

The refund doesn't cover:
Restaurants / meals
Tobacco products
Transportation
Alcoholic beverages
Certain services (entertainment, parking, shoe repair, etc.)

Auto repairs (but it does cover parts)
And no such luck -- it does not cover fuel, food, camping, cruising, or rentals.

Does that thoroughly confuse you? Well, don't panic. Keep your receipts; the GST tax is listed on it. If you don't understand it, they are most gracious in helping you claim your refund at any participating Canadian duty-free shop. You can also do it by mail with the appropriate application. There are many stipulations. Pick up a brochure with all the details so that you will know what is covered and what is not.

Cassiar One-lane Bridge

OK, I'm brain weary again. I'll mention other things as we get "on down the road." If this doesn't make sense, let's discuss it in a month or so over milk and homemade pie at the Seaview Cafe in Hope, Alaska.

Drive with your lights on at all times.

Salty Dog, Homer Spit

Beautiful
British Columbia
1996

I have crossed borders at Oroville (Osoyoos, BC), Sumas (Hunting-don, BC), and Blaine (Vancouver, BC), in Washington. It was the quietest at Oroville but not bad at Sumas. It was a zoo at Blaine since it is near Vancouver; however, it was noon, and I usually cross as early in the morning as possible. Sometimes the chaos is part of the fun.

Many routes lead to Prince George, British Columbia. This is the jumping off place and decision time for anyone going to the Alaska Highway via Dawson Creek from the south. Anyone coming from the East through Edmonton, would likely go directly to Dawson Creek. Don't be confused by the two Dawsons. Dawson Creek is in BC. Dawson City is in Yukon Territory, 1,195 miles farther northwest.

A number of interesting attractions are in lower BC, but I have rarely looked them up. I can see this area sometime when I am not going the long distance to Alaska. If you have plenty of time and you want to see everything as you travel, read The Northwest Milepost or the CAA (Canadian Automobile Association) TourBook. They will give you all the information you need.

Since I had traveled on the usual roads going north and south on other trips, In 1996, I took alternate routes wherever they presented themselves. The first one was going north from Sumas to Mission, BC, and turning right on Highway #7, eventually meeting up with Trans-Canada Highway #1, near Hope, BC.

Mission was experiencing springtime in full April bloom. I looked and sniffed and enjoyed. With heading north, I knew I would see little of spring again until June. Highway #7 is a leisurely route following the north side of the Frazer River. Both #7 and #1 to Hope go through beautiful farming country. I had every intention of stopping in Hope on my way back to see the wooden chainsaw sculptures the town is famous for, but I returned a different route. Ah, another time.

I was on a decided high after crossing the border. The clouds were playing hopscotch in the blue skies as I drove through the Frazer River Canyon. Cement barriers kept the road out of the river and spring landslides off the road. A fresh dusting of snow crowned the mountaintops. The afternoon warmth added more snowmelt to falls already gushing down every gully, gap and crevice.

At Old Alexandra Bridge, I hiked over the Frazer River near Hell's Gate, the narrowest part of the canyon. This beautiful old rainbow bridge is only for walking across since the new bridge was built in 1962. Giant logs and debris swirled in runoff turbulence, a little unnerving with major cracks separating one bridge end from the riverbank.

Hiking unknown territory is like driving down a new road. A short hike becomes "over the hill and around the bend" to see where the path leads. This led to a gigantic landslide and washout. On the way back, I found a Jeep parked with its lights on and all the doors locked. I hoped someone wasn't hiking back to a dead battery.

Canada's provincial parks are great. I often pull into campgrounds to see what they offer even if I'm not staying. I took advantage of dumping and filling with water at Skihist Provincial Park. Firewood has been provided free in the past, usually in large pieces. *(In 2001, scuttlebutt was that Canada contemplates a firewood charge.)* Some parks have a camping fee; some are free; others are on the honor system.

The warmth of mid-day drew me to an early stop at Goldpan Provincial Park on the Thompson River. After collecting tinder and kindling, I sat beside a crackling fire and enjoyed the surrounding scenery. Trains running occasionally alongside the river weren't obnoxiously noisy, just interesting, perhaps because I was in a state of euphoria.

It was really cold in the night. Flannel sheets kept me cozy and nobody, except God, knew I was sleeping past 6 a.m. I prayed for everybody in the world, so I could stay in my comfortable warm bed a little longer without feeling guilty. Guilt is a strange taskmaster.

I wear three sets of clothing in a day's time. I dress for the day, change into ratty clothes for dirty chores, and wear still others for stoking smoky fires. Three pairs of shoes also got a workout. I was breaking in hiking boots that I wound up wearing almost the entire trip. A pair of scroungy campfire tennis shoes lounged by the door. Black boots were at the ready so I could look like something other than a bag lady if I wanted to dress up. Dress up, meaning a pair of clean Jeans and a reasonably unratty sweatshirt, or a long skirt and top for church. They aren't too formal in the North Country (neither are most full-time RVers).

A train came along as I stepped out the door for a walk. The engineer opened his window to wave at me. It was a nice communication for 7 a.m. in a strange place. Bouquets of growing daisies made me aware of spring wonders. Snowplows coming south just made me wonder.

It was a magnificent first full day in Canada. Orchards hovered on the edge of the Thompson River Valley's curvy canyon route. Smoke shivered and curled from cabin chimneys into the cold morning air. Cowpaths wandered through the meadows looking for cows. A tiny church awaited Sunday. The wind tilted at windmills. One white-paddled windmill, more patriotic than the rest, proudly sported a red Canadian maple leaf in its center.

In 2001, I crossed at Osoyoos. Turning off #97 south of Kelowna, I took 97C west through beautiful mountain country to Canada #1 and stopped for the night near Spence's Bridge. For a $5 (Canadian) fee, I had a clutch of aspen trees almost all to myself. But I didn't learn from the first time I camped there. I had forgotten that train tracks crawl along both sides of the valley. Trains are often and engineers blow their horns all the way home. As I continued into this fourth trip, it was fun recognizing villages or countryside where I had traveled previously.

A hitchhiker gave me a beautiful smile. I waved. No way, Jose. On the other hand, if he had been a little more appealing -- say with gray hair and blue eyes. A caution sign warned of mountain sheep on the highway. Immediately beyond the curve, two sheep munched by the roadside. Obviously, they read signs in Canada, eh? I knew I was deep in Canada. I stopped at the Goldpanner Restaurant for breakfast, and the owner's sentences all ended with "eh?" I was in Canada for sure!

North on Highway #97 at Cache Creek, I saw black plastic mesh tarps covering crops of North American Ginseng. I hadn't seen ginseng growing since a trip to Korea. A sign, "Cariboo Community Project," preceded miles of people clearing roadside debris.

Many towns along here were stagecoach stops. Their names reflect the distances along the Cariboo Wagon Road to the goldfields from Lillooet, i.e., 70-Mile House, 100-Mile House.

Friday, May 18, 2001, had special significance. Between those houses this trip, the Sprinter's odometer turned to six nines, then six zeros, with the one slowly turning to two. He started on his third 100,000 miles. We toasted with a Pepsi and milk cocktail. His miles-per-gallon increased from six to seven.

Fuel and rest area stops are good times to clean the windshield and fill the windshield washer reservoir. While you're at it, wipe off your headlights, back lights, and reflectors.

At Williams Lake, the sign over a deeply wrinkled, flashy red Mustang, said, "120 -- 0 in 3.1 seconds. Speed is killing us."

Animals are another reason for traveling in early spring. Deer and moose-warning signs cropped up at about the same time. A tiny colt tried his newfound legs. A horse ran down a hill with a long stick in his mouth, playing like a dog.

Quesnel is a bustling community in historical Cariboo gold territory. The information center museum has the history and artifacts. I once met Santa Claus there! The town celebrates their annual Billy Barker Days in July, commemorating this Cornish miner's first gold in the rush of 1862.

This is a decision stop for an interesting side trip east to Barkerville Provincial Historic Park, on Highway #26. Tours are available during the season. It is a beautiful 102-mile round trip through Devil's Canyon and along the shores of Jack-of-Clubs Lake. It also passes Cottonwood House Provincial Park that includes a restored 1864 log roadhouse.

Barkerville is a restored Cariboo gold rush town. When I visited in 1992, CBS was shooting a TV special, Jack London's "Call of the Wild" with Ricky Schroeder. The park is open all year. The buildings and history are interesting, but the bakery has fresh goodies and coffee (even more interesting). During the season, costumed interpreters and street performers add to the daily drama. It is worth a side trip.

The road to Barkerville also leads to Bowron Lakes Provincial Park, a place I'd like to kayak (when I find a partner...or a guide). It is a series of connecting lakes creating a 72-mile, canoe-kayak loop trail.

A favorite stop is north of Quesnel at Cinema Second Hand. It is an unassuming general store with groceries, new and used furniture, movie rentals, and souvenirs. They offer free camping and the coffee is always on, but what has taken me back repeatedly, is the friendliness of the owners, Vic and Theresa Olson. Their own RV lives in the back yard.

The store is open every day from 9 to 9. They enjoy people and think it is fun offering a freebie. Of course it is impossible for RVers to bypass browsing any more than I did. I only had US funds, but Vic paid me the exchange rate. Most businesses take a percentage if you don't have their currency. Vic said he didn't think it was right when his fellow Canadians didn't give the exchange rate. God bless him.

In 2001, it was my first time to arrive late enough in the season to enjoy the evening campfires where neighbors and RVers get acquainted and tell tall tales, the usual campfire stuff. Even with blankets though, it was very, very cold. As I pulled away the next morning, Theresa waved from the window. It was beginning to feel like family.

Prince George is a city of 76,000, and the last really big one until you reach Fairbanks (85,000), or Anchorage (260,000). At this point, continue on Highway #97 to Dawson Creek, the beginning of the Alaska Highway, or turn west on Yellowhead Highway #16 and go north on the Cassiar (Highway #37). The Cassiar is a shorter route by 123 miles, but it works well to go up one direction and return the other. For first-timers, I recommend Dawson Creek first.

April, 1992

I drove west as far as I could go to get a look at Prince Rupert, BC This city of 25,000 is a main port for the Alaska Marine Highway and BC ferries. It is an alternate route with connections, rates, and descriptions well documented in the Milepost.

From Prince Rupert I returned east along the beautiful Skeena River and headed north on the Cassiar Highway (Highway #37). April was too early in the season for anything to be open and Meziadin Junction Provincial Park was deep with snow. This campground is at the junction where you turn to go to Hyder.

Hyder, fall, 1996

Don't miss going to Hyder, the Friendliest Ghost Town in Alaska, and the southernmost Alaskan community you can drive to, 900 miles from Seattle. The only way to reach Hyder, except by water, is to drive through Stewart, BC. Following the cliffs, the paved road ended at the Alaska border and beyond was a dirt, potholed road. The sign said 20 mph, not that you could go any faster.

Friendliest Ghost Town. Hyder. AK

Stewart and Hyder are at the head of the Portland Canal, a 90-mile saltwater fjord, and natural boundary between Alaska and Canada. It follows the Misty Fjords National Monument Wilderness all the way from the Pacific.

Friends would love to see me do something that has been popular in Hyder since the 1800s, and that is to get "Hyderdized." This involves downing an ounce of whiskey in one gulp. I would be dancing across the Portland Canal without benefit of a ship.

In Hyder's Home Town Cafe, I asked the lady who was cooking, if she was Laura Lee. I didn't expect her to remember me from 1992, but she said, "I know exactly who you are." She pointed to the bulletin board behind me. One of my yellowed columns was pinned to it. "I wasn't sure you'd still be here." "We've been here 25 years and we'll be here forever." I left my copy of *RVing North America* so she could read about Hyder. Susan at Northern Stars Gift Shop said a moose and a bear were hanging around town. The week before the bear had come halfway through the shop's doorway. She yelled and he scrambled back outside. Mothers have special voices for expected behavior and he had heard that tone before.

Susan said a customer had given her a copy of a magazine with Hyder on the cover. It was the Escapee magazine with a Hyder Street scene on it that I had taken in 1992. I gave magazine copies to both Susan and Laura Lee. They were thrilled. They love their little town and I don't blame them.

I had been on Salmon Creek Road to the mine sites, and above the

Salmon Glacier, with the Cushmans in 1987. In 1992, I started up with the motorhome and changed my mind (unusual). It is narrow, steep, winding and worth a trip, but it is safer in a car or truck. If the snows are melting or it has been raining, the gravel road has many washouts. Tours are available to the mines and glacier.

I parked at Fish Creek Bridge and worked for a couple of hours, hoping to see bears catching salmon. They must have stayed in for dinner that night, but it is a popular spot for watching bears and bald eagles.

I went back to the Home Town Cafe for a halibut dinner. I felt like a celebrity. Laura Lee had told her friends about the books. We had a question, answer, and autograph session before dinner.

As on earlier visits, everyone was friendly. I felt warm and fuzzy, and hated to leave, but Hyder winters are legendary. I've heard stories about walking out second story doors and tunneling out at ground level. As nice as they were, I wasn't prepared to stay for the winter. Actually, I'd like to see it in the winter. I filled with gasoline at Hyder's only gas station, and stopped at Canadian Customs. This was something new. Customs were not there during previous visits.

Hyder and beyond, Spring, 2001

In 2001, as in 1992, I drove the Cassiar first and I discovered that leaving in mid May rather than the last week of April, I was meeting more people. I camped at Meziadin Junction Provincial Park, 96 miles north on the two-lane Cassiar Highway.

Drizzly rain accompanied my trip into Hyder. Driving toward the coastal mountains was a study in black and white with snow and trees and a few spring green leaves thrown in. Snow, rock and dirt slides had come down the mountains with such force that trees were broken off like matchsticks. I wondered why a van was stopped in the road leading to the wayside view above where Bear Glacier calves into Bear Lake. I went around him and found a snow-blocked entrance.

From the highway, I saw where new calving had left pristine, blue-tinged, Bear Glacier ice. The lake was melting but still covered with floating ice. It didn't make sense that a house was being built immediately next to the glacier and in proximity to many slides. I discovered later that it was part of a movie set, eventually to be blown up. So much for the delicate environment.

Bear River winds its way through the canyon. Beavers had created dammed lakes alongside the elevated roadway. Sturdy cement electric poles were further sturdied by enormous rock piles around their bottoms in this active avalanche area. Clouds danced around the mountain peaks still deep with snow, spring falls dove dramatically off rugged rocked canyon walls. A bald eagle flew across my eye line. Wow.

At first glance, Hyder hadn't changed much. The new gas station had closed since I was there last. Much to my distress, the one local landmark that I returned to each time, the Border Café, was now a rented house. Tourist shops where I had become slightly acquainted were either not open yet or closed permanently.

Hyder post office gets mail only on Tuesdays and Thursdays. It was Tuesday. I hoped for Priority Mail but it was not to be. I had it forwarded to Tok. Chatting with the Postmaster, I discovered things weren't as bad as they looked in Hyder. A new water plant is almost a sure thing and will bring lots of jobs with it. I hoped for it too because I'd hate to see this charming little village go down the tube after all its historical years.

I stayed two nights in the seldom full, 46 multi-level-site campground, each with a great view of Meziadin Lake. The second afternoon, what should pull in but two RVs that had been at Second Hand Cinema.

Vern and June Lawton were traveling in a blue converted bus. Their friends, also in a motorhome, were Judy and Terry Huegli, all of Yuma, Arizona. I went to say hello and they invited me to a campfire. A couple from England and the campground hostess joined us. She kept us entertained with her stories of living in the North Country.

The next day I continued along the Cassiar, remembering. I drove it through a whiteout blizzard on May Day, 1992. I also remembered the milk and mustard I cleaned up when the refrigerator contents went topsy-turvy on the rough road.

I spent the night near Dease Lake beside a roaring stream. I still hadn't decided whether to drive to Telegraph or not. The road was open, and it hadn't rained for a couple of days. It was the right time. After filling with gas, I decided to go for it. I wasn't sure I had made the right turn. I asked a lady walking to work alongside the road. She said, "You're on the right road but be careful, I hear it is awfully windy and steep."

The first sign I saw on Telegraph Creek Road was "Check your fuel gauge." Fortunately, the Sprinter was already gassed up.

Two creatures, one a bit smaller than the other, were in the road ahead of me. Binoculars confirmed they were lynx. The second and third I'd ever seen.

The first part of the 70-mile drive was a good gravel road with occasional glimpses of the Tanzilla River, which eventually joined the Stikine River. Somewhere the Tuya River and the Tahltan River connected with the Stikine, too. It went through an old burn area and I had great views of snow-covered Mt. Edziza. I thought, "If this if is all the road is going to throw at me, I've got it made in the shade." When will I ever learn?

About 45 miles in, I hit the first 18% grade with narrow switchbacks that took a sharp turn to cross a bridge. I'll mention here that this road isn't recommended for large RVs or trailers. I don't consider the Sprinter a "large" RV so I didn't plan on any problems. However, 18% is steep, and what goes down must come up. I thought about that as I drove on.

The next downhill grade was 20%. The Sprinter had tears in his

Sealbeams. "What's wrong, Sprinter?"

"You promised, no more gravel roads."

Yeah, but this is such a good one.

"With 18 and 20% grades? Lucky you don't have to hold this load back or pull it up."

"You're a good boy and I'm lucky to have you. It could be worse, remember the 26% grades on California #108?"

Road to Telegraph, BC

Believe it or not, right then a rest area appeared! I drove through a herd of munching horses who gave me a rather confounded look. I parked, found my walking stick (actually a broken hoe handle I threw in at the last minute – hey, I put a lot of thought into my adventures), and went down the steep path to a plateau above the river gorge, not realizing much better photo opportunities were further on. However, I would have missed the good conversation with the horses and the French three-some who also stopped there. That wasn't much of a conversation since the only French word I could remember was "Frommage" and I knew that meant cheese, only appropriate if I were taking their picture. The road wasn't through with me yet. After following a ridge above the Tahltan and Stikine Rivers, I finally got a good view of what is called the Grand Canyon of the Stikine and some neat pictures. Then I had a glimpse of the next 18% downhill grade. This time it made a sharp right turn across the Tahltan River. The road passed by some Indian smokehouses and from there continued to be a much narrower road with most of it right on the Stikine Canyon Wall, making for some hairy driving. This could turn hair gray but since mine was already there, no problem. I thought this group of buildings was Telegraph but then looked at the odometer and realized I still had 14 miles to go.

Given the narrow, winding, steep road with no place to go but down, I found some very good photo ops and it was worth the drive. Passing through another Indian community, I went one last narrow, downhill distance into Telegraph. A road continued on to Glenora but I had reached Telegraph, and that was picturesque enough. I parked at the Stikine River Song Café, Lodge, and General Store but it wasn't open. Actually I don't think I could have parked my "small" rig anywhere else. This building is a renovated 1898 Hudson's Bay Company building.

Houses literally perched on the mountainside. Most were empty and dated back to the gold rush era. Coming up from Wrangell on the Pacific Inside Passage, this was one of the "all Canadian" routes to the Klondike goldfields, though it was discovered, one of the more difficult ones. Telegraph was also one of the telegraph communication terminals that linked Dawson City with Vancouver

As I walked along the riverfront, I wondered if I had stepped "back in time," but late-model trucks were parked here and there. Nothing was open (May 24) and I didn't see a single soul working or walking or driving. Even the local RCMP building was locked. I guess it was a good thing I wasn't in trouble. Tiny St. Aidan's Anglican Church had a note on the door that the Priest would be there for Holy Days and Special Occasions. My arrival didn't count as a Special Occasion.

I had to face it, nobody was home in Telegraph – either that or I was a lot more threatening than I felt. Nobody wanted to sell me a T-shirt or a hamburger or a boat tour. The Stikine River and I were the only ones moving. I would have thought I was in a ghost town except for one porch light that was lit.

On the way out, on one of those narrow curves with nowhere to go, I came nose to nose with a car. The lady in the passenger seat gave me a wide-eyed look. They pulled into the turnout to let me ease on by.

A calcium chloride tanker was parked near a bridge. He could see me coming for at least a mile. I waved as I passed him and did an immediate right to go up the 18% grade, trying to get up speed on the curve. As I rounded the corner, I realized a grader was working on it. He had piled about 1½ feet of dirt and huge rocks in the road's center. The road was narrow enough I had to straddle the hump and I couldn't stop or I would have been stuck. The grader quickly backed up so I could continue at full speed. I grappled the Sprinter to the top and stopped. I checked the Sprinter's undersides but didn't see anything broken. The Sprinter didn't say a word. I was furious.

I'm sure it wasn't in the tanker driver's job description to get out and stop me but it would have been nice if he had gotten off his duff long enough to warn me a grader was working around the curve and up the hill. If I had broken the oil pan or anything else, I was mad enough to go back down the hill and wrap it around his neck. Road rage at its worst.

After breathing a sigh of relief and managing the various steep grades on the way back, I had one major thought as I turned north along the Cassiar. I'll bet the people at the end of that road don't drive out for a quart of milk.

Telegraph

In 1987, the Carrs and Cushmans pulled into Mighty Moe's campground on Cotton Lake. Mighty Moe took me up the Dease River and dumped me and a 15-foot canoe, with several big logs for ballast, and I paddled back to his camp-ground in my first solo canoeing experience. Perhaps that short two-hour but peaceful isolated wilderness canoe trip planted a seed for tackling the Mighty Yukon nine years later.

Mighty Moe was an eccentric backwoods Canadian character who entertained the campers in his primitive campground with questionable stories and songs played on the backside of a frying pan. In 1992, I made an emergency stop there. Mighty Moe wasn't home but the Sprinter and I stayed the night, entertained by moose and beaver in his absence. In 1996, the place was called Moose Meadows. Mighty Moe was in a nursing home and I never saw him again.

The campground has changed. Most people would say it is nicer and I suppose more people will be tempted to stop. I hope you will, but keep on the lookout. I have a strong feeling that the slightly off-kilter, free spirit of Mighty Moe, who called himself, "The Godfather of Highway 37," will always roam the shores of Cotton Lake.

Though I love traveling the Cassiar, I think all first timers should travel the Alaska Highway the first time so let's go back to Prince George.

Prince George to Whitehorse

Spring, 1996

Leaving Prince George, I continued on Highway #97 (Also called John Hart Highway), toward Dawson Creek and the Alaska Highway. All the highways you'll be on are named after someone; but they also have number names. It can be confusing.

This is a good time to tell you that I avoid cities like the plague unless there is something within its limits that particularly calls to me. I prefer small towns, villages, and the country; therefore, my stories tend to cover those areas.

I was seeing the first frozen lakes and ice-clogged streams. The rock and roll had begun. The bad spots were flagged. I knew from that point on I'd have to pay close attention to the road ahead of me.

Mackenzie

Have you ever noticed how we North Americans always have the tallest, lowest, highest, sweetest, biggest, or mightiest? Mackenzie's population of 6,000 is no different; they think big. They have two claims to fame: North America's largest man-made reservoir at the south end of Lake Williston, and another that I wanted to take with me.

The Latourneau Tree Crusher is the World's largest tree crusher. It is a big yellow hummer that weighs 1,175 tons (about the same as the Sprinter, loaded), and powered by two Cummins V12 Diesel engines. It was built especially for crushing trees and undergrowth beneath its massive rollers to clear the flood plain under what is now Lake Williston.

I envied its 1,880-gallon fuel capacity, but I suppose signing a VISA slip for filling it would bring on instant cardiac arrest. I envisioned my Latourneau Diesel Sprinter scaring little old ladies who pull in front of me going three miles an hour. On the other hand, now that I am one, I might have to revise that whole train of thought.

Turning north again on Highway #97, I followed two small moving vans and a car who were traveling together, s l o w l y. I didn't really mind, since giant Cats lurked on every curve across Pine Pass and snail's pace driving was necessary. They were pushing aside mud and snow and building a new road.

Another reminder, don't Tailgate! It is irritating to have someone chewing on your bumper, not to mention dangerous. If possible, pull over and let a tailgater pass. If you have even a small train of vehicles behind you, allow them to pass.

The neat thing about RVing is that after a spell of white-knuckle driving, you can stop in one of many pull-offs. Notes from my log:

Time for a coffee break. Took garbage out and boy is it cold out there. Sunshiny day, hot cup of coffee, bumpy roads, fantastic scenery, what more could I ask for, except maybe a moose, but please, God, not right in the center of the road, unless I see him first.

It was 30 kilometers into Chetwynd when I saw the herd of buffalo. I had two thoughts, buffaloburgers, because I was hungry; and if I ran out of gasoline, I could become Buffalo Gal and ride one into town. Let's see, if I guessed right, I had roughly seven gallons of gasoline times six miles per gallon. All right. I would have about a 22-mile leeway.

The gas pump wasn't working right. I kept the young lady company for the 45 minutes it took her to pump gas into the Sprinter. She was from Russia. I noticed she didn't mind the bitter cold. She said that Pine Pass was a super highway that day compared to what it was throughout the winter. Good grief.

Dawson Creek
I forgot to tell you to take stock in Kodak or Fuji as one of your preps for this trip.

A major Kodak Moment is having your picture snapped in front of Milepost "0" on Tenth Street near the traffic circle. The Visitor Infocentre, in a restored railway station, and the Dawson Creek Station Museum, are nearby in NAR Park at Tenth Street and Alaska Avenue. A neat stop is a restored wooden grain elevator turned into the Dawson Creek Art Gallery. It was rescued from demolition for one dollar and revamped to the tune of $250,000. The Alaska Café has good food and live nightly entertainment (in season).

Often people spend a few days making sure everything on their RV is copacetic with the long trip ahead. This is where the caravans often gather their RV trip people.

Chetwynd

Since the 1996 trip was one of exploring new routes for me, let's return to Chetwynd where I turned on to Highway #29, the Hudson's Hope Loop route and follow the Peace River. Many turnouts beckoned. I stopped on the frozen Moberly Lake shoreline and stayed long enough for lunch and a VCR movie.

Confused Canada geese with ruffled feathers, wandered about looking for open water. I overheard one of them, "I told you so, Myrtle. We're too early. We're just too early! We could still be paddling..."

Deer were everywhere! Huge deer herds roamed throughout the Peace River Valley. Individual deer grazed peacefully with horses or cows. This would not be a road to travel at night.

A side road led to the Peace Canyon Dam. At Hudson's Hope, it was a 15-mile drive off the loop to the 600' high W.A.C. Bennett Dam that holds up the eastern arm of Williston Lake. It is one of the largest earth-filled dam structures in the world. Lake Williston is BC's largest body of fresh water. Again, the "biggest and the largest."

The Hudson Bay Company opened its first trading post at Hudson's Hope in 1805. That was well after the mammoths called it home. The museum with the artifacts, the fossils and the 11,600-year-old mammoth tusk, was closed. Instead, I took pictures of the little log St. Peter's Anglican United Church next door. An automotive shop had a sign, "Grizzly Repairs." I'd like to see them repair a grizzly...or could it have referred to the results? Hmmm.

I thought I had found the perfect place to camp on a cliff above the river, well away from the road. There were trees and a place for a fire, but then I discovered a smelly deer carcass thrown over the edge. It was a little too fragrant for my taste.

A 10% grade took the Sprinter past some major washouts to a nearly 3,000' elevation, with a magnificent view of the Peace River Valley and the snow-covered mountains.

The Sprinter and I junctioned with the Alaska Highway. It saved 23 miles but it was more about exploring a new road than saving miles. As you came out of Dawson Creek, did you stop to see the (didn't I tell you about this tendency to hyperbolize?) World's Largest Glass Beehive in Fort St. John, north of Dawson Creek?

I stayed in a rest area for the night and woke up to several inches of snow. I stayed put until about ten o'clock. A snowplow came in and when he left, I followed. How much safer could I be? He turned around about three miles up the road! I ran in and out of heavy snow, according to the elevation I was driving. It was May 1, and shades of the Cassiar Highway and the blizzard I drove through on May Day 1992. The weather wasn't my worst problem; the brakes were failing.

At Pink Mountain, the mechanic said the Sprinter might need brake fluid. He said the place to check it was up under the side of the motorhome, and he couldn't do it in that weather. I couldn't blame him for that but I was just as sure the brake fluid reservoir was inside under the doghouse. Alas, I wasn't going to argue with him, and it was against the law to put a gun to his head. He said he didn't know anywhere I could get help before Fort Nelson. That was 143 miles away. I asked him if there were any really steep hills in between (since I didn't remember). He said the only bad one was about 12 miles ahead. He didn't tell me it was Suicide Hill. With hot coffee in hand and a prayer on my lips, I took off.

The snowflakes were getting bigger. One great flake covered the entire windshield, not to mention the medium-sized flake behind the steering wheel. A truck flew by throwing rocks and just missing an oncoming car right off my bumper. Where is the World's Largest Tree Crusher when you need it?

Signs warned of dangerous curves, avalanches, and breaks in the pavement (as in, the pavement disappeared entirely). The wet gravel was slippery. A heavy snow sheet slowly slid off the roof, loading my windshield wipers to the point they were doing little work. Other than the slippery mud, curvy roads, steep hills, the blizzard, and my brakes going out, the Sprinter and I were cool. We maneuvered down Suicide Hill. I just hoped it wasn't a harbinger of things to come. Before modification through the years, the original Suicide Hill had a sign posted, "Prepare to meet thy Maker."

Obviously I survived Suicide Hill, but by the time I saw the Buckinghorse River Lodge, I figured it was time for some C & C (company and coffee). Here is a good time to share one of life's lessons.

If you find lemons in one place, drive down the road 30 miles and you just might find a lemon drop.

Over a delicious cup of hot coffee served by Dave, I shared the whimsical view of my day thus far. He worried about my trying to make it all the way to Fort Nelson. "Why don't you let me look?" he said. As I thought, the reservoir was under the doghouse, but in a very awkward spot that I couldn't have reached if my life depended on it (and it did!).

He used his own equipment and brake fluid. It was only a little low. As we walked by the hood, he asked if I had checked the engine oil. I guess he figured if the brake fluid was low, I hadn't checked anything else either. I can *reach* that.

He refused to allow me to pay for his time or the brake fluid. In the course of further conversation, he discovered I was a writer and wanted to see my three books (at that time). I bought coffee and postcards and he bought a book (I tried to give it to him, but he refused). We both paid in Canadian, but somehow I think I got the best of that deal. I meet the nicest people. By the way, they also offer free camping for the night at Buckinghorse River Lodge. I looked at the sites as I pulled out. They were deep with snow.

Unfortunately, the brake light came back on. Fluid wasn't the problem. I continued to Fort Nelson.

At Trutch Mountain, the powers that be have eliminated the route over the top. At 4,134', it was the second highest summit on the Alaska Highway. As so much of the original road has been straightened, leveled, rerouted, or improved, so this mountain was bypassed. With the Sprinter in his brake-weary condition, I should have been grateful.

It's unreasonable I know, but I feel that every curve that is straightened and every hill that is cut down, somehow takes away from the adventure of traveling it. Case in point, 132 curves were eliminated in one area between here and Fort Nelson. Certainly no one could drive it with a RV if it hadn't been improved immensely since 1942, but hey, don't get carried away. By the way, if you don't know Alaska Highway history, take time to read the various signs or stop at the museums that offer it. It is fascinating.

It was 4:30 by the time I reached Fort Nelson, too late to get anyone to fix the brakes even if they were so inclined. Now I'll share another traveling lesson with you.

Whenever I am in strange territory (most of the time) and I need repairs, I stop at a parts store, usually NAPA, for their recommendation of someone local.

This has never failed me. They gave me two names. I hit the jackpot with Harry's Auto Repair, Ltd.

I figured the brakes would get fixed about three weeks from the following Tuesday. Smack me for being so negative. Harry Clark scheduled me in for 8 a.m. The shock must have been evident on my face. He said he keeps one bay open for people passing through. He gave me permission to park next to the shop for the night.

I cooked dinner and watched TV. The weather outside was frightful but the RV was cozy and delightful, at least until 2:30 a.m. Two youngsters banged on my door. Another lesson:

Don't ever open your door to anybody unless you know who it is.

I opened the window a crack. They asked for a tomato. Several other kids lurked in the shadows. I said, "I just ate my last tomato. Go home!" I slammed the window shut. When I didn't act frightened or rise to their bait, apparently it discouraged them. They left. Another lesson:

Park so you can move forward in case you need to make a fast getaway.

Harry's crew began work at 8 a.m. Once in a while one of the guys would show me what needed replacing or tell me what they were doing. By 4 p.m., they had replaced one drum completely; replaced pads, rear shoes, and seals; cleaned my windshield and wiper blades (he said I didn't need new ones), and declared the Sprinter roadworthy once more. A spring had lost its clamp. He showed me where it had rubbed against the tire. They fixed that, too.

Since I knew I was leaving the territory, I requested a test drive with Harry as my passenger. Wow! I had brakes. I didn't realize how bad they had gotten. When I pulled up to let him out, he said, "You know how to handle this thing pretty well." I considered that a high compliment.

The bill, $936.95, translated to $693.02 US. On returning to the Canadian border the end of September, the entire GST tax was refunded.

In my defense, several months before I left for Alaska, on my list to be checked, were the brakes and the brake fluid. It was my fault for not asking, but only the brake *fluid* was checked, not the brakes. Lesson:

Start making a list and checking it twice...

Once when you take your RV in to be fixed,
And once when you get it back.

It will make a difference in whether your trip is naughty or nice.

The next 100 miles didn't disappoint me. The jagged peaks of the Rocky Mountains were smothered in snow. Streams breaking loose from their icy shackles were making their way through deep mounds of snow and ice in the valleys. Drunken sailor-type animal tracks wandered across an ice-covered lake. Caution signs warned of caribou, but the tracks were empty. They don't read as well as deer.

I drove in and out of paved highway and gravel road. Did I mention steep and winding, my favorite kind? The Sprinter groaned a couple of times in the soft dirt. The Cats were busy again, reworking the road and rescuing it from winter ravages.

Summit Lodge advertised grizzlyburgers. (I've had grizzly burgers before but that was the result of my own cooking.) My stomach growled and I looked forward to a treat. The lodge, the highest point on the Alaska Highway at 4,250', was closed tighter than a drum. Most Provincial campgrounds were sleeping in deep snow.

It was extremely cold hiking near the stream at 113 Creek Provincial Campground (more of a rest stop next to the highway), where I parked for the night. I thought I was going to have it to myself, but before I went to sleep, a motorhome and a truck camper pulled in.

I love getting up in the early morning. Actually, that isn't true. I like *being* up in the early morning. The physical act of *getting* out of a warm, cozy nest is questionable. In this case, I had help. It came about 3 a.m. in the form of another adventurer off to see the world. This traveler was tiny compared to humans, and carried his own warmth on his back. He wasn't an animal activist; his coat was genuine mouse fur.

Although I'm usually a friendly sort, I draw the line at middle-of-the-night visitors. Having had major experiences of this type previously, the wee scrambling sounds in my rolling mansion brought a whimper to my lips and a groan, "Oh, no, not again." I prayed that I was wrong, that I merely had an overactive imagination.

Finally I got out of bed, turned on the light, and there he was in the middle of the motorhome. We stared at each other. He moved toward me. Now, I am this fearless, brave, I-am-woman type traveler, right? Wrong! When he headed toward me, I screamed and climbed up on my bed. There was no way I was going to take a chance he would run across my bare feet. When he disappeared, I put on my hiking boots, and went out in the frigid cold to fetch the mousetraps from the hold.

He avoided my traps and continued to make so much noise, I wondered if he was accompanied by a herd of elephants, but then I concluded there was more than one mouse in my house. I filled a wastebasket half way full with water and pasted some cheese on one side, posted a "Ye Olde Swimming Hole" sign, and hoped the whole gang would go for a dip. Fat chance. By 4:45 it was getting light. Since I couldn't sleep, I took off.

Despite everything, it was a gorgeous morning. The sun painted the mountain peaks with pink frosting. The sheep, caribou and moose were hiding, probably because of the deep snow. I followed the Toad River until it turned. I traveled on alone until I reached Muncho Lake. Its frozen surface was no surprise.

This has to be one of the most beautiful areas I have ever seen, in any season. The elevation here is almost 2,700' with the mountains above it ascending to 7,000'. The road barely has room between the lake and the cliffs. When the lake is clear of ice, it is an incredible turquoise blue. Given the terrain, it isn't surprising that it is avalanche country. I parked to use a litter barrel and was startled by rocks scattering across the road. I got out of there.

I hadn't caught a mouse yet but as I rearranged the trap under the bed pedestal, my flashlight beam caught him staring at me. He was blatant and I told him so. Just because I jumped the night before was no sign I was going to continue being a wimp.

Major beauty doesn't stop at Muncho Lake. It continues. That morning several caribou ran across the road. I preferred them to a belligerent mouse. With no traffic to annoy me, I stopped in the middle of the Liard River Bridge. Ice chunks floated between thickly iced banks that extended well into the river. The owner of the Liard River Lodge said the ice had broken up with great rumbling and drama the night before.

Over coffee she told me they were trying to sell the lodge. I fell in love with the lodge and the Liard River and couldn't understand their giving it up; but then I hadn't dealt with tourists for eight years. I relayed my Mickey Mouse tale to her, hoping to find peanut butter in the small store, but their inventory was depleted. She gave me two peanut butter packets usually given out with breakfast toast.

I returned to the motorhome. A mouse was in the trap. Ha! He was a big hummer, almost the size of that World's Largest Tree Crusher. In case he wasn't the only one, I smeared peanut butter on top of the cheese for good measure, and in sadistic delight. They can't resist peanut butter.

One place you must never pass by is Liard Hot Springs Provincial Park. Usually moose are everywhere, last time even *in* my campsite. I must have parked on a moose trail because he was there the next morning, too. It is at least a 1/4-mile walk along a wide boardwalk to the first pool. Moose frequently feed in the wetlands nearby, but nary a moose showed his hide this time.

The hotsprings are heavenly. Alpha pool is the first one, more like a widened stream. Beta pool, a 1/4-mile farther through the woods, is larger and deeper, with a view of the mountains. Another boardwalk leads to the hanging gardens. Spring plants were tiny and nothing was blooming yet. A little snow here and there had survived the warmth.

Both pools have change houses and decks. Long wooden benches in the pools are great for stretching out on. Oooh baby, wooonnnderful. The third time I went in, sleet and snow melted into the hot pool around me. Cool. Very.

The campground has excellent dry-camp sites. It is open all year. The $15.50/night is fair, considering the hot springs, the fun, and informative interpretive programs during season. The campground fills early in the day. It is wise to plan ahead for this stop. Bear warning signs were tacked everywhere. It is safer to *always* be on the lookout for animals. This is wild country.

Less than 50 miles up the road, I parked in an undeveloped campground on a Liard River bend. I sat on rock formations that looked like God upended them on a restless day. Last trip I was invited to share an evening campfire with two couples. They had seen a bear run through my site while I was sitting on the rocks, as I was doing now.

I have had two letters from the North Carolina couple. When they first wrote, they said, "You probably won't remember us, but..." I could even pinpoint the date. They were in my notes, another good reason for keeping a log.

Mice were on the loose again, but I slept like limp spaghetti, a combination of no sleep, mice, and hot pools. Mouse #2 bit the dust. When the traps snap, it usually awakens me. I throw the culprit out the door, wash my hands, go back to bed, and reclaim the trap in the morning.

At a high point above the Liard River, I took my coffee outside to admire the view, and talked with a burly, full-bearded fellow from Hay River, in the Northwest Territories. I had wanted to drive there this trip, but decided against the turn near Fort Nelson because of the Mackenzie River. He confirmed the ice bridges were closed.

He suggested I come in early fall. I asked him what people do during the two-month interim between ice bridge and ferry. He said distances were so great that people fly in and out most of the year. Airplanes are the major transportation in the North Country.

Fritz came from Germany, had traveled the world, and raised nine kids alone, giving them all college educations. As we surveyed the magnificent scenery in front of us, he said, "I don't understand people looking at something like this, and not believing in God." Amen.

While we talked, his friend who had been down by the river, returned with two five-pound pieces of jade and other unusual, colorful rocks. If he did that at every stop, they were going back with a lot of weight.

Mile after mile of blackened trees were evidence of a 1982 fire that destroyed more than 400,000 acres. Often signs tell the fire stories. It is interesting to know when fires occur, when the land is replanted, and how long it takes for the forest to grow back.

Although history reveals that fire is nature's way of cleaning house, don't be guilty of starting one through your carelessness in campgrounds or along the road, please.

From spring through fall, the fireweed flowers are in some stage of beauty. They are the first to show promise after fires burn and blacken the countryside.

Watson Lake was flying both the American and Canadian flags on every pole. Neat.

Signpost, Watson Lake, AK Highway

Decision time

Skagway, Whitehorse, Tok, and Fairbanks, continuing on the Alaska Highway or North to Dawson City and Top of the World Highway to Chicken and Tok via the Campbell Highway.

We're going to do both.

2001

We'll fast forward to Mukluk Annie's on the Alaska Highway, 785 miles northwest of Dawson Creek on the Alaska Highway. Isn't this electronic age marvelous!

On previous trips, it was either too early or too late to take advantage of Mukluk Annie's free RV dump, free RV wash, and free camping. I found three levels of wooded campsites overlooking Teslin Lake and beyond to the snow-covered Coastal Mountains. They also offered powered pay sites, hot showers, a motel, gift shop, and a Laundromat with a floor so squeaky clean I hesitated to step on it.

A free evening ride on their 35-passenger houseboat was available if you partook of Mukluk Annie's Salmon Bake. Teslin Lake was icebound but they gave me an icecheck for a ride on my return in early September (With a flip of that special full-time RVing coin, I changed directions, but I'll tell you about that later).

The college student chef and waiter from Saskatchewan were talkative and interesting. The mini salmon steak and Bar-B-Que ribs combination with baked potato, salad, hot rolls, and an outstanding chocolate-plus-chocolate brownie that guaranteed a 3 a.m. headache, were mouth-watering.

A blue converted bus and a motorhome rolled in. I'll explain something I have observed over and over. Meeting RVers for the first time is nice, but it's unlikely names will be remembered 10 miles down the road. The second meeting is pleasant and address cards are exchanged. The third accidental meeting is like old home week.

I invited them to a campfire at my "digs" but I almost regretted it when all I could find was tinder and kindling firewood with nothing for fuel. Scouring the beach, I several times drug back as much as I could carry for two blocks and back up the hill. By that time I wished I hadn't made friends with anybody.

Ralph and Karen Gillespie from Colorado, had seen my Family Motor Coach emblem, found my name in the directory, and came down the hill to say hello. They were also fellow Escapees. I invited them to the fire, "For as long as it lasts," explaining that I was at a loss for enough large pieces. That was no problem, Ralph brought his trusty hatchet. I also invited Eldon and Margaret from Calgary, Alberta, to the fire, "For as long as it lasts." Al and Ralph scouted out tons of beach wood. I felt a little like Tom Sawyer. It needed cutting up but instead, I fed the big pieces into the fire foot by foot.

A Mississippi couple dropped by and soon the Arizona four came. It wasn't easy for Judy to get down the hill. She had broken her ankle several weeks before and hobbled about in a boot with crutches. Eventually, Jared and Shirley Johnson from Oregon joined us too. As they came, they introduced themselves and soon the perfect May evening was abuzz with getting acquainted and talking about where they had been or what they had experienced and asking questions.

"Have you seen very many animals?"

"Well, not this time, but in '96 I saw a black bear with triplets."

"Did you guys get "Hyderdized" at Hyder?"

"What kind of gas mileage do you get?"

"We found a great mechanic back in..."

"The time we went, it was covered with snow."

When they left three hours later, the Girl Scout in me stirred the fire with water until it was completely out, then took my tired body and put it to bed, a fantastic evening.

But that wasn't quite the end of it, Mukluk Chuck (He's like, you know, Mukluk Annie's husband) has an All-you-can-eat Unique Yukon Breakfast. This involved oversized blueberry pancakes with scrambled eggs, bacon and sausage. The whole gang was there to eat with the same buzz of conversation. We parted in the parking lot amid hugs and goodbyes, with most of us continuing North to Alaska.

As I sit here in February of 2002, typing stories like this one from the last trip, I smile and remember with great joy, and you will too. There is magic in that phrase, "North to Alaska" as it was for all those adventurers before us. And hug memories from new friends doesn't exactly detract from my warm fuzzies either.

A landmark on the Alaska Highway, Jake's Corners, was being sold but I could still buy gas there using a cardlock. The owner saw my puzzled look. He came over and made me do it myself because, "You may need to know this somewhere else." I finished and then couldn't get the receipt for the life of me. He pulled it out. I had been trying to lift it up. He said, "This is the technical part," laughed and gave me a hug.

With a full gas tank, I turned toward Atlin and 58 miles I hadn't traveled before. It was very good gravel road for about 40 miles, and paved the last 18 miles into Atlin. Dall sheep rested on a ledge around a rock corner. I pulled out of a rest area and saw a bear ambling up the highway. He kept looking back toward me but continued in the middle of the road. He finally ducked into the woods when a truck came barreling through.

I had a beautiful view of 85-mile-long Atlin Lake, BC's largest natural lake, and snowy Atlin Mountain at Norseman Adventures RV Park. I walked a back path into town and wandered around Atlin's picturesque old houses, many freshly painted in bright colors. The Pine Restaurant put out a mean hamburger and fries. The Globe Theatre and M. V. Tarahne are restorations are in progress. If I had time to return to all the places where I'd like to stay a while, Atlin would be one of them.

Atlin Mountain, British Columbia

The next day I didn't move too fast. It was raining and cozy to stay in bed. The people who owned the park stepped out on their porch to wave goodbye as I took off. After traveling through cattle, reluctantly moving calves and horses, I saw several abandoned mining buildings and Pine Falls, none of which I remembered seeing on my way in. Crossing a bridge that dammed a lake and starting up a narrow steep hill, which I also didn't recognize, I realized I was on the wrong road. The name of the Lake at the top of the hill was Surprise Lake – and was it ever. After checking the Milepost, I realized I had inadvertently taken the Discovery Road out of town. It ends at 11 miles and I had thought about going on it and the only other road out of town but the weather was so bad, I decided against it. However, with my knack for getting lost, I did it anyway. It was an unexpected adventure.

I don't often stop to visit people but Rena and Reub Fendrick, neighbors from North Ranch, had invited me to stop when I drove through the Yukon. I met their son and grandchildren and enjoyed my first moose roast that Rena fixed. Delicious!

Reub built their beautiful house overlooking Marsh Lake. They love it and so did I. I hinted but they didn't seem interested in adopting me. Reub retired from the Royal Canadian Mounted Police after 33 years of service. They told stories and showed slides of being stationed all over the Arctic including Inuvik where I had visited in 1996. I loved every minute of it. They lent me many Yukon history books, especially about Dawson City. Over the next few months, I literally inhaled them. They are very interesting world travelers and knew the owners of my favorite RV park in Sayulita, Mexico, where I stayed in 1989.

About 15 miles south of Whitehorse, we'll turn off the Alaska Highway for **Skagway, Alaska, and The Golden Circle Loop trip**.

Big Blue Canoe Deck, Skagway, AK

The Golden Circle Loop

and

On to Fairbanks

1996

I have traveled Klondike Highway #2 to Skagway four times, in May snow, twice in June green, and lastly, in a 2001, multi-colored September. Springtime 1992 road crews knocked loose rocks off the mountainsides and "netted" the cliffs so debris wouldn't fall on tourists who would come later in the season. Yellow Cats cleared rockslides.

Other tracks were deep indentations in the snow on their way to places I couldn't follow; filled with animals I couldn't see beyond the ridges and rocks. A perfect stranger (He seemed perfect at the time) I met at a pull off, offered to let me borrow his cross-country skis and return them to him in Whitehorse. I declined but appreciated the trust. In 1996, I carried my own cross-country skis for 10,000 miles and never used them.

Carcross is on the banks of Lake Bennett, part of the waterway the gold rushers used to eventually reach Dawson City. It was also a stop for the railroad to Whitehorse until service stopped in 1982. Although I haven't taken the time to do more than read about Carcross, its history is extremely interesting.

In May, the lakes, including beautiful Emerald Lake, were under a deep blanket of snow. The winter scenes were great for slides, but most people would prefer coming when tourist attractions are open in June.

The Yukon/Alaska border at the top of White Pass is open 24-hours during the season. Tall poles outlined the road for snowplows pushing through the deep snow. From White Pass, I could see the coastal mountains still in winter sleep. I started the 11.5 mile descent into Skagway and spring.

Skagway and Dyea

Don't shortchange Skagway; it exudes history. A good hike will take you to see most of it, but everything can be driven to as well, including the Klondike Gold Rush National Historical Park Visitor Center, a good place to start. I parked at the Pullen Creek RV Park by the small boat harbor. It was a convenient walk uptown or to watch the cruise ships come into the Lynn Canal.

Skagway (Haines) is the northernmost stop for the Alaska State Ferries (Southeast Route), following the 1,000 nautical miles on the Inland Passage from Bellingham, WA.

The former Dyea townsite is at the head of Taiya Inlet, an 18-mile round trip. It's a gravel road, curvy, scenic, and narrow in spots. I caught up with an organized hike. The ranger explained, "Dyea mostly washed away in the 1950s with flooding and the changing of the river's course. An archeologist witnessed pine boxes washing out to sea but was powerless to stop them. A few graves were removed to Slide Cemetery."

Dyea was an 1897 trading post and Native camp. With the Klondike Gold Rush, Dyea swelled to 8,000 and became a major port city for the stampeders. The poor harbor in Dyea, and the building of Skagway's White Pass and Yukon Route Railroad, led to Dyea's short life. The "Slide" cemetery is the burial site for victims of the April 3, 1898 snow slide. Inexperienced gold rushers paid dearly for their eagerness to get on the gold trail when others wisely waited.

Bits and pieces of Dyea surfaced as we poked through the woods. Everything is part of the historical site, and protected. Do not remove. The pilings of a huge warehouse are stark evidence of long ago prosperity. Remains of cabins and barns are all that are left.

The Chilkoot Trail trailhead is nearby. It was a major trading route between Indian tribes until the gold rush. The Canadian government required each gold rusher to have supplies for an entire year before entering Canada. On the Chilkoot Trail, it was 33 miles to Lake Bennett, but it included a 45-degree climb to Chilkoot Pass. These supplies all had to be carried up "The Golden Stairs," steps carved in the ice and snow. The rushers had to step up more than a foot for every one foot forward - almost like climbing a ladder.

Gold rushers built boats and continued by water to Dawson City. If they survived the arduous Chilkoot Trail, the winter, and the Whitehorse Rapids, they went on to Dawson City where they found for the most part, that the gold claims were already gone.

The Chilkoot Trail is "The Longest Museum in the World." The ranger told us, "When the snow melts, you can see everything from the soles of old shoes to steam engines."

Spring was in Skagway, but I couldn't leave well enough alone. I went looking for winter again. The White Pass & Yukon Route Railroad was finished too late for the gold rushers, but it kept Skagway alive, and today it is a great trip to the top of White Pass. Most of the way we chugged along the Trail of '98. Over 3,000 pack animals died at Dead Horse Gulch attempting to reach the top. Overloaded and neglected, they died without so much as a kind bullet.

The narrow-gauge railroad goes up one of the steepest grades in North America. The track climbs 2,885' in 20 miles to White Pass Summit. I went from spring to snow mounds higher than the train. We waited for a snowslide clearance, went through tunnels, over bridges, and looked back from Inspiration Point toward the Lynn Canal, the Harding

Glacier, and the Chilkat Mountain Range. Spectacular. It is three hours round trip and well worth the adventure.

The Arctic Brotherhood Hall has 20,000 pieces of driftwood nailed to its front, and the Red Onion Saloon has "ladies of the evening" flouncing around in the windows, wearing fancy clothes. These "painted ladies" are just that, painted on the windows. The stories are many; Mollie Walsh; Harriett Pullen; Jefferson "Soapy" Smith and his gang; and town hero, Frank Reid. You'll hear their names over and over. If you want to say hello, walk around the Gold Rush Cemetery.

Personally I love walking around old cemeteries reading gravestones, visiting and absorbing history. If you do, too, please remember to treat the grounds, graves, their inhabitants, and historic artifacts with respect. Someday, we'll all be subject to grave walkers.

Boarding Ferry, Skagway, AK

Well, I won't tell you all of Skagway's secrets. Take your time. When you leave Skagway, either return along the road you came in on or take a ferry.

I took the Sprinter for a ferry ride to Haines, Alaska. It was a great hour-long trip down the Lynn Canal, the continent's largest and deepest fjord. Fort William H. Seward and the Chilkat Mountains are the backdrop for Haines, and what a view that is coming into the harbor.

Most of my time was spent seven miles out of town at the Chilkat State Park on Mud Bay. Other than the hosts, Shirley and Victor Keitel of St. Louis, Missouri, I was the only one there. They kindly shared campfires and information with me. During the day, I parked near the water across from a hanging glacier. Porpoises played in the inlet and thousands of Arctic terns gave me background music to work by. *(In 2002, I still hear from the Keitels. Their travel adventure letters wear me out!)*

Eagles return to the Alaska Chilkat Bald Eagle Preserve just outside of Haines. I saw a lot of eagles but the preserve in October, is far more dramatic. Four thousand American bald eagles gather along a five-mile stretch of the Chilkat River each fall. It is the largest gathering of eagles in the world. Warm water upwellings in the river bottom, keep stretches of the Chilkat river ice free through the winter, providing salmon carcasses when food supplies elsewhere are exhausted.

The adult eagles have the distinct white "bald" head and tailfeathers but the immature eagle has mottled brown and white plumage. They can fly at 30 mph, and dive at 100 mph. I thought about getting one to keep my in-house mouse population down, but then I discovered their wing span is six to eight feet, and their average weight is 13 pounds. So much for that thought.

Eagles are federally protected.
Possession of any parts, including feathers, is illegal.

During season, you can see the Chilkat Native Dancers and hear the Tlingit legends. A self-guided walking tour is available through Fort William H. Seward, a Historic Landmark. The military post, permanently established in 1904, has an interesting history.

Haines is famous as an Alaskan artist community. I watched Gresham Gregg woodcarving at the Sea Wolf Gallery. I also recommend the Sheldon Museum and Cultural Center for the pioneer history and Tlingit Indian Culture. They may serve you "Russian Tea."

It was early May as I drove Haines Highway (Alaska Route #7). The area was bursting with snowshoe hare that year and that brings on the lynx, I can vouch for it. A lynx bounded to the road's edge and braked at the same time the Sprinter did. His blue eyes met mine for a thrilling instant, then he was gone like a shot.

I took off on a side road to Mosquito Lake and found a delightful State Recreation campground to wile away a few hours. It was too early for mosquitoes or maybe they were taking pity on me.

The scenic Haines Highway goes past the Tatshenshini-Alsek Wilderness Provincial Park, over Chilkat Pass into British Columbia, then into Yukon Territory, following a portion of Kluane National Park Reserve. Dezadeash Lake is a good place to stop, and don't fail to walk the boardwalk at the Million Dollar Falls. Both places have campgrounds.

Whether you camp or only admire the scenery, stop at Kathleen Lake. When Perry Como sang, "The bluest blue is in Seattle," he obviously hadn't been to the North Country. It is an incredible turquoise blue, glacier-fed lake. The setting is exceptional.

At Haines Junction, stop at the Kluane National Park and Yukon government visitor information centre. Always take the time to drive around these small towns. You'll always see something of interest. Many leftovers from the Alaska Highway construction have been used in unique ways. Our Lady of the Way Catholic Mission is in a Quonset hut surrounded by flower gardens.

I returned to Whitehorse on the Alaska Highway, completing "The Golden Circle Route" (Whitehorse, Skagway, Haines Junction -- approximately 362 road miles).

Whitehorse

With a population of around 24,000, the capital of Yukon Territory, Whitehorse, is the biggest city until you get to Fairbanks. Whitehorse was named after the frothing, churning Yukon River rapids that resembled charging white horses. If you're into hiking, trails lead along both sides of Miles Canyon with a connecting bridge.

Those rapids put an end to getting-rich dreams for many Klondike gold rushers who chanced going through Miles Canyon rather than portage around it. Some gave their lives to it. The rapids disappeared when the river was dammed to form Schwatka Lake. I've cruised the lake in the M. V. Schwatka. It is a pleasant, scenic, two-hour trip.

You can find just about anything you need in Whitehorse. They have nice campgrounds, restaurants, and entertainment. The stern wheeler, SS Klondike, is permanently berthed on the Yukon River bank. It plied the Yukon from Whitehorse to Dawson City from the mid 1930s until the 1950s. It is a National Historic Site and tours are available.

I always enjoy the live shows. The Frantic Follies is a vaudeville revue with music, dancing, singing, comedy, Robert Service skits and poetry. There are other shows, as well.

The MacBride Museum has exhibits of Native culture, the RCMP, wildlife, and the Klondike Gold Rush. They also have an outdoor museum that includes Sam McGee's cabin (The Cremation of Sam McGee), stage coaches, and steam engines.

I like the log skyscrapers downtown and the Old Log Church Museum. The church is a Territorial Historic Site. Episcopal services are held there on Sundays.

You won't want to miss the Yukon Transportation Museum with the amazing Alaska Highway construction story and other methods of northern transportation, including dogsleds, stagecoaches, planes, trains, and riverboats. It is impossible to miss this place. It is on the Alaska Highway, across from the Whitehorse International Airport. You can find that by the weathervane in front, a Douglas DC-3 on a stick.

If you've not read the Alaska Highway history, take time to do it. It is absolutely amazing. The U. S. Army Corps of Engineers built 1,523 miles of road across Canada and Alaska in eight months.

North to Fairbanks

2001

It is 633 miles from Whitehorse to Fairbanks. The Alaska Highway ends at Delta Junction. The Richardson Highway goes on into Fairbanks. You'll often see signs for "old" sections of the Alaska Highway.

From just short of Haines Junction, the road was really bad. It was bad in 1987, 1992, and I heard it was bad in 1996! In 2001, it was still awful! and except for some good areas well on the other side of Haines Junction, the whole way to the Alaska border was a disaster. Road construction in the rain is not fun. A gravel section was all washboard and the usual just plain bad areas were exacerbated by rain.

The sign ladies stopped me to say, "Equipment might be on your side of the road. Stop and let them do the maneuvering." They were very up-beat and cheerful. That helped. Suddenly over a hill, I was confronted with several construction vehicles heading toward me in both lanes! One equipment operator turned on a blue light and indicated I should follow her. We wove in and out of the oncoming machinery. I played chicken with double-bottom gravel trucks loaded to the gills. I stopped at Haines Lake for a nap after the strain of what I thought was the worst of it. Ha!

Haines Ghost

Near Haines Junction, the fantastic Kluane National Park comes into view. You can sometimes see the Mt. Kennedy and Mt. Hubbard peaks of the Icefield Ranges in the park's interior. Spectacular mountain views, providing the weather is reasonably clear, will be with you for all the miles north. Kluane National Park, a World Heritage Site, has the highest mountains in Canada, the second highest coastal mountains, and the largest non-polar icefield ranges in the world.

You never really lose mountain views. The views will change. Eventually you'll see the mountains in the Wrangell-Saint Elias National Park and Preserve in the distance. This park includes nine of the 16 highest peaks in the United States. It is our largest national park, the size of six Yellowstone parks. The Bagley Icefield is the largest subpolar icefield in North America. In conjunction with Kluane National Park in Canada, it is also a World Heritage Site.

Then you begin to see the Alaska Range (Mounts Hayes, Deborah, and Hess). Look at your map; magnificent mountains are in every direction. Heck with the map, throw it away, and look out your window!

Look in your rear view mirror once in a while. The difference in your view can be startling (Especially if there is a semi in your sights).

Stop often. If you're like I am, you can't resist framing the spectacular mountain scenes in flowers, trees or clouds. Great photo opportunities are everywhere.

If you enjoy scenery, you could easily take a month driving from Whitehorse to Fairbanks. Campgrounds are available. Some are private; others are recreation sites near streams, lakes, or in the woods (Get out that gallon of repellent!).

There were miles of stacked trees cut out of the wilderness where they contemplate building more new road sans the curves. Sooner or later all the challenge will be gone and we'll fall asleep driving it. It would be fun to work on a project like that. I saw either girls with long hair working the equipment or else the guys had let their hair down.

Kluane Lake is the largest lake in Yukon Territory, and you will follow its beautiful shores for many miles. I turned off at Milepost 1020 to go to Silver City in 1992. It is a little over six miles round trip on a gravel road. There isn't a lot there any more, but the fireweed and the ruins of an early trading post, made for great slides.

You'll go through Destruction Bay and Burwash Landing. The Kluane Museum of Natural History is worth a stop at Burwash Landing.

Beaver Creek is Canada's most westerly community (100 miles west of Victoria, BC). Twenty miles northwest of Beaver Creek, you'll hit the Alaska-Canada International border. There is a pullout where you can see the narrow swath cut across the countryside to mark the border. Bill (Yukon guide) said they clear it every 10 years. You are also changing to Alaska Time as you cross the border. You're now four hours away from the East Coast. I drove an hour into Alaska and stopped to read and sleep in an overlook. A tiring day. This border is open 24 hours a day.

Outside of Tok about 15 miles, is the junction with Taylor Highway (toward Chicken).

Tok 1996

Tok is called, "Mainstreet Alaska." You can get most necessities there. It is a small community but it gets all visitors "coming and going," since you must drive through this town to reach the rest of Alaska. Tok is also known as the "Dog Capital of Alaska." It is a center for dog breeding, training, and mushing. The Burnt Paw gift shop has a free Dog Team Demonstration in the evenings at 7:30.

I had breakfast at Young's Cafe, and filled up with gasoline at Young's Chevron Service. I took them up on their offer of a free sewer dump and water fill-up. They also offer free RV parking. A number of campgrounds are in the area, Tok River State Recreation Site southeast of town, and Tok RV Village in town, among others. Tok Gateway Salmon Bake and RV Park offers a free night of dry camping with dinner. Sourdough Campground has a free nightly slide show. Check to see which one offers whatever floats your boat.

The Tok Mainstreet Visitors Center has wildlife displays, Alaska videos, free coffee, and a list of activities. There are telephones inside and outside. The Alaska Public Lands Information Center has a historical timeline room and displays, a wildlife museum, restrooms, pay phone, and message board.

Alaska Public Lands Information Centers cover National Park Service, U. S. Forest Service, Bureau of Land Management, U. S. Fish & Wildlife Service, U. S. Geological Survey, Alaska Division of Tourism, Alaska Department of Natural Resources, and Alaska Department of Fish & Game.

They are located in **Tok, Fairbanks, and Anchorage**. It is beyond my comprehension that government agencies have come together so you can get needed information from one place. Fantastic! If they don't have the information, they should be able to tell you where to find it.

Tok has several repair service centers, quick lube, tire centers, and places to have your front end aligned (should you have need).

South of Delta Junction there is a Bison Sanctuary. The only bison I saw were between Haines Junction and Whitehorse. Bill (Yukon Guide), as we drove from the river trip back to Eagle, told me about the roaming bison raising havoc with crops in the big Delta Agriculture Project. The Sanctuary has 90,000 acres, but so far the critters haven't read the fine print. They are still causing problems to local farmers. And who is going to argue with a 2,000-pound bison?

Stop at the Delta Junction Chamber of Commerce Visitor Center. Just as you had a picture taken at the beginning of the Alaska Highway at Dawson Creek, B. C., you'll want one taken in front of the "End of the Alaska Highway" monument. You can buy a certificate stating you have officially driven the Alaska Highway.

Rika's Roadhouse and Landing is part of the Big Delta State Historical Park. The staff wears period costumes. The Packhouse Restaurant is a good place to eat. This is the home of the Alaska Baking Company, known for their yum-yum bakery goods. Beware eating in competition with the tour bus crowd. When I was there, I could hardly find a place to sit, and it seats 150. The complex covers 10 acres. It is a fun place to walk around, and the shops have unusual gifts. A campground and a dump station are available.

One of the best views you will have of the Trans-Alaska Pipeline is at the Big Delta Bridge as you and the pipeline cross the Tanana River. There is a parking area south of the bridge with interpretive signs.

Santa Claus House in North Pole is billed as "Interior Alaska's Largest Gift Shop." I've always enjoyed wandering and looking; but beware, your credit card will wiggle until it gets loose. They have Santa letters for children (or adults) for mailing at the appropriate time from the "North Pole." This business has grown over the years and the story is interesting. They used to offer free camping. It is now a full facility Santaland RV Park and Campground, a Good Sampark.

Later, coming from a different direction, I'll give you an idea of what you'll find in Fairbanks.

For now, I'm taking you back to Watson Lake and the beginning of the Campbell Highway to Dawson City and over Top of the World Highway to Chicken. Hang in there. We want to cover all the roads don't we – so you'll know the choices!

The Spell of the Yukon

1996

My gold panning could hardly compare to any turn-of-the-century gold rushes. I haven't gone far enough into the wilderness to experience the loneliness, the madness (well, perhaps a little of that!) or the fear. I haven't wintered in the far North or walked in a whiteout snowstorm, but the spell of the Yukon, nevertheless, holds me in its grip.

My first knowledge of Robert Service, the "Bard of the Klondike," was through a former Alaska Territorial policeman, who held me spellbound with his poetry in Baja, Mexico. Now that I have traveled a portion of that wilderness, I am more enthralled than ever. The last four lines of "The Spell of the Yukon" explains very well how I feel.

> It's the great, big, broad land 'way up yonder,'
> It's the forests where silence has lease;
> It's the beauty that thrills me with wonder,
> It's the stillness that fills me with peace.

I equate the word "Yukon" with adventure. My heart rate went up at least two notches when the "Welcome to the Yukon" sign came into view near Watson Lake.

My spur-of-the-moment (the best kind) decision to take the Campbell Highway would cut off Whitehorse, and take me 373, mostly gravel miles, to connect with Klondike Loop (Hwy #2) to Dawson City. This was new territory. I was quite sure the road wouldn't be highly traveled...but then my transmission was only a couple of months old, and I had just had an entire new brake system installed. What could go wrong? (Always a dangerous question!)

My decision point was Watson Lake, Gateway to the Yukon. Watson Lake has a population of about 2,000. During the season, the Alaska Highway Interpretive Centre is an interesting place to visit. They have displays, photographs, and a video on the Alaska Highway construction. It was closed. Watson Lake is the home of the famous Signpost Forest, and it is always open -- out in the open. The icy wind whipped around the poles holding roughly 30,000 signs.

If you've ever gotten lost because of the absence of a signpost, it is probably here. This amazing collection represents States, counties, towns, and most foreign countries. The tradition of leaving a geographic momento began with Carl Lindley, a WWII soldier, who worked on the Alaska Highway in 1942. Legend has it that he was so homesick, he posted a sign giving the distance from Watson Lake to his hometown in Danville, Illinois. You wouldn't want to break tradition. Tack up an old license plate or homemade sign and leave your mark.

The Signpost Forest is at the Alaska and Campbell Highway junction. It was three in the afternoon when I turned northwest. I hadn't gone a half-mile, when I drove head-on into a blizzard. By the time the paved road turned into gravel, the snow stopped and blue skies prevailed. I berated myself for even *thinking* of turning back when I hit snow.

The entire route followed one river or another. All the lakes were frozen. The rivers were running through and under great depths of ice. It was a month and a half before I again saw completely ice-free water, especially in shaded areas.

The bad road sections were flagged; but this time of year, the road was more bad than good. It was wet, slippery, and the outside edges were soft. It was narrow, often one vehicle wide, and I filled it. The road was built up several feet to avoid the water that was usually on both sides. It was abundantly clear that if I didn't want to become a houseboat (or icehouse), I was going to drive in the middle except when I saw another vehicle.

I needn't have worried. It was slow going, but not due to heavy traffic. Over the next two and a half days, except for stops in the towns of Ross River and Faro, I saw ten cars and trucks.

The main road through Frances Lake Yukon government campground was plowed, but the sites were snow filled. At the boat launching pad, I found a level space next to shore. What a view it was of one of the Yukon's largest lakes. It wore a thick mantle of snow, as did all the surrounding mountains. I was quite certain I wouldn't be in the way of anyone launching a boat.

That night I caught mouse #3, the last one. I opened the bed pedestal and foamed it nearly full, missing the space for the waterpump, house batteries, and inverter panel. I foamed around the steering column. I had plugged this area during my last Alaska trip, but the carpet replacement had left holes behind. If they get through there again, they'll have two feet of foam to tunnel through. I didn't have problems with mice the rest of the trip, but it took a while for my paranoia to go away. Every noise was a giant mouse looking for peanut butter.

The one foray I made into the frigid mid-day brought me another startling noise. I thought I heard a motorboat! I knew that wasn't possible with lake ice several feet thick, then I spotted two mating grouse in the woods. They were the only signs of life I saw until my first moose (this trip). I always forget how big they are. He lumbered across in front of me, probably disgusted with the heavy traffic.

The Sprinter and I descended into a steep ravine. A black bear was across from me on the next rise, probably an eighth of a mile away as the crow flies. He stopped. Even from that distance and with the naked eye, he was huge. I watched him with binoculars. Wouldn't you know it; with virtually no traffic at all, a truckload of people came from behind him.

They were going like a bat out of a hot place, laughing like mad when they passed me, and probably thinking it was neat sport to chase that big bear into the woods. In my disappointment, I wished a pox on that load of hyenas. Another black bear and another moose eventually healed my road rage.

Only a few of Ross River's 400 residents were out in the cold as I went through town. I parked in the gravel lot near the Pelly River where RVers are invited to park overnight. I bundled in layers against the Arctic air and walked across the suspension bridge. The swollen river swirled ice chunks in its current and pushed them toward the Yukon River. The bridge groaned and creaked as I made my way across to hike the mile to an abandoned Indian village on the Ross River.

It was a steep path at first, but one of those narrow ones like a cow path, that fascinates me. It wound through the trees above the river to a small cemetery where I visited for a while. I saw the village in the distance but the extreme cold turned me back.

The gas station wasn't open in mid-afternoon. A sign pointed next door for service. On the way, I ran into the attendant. The big news was out; a customer was at the pumps.

Faro had about four times as many people as Ross River and was quite a bustling community. Friendly people gave directions to the driver of this usually lost "rolling igloo." They call the Discovery Store, the Case Place. They don't buy a bottle of catsup or a can of fruit in these isolated communities. Food is sold by the case.

People were walking to the movies or other activities. I couldn't believe they were out just for exercise in that frigid evening air. It might have felt like spring to them.

On previous trips I had seen the yellow Yukon Alaska Transport trucks, called "B-trains," originating from the Faro mine and making their way to Skagway. The Faro mine is said to be one of the largest producers of lead and zinc concentrates in the western world. They travel 40 minutes apart, 24 hours a day, taking their loads to port. These eight-axle beasts are 85 feet long and carry up to 53 tons of concentrate. (*By 2001, the mine had shut down and the B-trains were no longer running.*)

I stayed the night beside a half-frozen stream. I left early and connected with the Klondike Loop north of Carmacks. I saw the Yukon River and my heart sank; the ice had already gone out. So much for seeing the river break up.

Every trip I stop at the interpretive overlook above Five Finger Rapids, fascinated with stories of the goldrushers who ran them, sometimes with all their worldly goods on their backs. This time there was a bluff viewing platform and another down near the rapids. The mile-long path between the two beckoned to me, although I knew the 219 steps would be more difficult to negotiate climbing back up.

Two black bears munched along the highway embankments a few minutes before. I decided it would be prudent to be watchful. During this brisk, lighthearted walk, my eyes roamed back and forth across the path and into the trees, for something black and moving. My ears listened for the telltale crunch of sharp teeth on my limbs, or hopefully, a noise more distant, like the cracking of a tree limb. My nose sniffed for pungency. Experts say that bears do not wear enough deodorant and tend to smell a great deal like skunk.

I wasn't wearing bear bells and my singing would have been rather tremulous. The tape recorder became my AWS (Advance Warning System). I reversed the tape a bit, then played it really loud for a few seconds. This I did several times. Probably all present bears disliked it as much as I did, but it made me feel safer.

This was the first heavenly springtime warmth since leaving southern BC. It was great. I glimpsed something big and dark and moving fast. My heart beat faster. I turned the recorder on loud and strong, only to realize what I had seen was across the river, a moose running. I wondered where he was going and what had startled him enough to travel that fast. I stayed for a while near the rapids. The miners named them Five Finger Rapids because they looked like fingers in a hand.

Since I hadn't seen evidence of any animals, on my return trip I was rather blasé about making noise. When I was near the steps, I turned the recorder on one last time. Something crashed through the trees. I clutched my chest. My life passed before my eyes. It was a huge snowshoe hare. I had scared him almost as much as he scared me.

I had only driven 30 miles when I turned on a narrow gravel road leading to Minto Landing. It was a Yukon government campground. *(In 2001, it was no longer listed.)* Having it all to myself, I picked a choice grassy area on the riverbank.

The lone cabin had suffered the ravages of time. It had fallen into itself, the last remnant of Minto Landing history, a halfway point for steamboats running the Yukon River from Whitehorse to Dawson City in the mid 1880s. Great ice rafts nudged the heavily ice-lined riverbank, pulling more sculptured chunks into its journey to the Bering Sea. The only sounds other than the river and the refrigerator, were the grass growing and the flowers opening.

The Sprinter and I were 11 days and 2,000 miles from Seattle, and with the warm, dry afternoon, it was an excellent time to do a more advanced "walk-a-bout." After checking all the fluids and thumping the tires, I cleaned 25 pounds of mud from the generator. I sprayed WD-40 on my hold locks, and caught up on my daily log via computer and solar energy.

The Sprinter was disgustingly muddy but I couldn't quite talk myself into a precarious 30' climb down the cliff for water, and possibly flipping myself into that swirling death trap. Lovely to look at but questionable for swimming.

I hiked upriver for a mile or so. The riverbank was grassy and the area open enough for observing. The bears were out of hibernation but I felt lighthearted and free as I collected firewood.

Since I had done my chores and exercised, I felt quite justified in sitting by the fire doing nothing. I kept a bucket of water, a folding shovel, and my trusty, recently sharpened hatchet nearby (always the Girl Scout). I poured myself a stiff drink of Nutrisweet-sweetened, calorie-free, sparkling-flavored, Sam's Choice Free and Clear White Grape. What a life!

I thawed chicken strips and cooked them over the fire. I rolled a potato in tin foil, but it didn't get done enough to suit me. I did what any self-respecting "camper" would do; I zapped it in the microwave. I had been so terribly good diet-wise, that I ate a banana with peanut butter and fudge on it.

The sun worked its way to the other side of the world. Its low light silhouetted the wild crocuses, outlining them in silver. Sunset was a mere rosy glow by eleven o'clock. The air was frosty and so was I. In my cozy house beside the Yukon, I awakened only once with a loud protesting of ice against ice. I wanted to stay awhile, but the Sprinter was in need of dumping and filling, and besides, Dawson City was calling.

Memories of previous stops gave me pleasant thoughts. I hungered for one of their delicious cinnamon buns and coffee; but alas, Moose Creek Lodge was closed. Compensation for everything being closed was that I wasn't sharing life with bus tours, RV caravans or hungry bitey bugs. Among other pluses for going early, animals were everywhere. I made coffee in a pullout, sharing the space with a fat ground squirrel that rose up on his hind legs to check the great white apparition.

I almost creamed a ptarmigan. They will not get out of the way even when a RV is bearing down on them. I pulled off to watch a black bear. He went back and forth across the road into the woods three times. The last time, he stopped for a couple of seconds as though asking, "Why are you still here?"

At the junction with the Dempster Highway, I filled the Sprinter with gas and took advantage of their free sewer dump and water fill-up. The fellow who pumped gas said, "The river ice is still piled up at Dawson. The Klondike River just broke up and its pushing into the Yukon, something's got to give soon." I **wasn't** too late. Yessss! I forgot that it didn't automatically break up everywhere at once.

I arrived in Dawson City in the nick of time. The river ice had moved enough that morning to displace the tripod in the center, signaling the "official" ice breakup with bells and whistles and celebration. People for miles around buy tickets as to the day, hour, and minute the Yukon River breakup will happen. Somebody had already won a pot of gold. The main breakup waited for me.

Dawsonites believe spring has arrived when the ice moves downstream. In shorts and short sleeves, they were out in number to watch it. It was too cold for me. I guess when you are used to -50, anything above freezing is a heat wave. They sat on blankets and chairs on the earthen

Robert Service Cabin, Dawson City

dike that follows the confluence of the Yukon/Klondike Rivers. The dike was built to prevent another major ice jam flood like the one in 1979. The path along the top is a favorite place for walking, running, and biking.

Remember I mentioned Robert Service? Would you believe I shared the river watch with him? Wait you say, how old is this guy? He was really Tom Byrne, an actor and storyteller who relates Robert Service poetry at the Service cabin in Dawson City.

While we waited for the ice to do something spectacular, Tom regaled me with stories of local characters.

It seems one Captain Dick, offering the best drink in Dawson City, the "Sour Toe," lost the major content to a bender-bent imbiber, who drank the drink and swallowed the toe. The story was a bit hard to swallow, but Tom swore the toe was real. When that toe disappeared down the hatch, Captain Dick put an ad in the paper for another. Truth being stranger than fiction, he got it!

First light follows close after last light in the land of the midnight sun, and townspeople came early to check the rivers progress. By eight a.m., the ice moved. What excitement! Many people depend on the Yukon River for their livelihood. The river breaking free means a great deal to them. It jammed at the bend and water backed up alarmingly fast. It subsided as the chunks broke free.

The water mingled forward and backward, swirling, groaning, moaning, and pulling trees grabbed from distant shorelines and river-size icebergs, into its wild journey. Desolate and dirty ice clung to the gravel bars, stranded and left to melt in the warming sun. Locals told me it was less than a spectacular break up, but it was exciting to this Midwesterner, as is almost everything about the North.

Nearly a 100 years ago, August 17, 1896, George Carmack, Skookum Jim, and Tagish Charlie discovered gold on what became known as Bonanza Creek. They staked the first claims and made the history that Dawson City celebrates, the great Klondike Gold Rush of 1896-98.

As a matter of fact, once these Canadians get a party started, it's hard to stop them. They are celebrating right on through 2003 with centennials of the Palace Grand Theatre, the post office, the Carnegie Library, plus numerous other anniversaries.

Over 100,000 dreamers set out to make their fortunes; perhaps they were your relatives. About 40,000 survived carrying their goods over the Chilkoot and White Pass Trails from Skagway and Dyea, Alaska, and the Yukon River Whitehorse Rapids to the gold fields. By the time most of them arrived, the creek beds had already been staked with claims from end to end.

Relatively few became rich with first-hand gold, like the 72-ounce gold nugget that, with today's prices, would be worth $30,000. Second-hand riches were made in services, uh, some unmentionable here. Saloons, restaurants, and shops opened, and Dawson City transformed from a tent city to the largest city north of San Francisco. It had running water, telephones, and electricity. Good gravy, we didn't have those amenities in the southwestern Michigan log cabin where I was born, a whole lot (a whole lot) of years later.

A good place to learn the details is at the Dawson City Museum. The movie shows Dawson during the Klondike Gold Rush days after it had fallen into decay, and during its slow restoration.

A few historic ruins are precariously propped with posts. Walking the boardwalks to avoid the dust and/or mud, you would never guess that behind business walls, lurks a computer age on-lining its way through the 21st century. The 1898 population of nearly 30,000 people, has stabilized to a lively 2,019 (The population of the entire Yukon is only 31,349).

In the meantime, I met several people at the Community Gospel Church and through a writer's group at Yukon College.

Jack said his family had owned a gold mine for many years. "They exposed old sealed mine shafts tunneled through the pay gravel. They found a post with a hat still hanging on a nail and tools leaning against the wall. In the frozen muck were perfectly preserved cans (with readable labels) which rusted immediately when exposed to air. A man's boots were beside a woman's tiny high-button shoes. A variety of bones have appeared as well." History reveals itself.

Doreen was a retired teacher and world traveler. We became friends and went to an Up with People program together. This was a first for that kind of production in Dawson. We couldn't get much more uplifted than by this group of talented students who were pure dynamite. These performers, ages 17 to 25, travel all over the world, singing and dancing in traditional costumes that represent 20 different nationalities.

We attended the season's opening and the silver anniversary of Diamond Tooth Gertie's Gambling Hall. The Can-Can Dancers did somersaults, back-bends, splits, and, of course, the can-can. My back sprained just watching them. The always-buxom Diamond Tooth Gertie, belted out songs to knock your socks off, but I didn't see a diamond between her two front teeth.

The Gaslight Follies at the Palace Grand Theatre opened. Tales of

Arizona Charlie Meadows, who built the Grand Opera House in 1899, claim that when things got dull, he invited his wife on stage and shot glass balls from between her fingers.

Although he was a "crack" shot, one night he shot her finger off and she insisted they drop the act. Hmmm. Could it have been a finger, and not a toe, in that famous "*Sour Toe*" drink?

I talked with Vancouver (BC) visitors. He was very positive, loved every minute of their trip, and would have enjoyed staying longer in Dawson City. She, on the other hand, was the kind that gives tourists a bad name. Of course I was raving about the place when she said she couldn't wait to get away. I asked how long they had been there. With a definite facial grimace, she said, "Since yesterday afternoon!"

She didn't like the dirt streets or dust and said there was nothing to do. She said, "Dawson isn't anything like I expected. I love big cities, and I can't wait to get to Anchorage." She also griped about the nearly 24-hour daylight. I asked (not as sarcastically as I wanted to), "What did you expect in the Land of the Midnight Sun?"

It was totally beyond me how she could be there less than 24 hours, visit none of the attractions or shows or goldfields, and judge Dawson City in that fashion. Only in my wildest thoughts could I imagine what she would think when they arrived in Chicken, Alaska, their next stop. Please don't go from Whitehorse to Tok via Dawson City expecting metropolitan fare. It won't be so, and I'm grateful.

People in the North Country either love living there or they hate it with a passion and feel trapped. An interesting comment from a 16-year-old who pumped gas was, "I want to move to Ontario where I can be closer to Florida." (I thought about leaving him a map.)

I drove the steep winding road up to The Dome each night, 2,000' above Dawson City, and backed into a gravel area just below the dome. Spectacular sunsets reflected in the Yukon River bend close to midnight. It was a marvelous place to hike early in the morning. The wind threatened to unwind my muffler. Ravens flew about asking my intentions, then gathered with colleagues on tree limbs, discussing my answers.

Sometimes when I walked to the top of the dome, I was in an island of fog. Other times it was clear and I could see deep winter snows still hugging rugged mountain ranges. Below me great long mounds of gold mine tailings, wormed their way through the goldfield valleys.

Once I awakened to several inches of new snow. It wasn't a hard decision to stay there for the day. I had enough propane, groceries, and water in case the snow didn't stop. That late in the season, surely it would melt in two weeks at the latest.

Campgrounds finally opened in Dawson, but I preferred The Dome. During the season, I'm sure they wouldn't allow anyone to park there.

Only once did I think I might have a problem. I was reading late in the evening when a pickup truck made a beeline to the driver's corner of the Sprinter and slid to a stop just before it hit the bank. I stared at the two of them for a couple of seconds. They backed out and left. My kids said nobody could withstand "The Look," but what do they know.

**Signs throughout the Yukon
said it all,
*"Bears dump in the woods...you don't have to."***

Young people (usually college students) come to Dawson from all over North America and beyond. If you see familiar faces in The Farmer's Market grocery store, Maximilian's Gold Rush Emporium, or Klondike Kate's Restaurant, you probably are. Most students have two jobs. They use their evening talents as dancers, singers, waiters, or musicians at Diamond Tooth Gertie's or the Palace Grand Theatre.

I had quite a few groceries. I bought supplemental milk and bread. Milk was $6.14/gallon. With the exchange rate of 34 to 1, it was $4.10 U.S. Not everything was that high but it is more understandable when you realize shipping logistics.

A Jack London cabin was discovered in 1936 and brought in log by log, from "the left Fork of Henderson Creek." Two cabins were built using the original logs (and a few new ones). One is at the Jack London Interpretive Centre in Dawson and the other in Jack London Square in Oakland, California. Maybe my love of the North started way back when I read the exciting books, *Call of the Wild* and *White Fang* in my Michigan cabin on the Dowagiac Creek's western bank.

The two-room Robert Service log cabin snuggles against the hillside among the willows and alders overlooking Dawson. He wrote his first novel there, *The Trail of ninety-eight,* and continued writing poetry. As he created, he wrote notes on the wallpaper. He was one of the few people at the time that could afford a telephone. *(Writers must have made more money then!)* According to Robert Service himself, "Everything was snug and shipshape...I would not have exchanged my cabin for the palace of a king..." Maybe Jack and Robert are my kindred spirits.

Tom Byrne mesmerized all of us with his readings of *The Cremation of Sam McGee* and *The Shooting of Dan McGrew.* He sat on an old rocker with a huge umbrella over it. In his distinct Irish accent, he wrapped the audience in his oration. His dramatic whispers were clear as a bell. His hand movements and eye contact kept us watching every minute. I was only vaguely aware of the small birds singing in the trees above and the ravens calling to each other a block away.

Tom owns his own cabin in Dawson. "Outsiders," as people in Alaska and Northern Canada call anyone from the "lower 48," aren't aware of the enormous permafrost problems. Tom said part of his cabin floor was rotten. He tore it out. Under that floor, he found joists of another. Before he was through, he found three floors had been built over each other as the cabin sank.

He raised it rock by rock with jacks until he finally hit bedrock, and the jacks started lifting instead of sinking. After he had made some headway, three buddies offered to help. When he told them to stop jacking, one continued, and suddenly the whole thing squeejawed into itself. He said, "If the cabin hadn't been dove-tailed and pegged, it would have fallen apart." Tom started over again with jacks and a come-a-long, until eventually he made it level (by himself).

There are a number of places you can gold pan commercially. The Klondike Visitors Association allows you to pan for gold on your own at Claim #6, above Discovery.

You can also drive yourself via a 60-mile loop or a combined 102-mile loop along Bonanza Creek Road, Sulphur Creek Road, Dominion Creek Road, and Hunker Creek Road. You can visit Dredge #4, the largest wooden hulled, bucket line dredge in North America.

Worn-out rusted trucks; Cats, pipes, and pumps compose a living history of mining claims. Tailings with full-grown trees growing in them evidenced the passage of time. Little cabins, houses, or mobile homes overlook mining claims. One claim had a skull and crossbones displayed at the driveway. It isn't wise to walk where you don't belong. You'll understand when I say the gold is still being mined to the tune of nearly $40 million a year.

I did part of the route but it was springtime and the road was washed out. If you don't want to drive this narrow, winding gravel road yourself, commercial tours are available.

I visited the mountain cemeteries above the town and Crocus Bluff. Carolyn and Barb from church took me on a long hike on the Sancho Park Historic Trail System above Dawson. It was a great hike. Going across the old rockslide, one misstep and I wouldn't be writing this.

You can hike to (with permission from the local Indian band office) or take a river tour to the village of Moosehide. Where Dawson is now, the Han Indians once lived. Once upon a time the village was below the rockslide that I crossed.

Dawson is one of the few places that is a bustling tourist town, and yet maintains its historical flavor. I felt I stayed long enough to feel that flavor.

Doreen invited me to dinner at her son's house. He was with the local RCMP. Doreen had spent a lot of time in Turkey. She asked me if I knew what happened to Mary after Christ died and rose again. I had never thought about it before. She said, "The disciple into whose care she was handed, set her up in a house with a beautiful view at Ephasis where she later died."

The Yukon freed itself of the last dangerous floating ice chunks. The George Black, the Canadian government free ferry, and the only transportation across the Yukon River to the Top of the World Highway, slid along its wooden track into the water. The season had begun.

I topped off the gas tank and boarded. I had mixed feelings about leaving friendly Dawson City. It was fun watching them erase winter scars and gear up for the tourists, but after two weeks in one place, my itchy wheels were singing,

Alaska!

Alaska!

Alaska!

George Black Free Ferry Crossing Yukon River

Flying with the Eagle-ites

1996

During the season, it is a good idea to get to the Dawson ferry early. It is busy and ferrying is the only way across the river. Top-of-the-World Highway has offered me foggy, muddy and slippery roads, snowdrifts, rain, and washouts, but this day it gave sunshine and flowers.

Driving on the ridge above the tree line, it feels and looks like you are, indeed, on top of the world. Although storms played in the distance, I couldn't resist stopping in an iffy pullout and hiking up to a pointy outcropping. Tiny yellow and red flowers reached toward the sun. The season is short. Even brave plants have a tough time growing.

My Julie Andrews' Syndrome took over. I felt like throwing my arms open wide and singing, "*The World is alive...*"

At the rest stop and highest elevation on the Top of the World Highway, 4,515', I could see the Alaska/Canada border ahead of me. It is not open 24 hours. Be aware of your timing and time changes.

I passed a sedan nosed halfway into a snowdrift with its windows smashed out and flat tires. It must have spent the winter. I wondered what happened to the people who were in it. This road closes when deep snow arrives.

This is the most northerly land border port in the United States. Population: 2. Elevation: 4,127'. The border guard came out of the Canadian Customs house, perhaps from sharing his morning coffee. He was not unfriendly, but very crisp. He wanted to know what I had brought in from Canada. I told him, "Dust."

People who have driven Top of the World and Taylor Highways, relate horror stories about road conditions. It was like a super highway, comparatively speaking, say with 1987. It had been widened, leveled, and most of it chip-sealed. (*They were heavy into road construction on the Taylor Highway in both 1996 and 2001. A few miles are still narrow, winding, and iffy.*)

Boundary has fuel. This would be rugged country to run out of gas. A friendly fellow, Pete, worked for his uncle at Boundary Lodge. When I walked in, he said, "Welcome to the top of the world." I said, "Thank you, again."

"Ah, you are a repeat offender." He said his uncle had bought the place. They were cleaning it up and residing the old buildings. It was one of the first roadhouses in Alaska. It is now a snack type stop, but it was warm and friendly. Motorhomers were there from Germany. Throughout the summer, I ran into many visitors from other countries.

Pete had a full beard and a head of black hair that was very long in the back, with short, sort of spiky hair all around his head. He looked like he was wearing a coonskin cap. He had friendly eyes and actually was quite good-looking, considering he slightly resembled a werewolf.

After the other visitors left, we chatted. I'm always curious about what it is like to live in the North Country. "I never watch TV. The view across the road is much better than TV. It changes constantly; it's never the same." He said he lived alone and liked it that way. He wanted to know how I came to be traveling alone. I said I had been RVing solo for many years. He said, "Sometimes it is better to be alone. You don't have to do what everybody else wants to do." We walked on common ground.

At Jack Wade Junction, I made one of those "Decision-time stops." Should I continue to Chicken, or head north to Eagle, and into uncharted Minshall territory? Yesss! Turn north to bumpier, narrower, more-like-it-used-to-be winding road. It was twistier than a drunken sidewinder. Land-slides were prevalent. This was springtime; slides were expected. The road was often one lane with a cliff to peer over. Taylor Highway closes in the winter and it hadn't been open very long.

Road to Eagle, AK, Taylor Highway

The road made grand sweeping curves in tree-less country where I could see forever or at least to Canada's Olgivie Mountains. I knew if I could see far enough beyond the mountains to the left, Fairbanks was about 200 miles directly west of Eagle on the 65th parallel. Then I dipped into valleys; "dip," meaning hairpin curves, steep winding roads, and thrills for the Sprinter and me.

At Fortymile Bridge, with a view of the rapids, lots of trees, and nobody to break the peace, I parked for the night. The sign said "No Parking" but there were two old trucks, one with a camper on it, and an old boat. They had flat tires, and foot-high weeds surrounded them, so I was sure they lived there. Somehow, I didn't think anybody would mind my parking. *(They were still there in 2001!)*

However, I minded it before long. A van pulled in with a couple and a dog. By that time I had eaten a fine dinner (well, I did cook it so "fine" may be an overstatement), and was settled for the night. The dog barked repeatedly with joy at his newfound freedom. I climbed back in the driver's seat and drove on.

It was about 11 p.m. but still light. If I hadn't taken off again, I would have missed seeing the big moose ambling ahead of me, and the little waddling porcupine. In a rosy sunglow at midnight, and accompanied by a quarter moon, the Sprinter and I settled into a gravel pit.

The road was narrow enough in spots that I would have needed a pullout for passing, but I drove for 45 minutes before seeing anyone. A truck driver waved. A fellow standing near a rare mailbox was startled, but waved and smiled. His tiny house was down a steep bank on the opposite side of the stream. I didn't spot his means for getting there.

Discovery Creek flows through this narrow valley. It was nearly solid with several feet of ice. What little water I saw, was bright red. I paused to take a picture of a hiker. His red coat reflected colorfully in a mudpuddle. He wondered what I was doing, and we started talking.

Jim gave me my first Eagle welcome. A native of Wisconsin, Jim had lived in Alaska since 1969. He said he walked every morning before the dust kicked up. "I usually carry a small gun, but today I brought a bigger one. There's a moose and calf in this area. You don't know what these creatures will do when they are calving."

I talked to him again later in the day, and he invited me to come for coffee and see his cabin. Jim grinds his own beans for fresh coffee and brews homemade beer. The log cabin had beams from a miner's 100-year-old cabin. The old logs were shaved to look new. It was a small cabin with an upstairs, about the size of the Sprinter by three. He slowly carved his existence out of the woods, finishing the cabin at his leisure.

I made my way down the long hill into Eagle. I found the post office first, then the Riverside Cafe. The cafe is in "downtown" Eagle, and has a marvelous view above a wide Yukon River bend and Belle Island. Marge brought me a true northwoods breakfast, big and hearty. With a touch of "outside," three weeks worth of mail, I was content.

Later, her husband, John, was doing laundry when I did mine. I asked him about the winters. "I love it," he said. "It's peaceful and quiet." I discovered that was the consensus. Eagle is at the end of the road, where they can go east, north, or west, and walk where few people have gone, and they like it that way. "We're quite proud of our little town."

With the road closed October through April, he said, "The school offers various activities, and families get together more often. The library is heavily used for books and tapes." The library is small by big-city standards. Hopefully, it will never have those standards. The barrel stove in the center, provides cozy warmth on those -60, long evenings in Eagle. What more could anyone want than a reading room, comfortable chairs, and a current book supply?

To learn more about Eagle, although I didn't have a card and didn't know anybody in town, Theresa graciously allowed me to take two books written by local people, whom I later met. *Life in a Small Alaskan Bush Community*, by Reverend David Stovner, the minister at the log church, was a very personal view of local life. Elva Scott's manuscript, *Historic Eagle and Its People,* was a wealth of information. She was acknowledged by the author in James A Michener's *Alaska*.

She gave the history of the Han/Athabascan Native Americans who live three miles east of Eagle, in Eagle Village. The population has dwindled to 17. The road follows the Yukon River upriver, and continues 10 more miles, to accommodate people building even farther away from what most people term, "civilization."

One of Eagle's most famous visitors was the Norwegian explorer, Roald Amundsen. He mushed overland from his sloop, Gjoa, icebound on the Arctic Coast, to Eagle, in December 1905, to telegraph news of his discovery. After two months of local hospitality, he returned to his ship and completed the first successful voyage through the Northwest Passage.

I learned a lot about Eagle as I wandered around, but a sign on the side of Elmore Enterprises, really caught my attention, "Raft through untouched Alaskan wilderness." Wow...Maybe...Do you suppose?

Bill Elmore, 46, former North Slope crane operator, jack-of-all-trades, EMT, and guide, didn't laugh when I poured out my soul's desire. "I want to canoe the Mighty Yukon River. I want to experience the wilderness. I want to see it, hear it, touch it, taste it, and smell it. I want to pit myself against nature." What I really wanted was to erase the look on his face that said, "This woman is a nut case."

Twice in the four years previous to this trip, I made plans to canoe the Yukon River with different male friends who were experienced in wilderness camping and canoeing (because I wasn't). Both times, they backed out on me. I finally figured this particular dream was never going to happen. Sometimes keeping "Your arms open to adventure" takes longer than usual. Even dreams happen in their own time.

Bill said he would "work something up." I had the choice of taking my own equipment and food or he would provide everything. Since I had given up ever doing this trip, I was not only unprepared physically, I had little of the proper equipment needed. When I left his shop, I was alternately elated with the *possibility* of canoeing the Yukon, and *terrified* it might actually happen.

By Saturday, I couldn't wait any longer. I went back. I was disappointed. No plans. He was busy working on a Memorial Day speech. Later, on the canoe trip, he confessed he hadn't taken my request seriously. I guess he thought it was a passing thought. Ha!

Eagle has two airports, one with a grass landing field and the other with a gravel runway for the four daily flights delivering mail, groceries, equipment, or parts. It is cheaper to fly necessities in, than drive the nearly 800-mile round trip to Fairbanks.

I crossed the grassy airport behind the "Beware of low-flying aircraft" sign, to reach the BLM campground about a mile from town. It was free. I settled in, only to have a knock on my door at midnight. The Sprinter's lights were on. At midnight in May, I didn't realize they were on.

On my daily mile-long hike through the forest, I watched for moose and sniffed for odor of skunky bears. Visitors to the North Country don't think of moose as being dangerous like bears. I guess it is up for grabs which is the most dangerous. Bears tear you apart and eat you for breakfast, lunch, and dinner, and moose gore or kick you to death and leave you wishing you had been more polite. Some option.

Carrying guns is as much a way of life in Eagle, as planes, snow machines, sled dogs, and four-wheelers, but I didn't have one. My only weapons were strong lungs and a tire-pounder. If nothing else, I could wedge it between the bear's teeth, while he ripped my arms and legs off, or maybe, break off the tip of a moose antler.

In my wanderings around town, I ran into one of Bill's four sons who said his dad was looking for me. You don't have to look too hard to find anybody in Eagle. He had the figures. He would provide all equipment, food, and guide service for $180/day for a two-week trip from Eagle to the Dalton Highway. He asked me to think about it and let him know.

Financially, at that moment, it was probably the last thing I should have done, but since I wanted the memory more than the money, I said, "Yes," immediately.

WOW! WE'RE GOING!

Eagle's Public Well

The Eagle Trading Company has groceries, propane, a motel, and RV hookups overlooking the river. The Village Store carries groceries and hardware. Gift shops feature creative stationary, basketry, leatherwork, beading, weaving, and quilting. The 160 residents are craftspeople, trappers, carpenters, pilots, miners, teachers, service people, and retirees. The Sundog Gift Shop offered chocolate frozen yogurt but I had to wait a few days. The seasonal shops were awakening after a long winter's nap, and the frozen yogurt wasn't frozen yet.

You'll find porcupine quill and moose poop jewelry at the American Summit Gift Shop. In talking with Jean, she said, "'Outside' people don't understand our need for the old-fashioned sponge bath. When you transport and carry your water from a shared well, you don't take numerous showers." She was just as unaware of boondocking in a RV, and taking a "bath in a teacup" to stretch the water supply.

The most important thing in Eagle is the public well. It was hand dug in 1902 and still used by 75% of its citizens. Since few have their own water, there are also more outhouses than in a "lower 48" village.

Eagle is unique. Jackie said they had to dig 20' through frozen muck to hit gravel for a septic system. Previously, her garden consisted of plantings in dirt-filled tires. The muskeg and trees were removed and the soil worked into a rich peat garden. The two months of daylight make up for the short growing season.

Gasoline was $1.83 a gallon. Washing clothes cost $4, $6, or $8, depending on the machine size. A quarter bought three minutes drying time. After $2, I finished drying in the Sprinter. It was the most expensive Laundromat I found. Even in the towns that had no roads leading to them, a load of laundry could be washed *and dried* for $3.75. Only the river trip drove me to do more laundry in Eagle.

On Sunday, I sat in the padless pews of the log non-denominational church, built by Presbyterians at the turn of the century. The original log city hall behind the church is still used. The school has 20 students, with a few other youngsters taking correspondence courses. Gold was discovered at American Creek, Fortymile and Seventymile Rivers. Other than privately worked claims, the only functioning gold mine now, is nine miles south of Eagle.

I started my historical tour going through the Wickersham Courthouse. Judge James Wickersham established the first Federal court in Alaska's interior, in Eagle, in 1900. The Third Judicial District covered 300,000 square miles. Eagle was conceived in 1897, and by 1901, became the first incorporated city in the Interior.

Phyllis Hyde followed her heart to the Yukon after reading *Coming into the Country*. As a volunteer, she guided me through the Historical Society's walking tour. Eagle-ites say they may have more square feet of museum displays than anywhere else in Alaska. I'll vouch for it.

She took me into Fort Egbert's six preserved buildings out of the original 37 military buildings. Fort Egbert was built in 1899 to maintain law and order and complete the Washington-Alaska Military Cable and Telegraph System (WAMCATS). By 1903, Billy Mitchell, known later as "The Father of the U. S. Air Force," built the final section, linking Fort Egbert to Fort Liscum at Valdez, and Fort St. Michael on the Bering Sea. The fort closed in 1911, leaving all equipment intact.

The fire station housed antiques. The 58-stall mule barn displayed big items like dogsleds and mining equipment. We stopped in the Customs House Museum by the river and found the unusual (usually what you expect in a museum), dog booties, a cabbage stomper, and an in-house, one-hole, corner-room toilet.

Phyllis pointed out Anne Purdy's tiny cabin, a young Missouri girl who came to teach school. She told her story in the book, "*Tisha,*" by Robert Specht, which I had read on an earlier trip.

Phyllis, who referred to Indiana as "Out East," had settled into Eagle's harsh life. Snowmobiling is not only a recreation but also a necessity to get around. A few still use dogsleds but they are mainly for recreation now. Phyllis told stories about breaking through "second" ice with her snowmobile, water that has frozen on top of the original ice. Both Jim and Phyllis came to share evening campfires with me, giving me a chance to get acquainted, and learn their views of life in Eagle.

Jim invited me to the seasonal grand opening of a tavern his friends owned, halfway back to the junction. Taverns aren't exactly my thing since I don't drink; but in the North, they are gathering places for a bit of social life. Jim asked if I knew what the bell above my head was for. I shook my head, thinking it was a decoration. He told me to ring it. I did, and all the locals laughed. It meant you were buying drinks for everyone. They didn't make me honor it since I was a greenie.

A busload of tourists stopped. Jim and the others gave them a bit of local color. For a while I felt almost like a local.

On Memorial Day, I went to the cemetery surrounded by the high white picket fence in the woods. The bugler played *America* and *God Bless America*. Bill (the guide) told a story about another bugler who lived at the Eagle fort in the early 1900s.

**"He came to visit in 1969 and told about playing his bugle when it was -79°. He claimed,
'It echoed off Eagle Bluff and straight to God.'"**

Bill said, "We should ask ourselves what we can do to help keep our freedom intact, to preserve what these people died for." He became quite emotional when he spoke of his father, who had been in three wars. You knew it all meant a lot to him; it wasn't just words. The bugler closed the ceremony, playing *Taps* over new graves and old heros. Afterward, Bill came to talk about the river trip itinerary. We covered a lot of territory in that short hour, enough that we felt we could survive two weeks together in the wilderness. I warned him again that I had done a lot of camping and canoeing, but nothing of this magnitude. He didn't flinch. He was a brave man.

I spent the week doing laundry, packing one tall but skinny duffel bag, writing columns ahead, and making phone calls to my daughters and brothers. They were excited for me, especially Janet, my oldest. If she could have managed it, she would have been right there in the middle of the canoe.

On my last evening, I had a panoramic view while eating my veggie-burger at the Riverside Cafe. Fresh snow covered a distant mountain. Storm clouds made quilted patterns of sunshine and darkness. Ice chunks still clung to the Yukon River shoreline. The spell of the North was upon me big time, and the next day I was starting the adventure of a lifetime.

The Mighty Yukon River
1996

From my roots in Michigan soil
I sought a wilderness dream
To canoe the Mighty Yukon
And pan In a rock-laden stream

I yearned to be in the bosom of the
Birds and the bugs and the beasts
To experience the wonders of nature
In endless and infinite feasts

Beyond the Arctic Circle I canoed
I found gold in the rock-laden stream
I'll always be grateful for memories
Of living my wilderness dream

Several sources gave the length of the Yukon River, anywhere from 1,979 to 2,300 miles long. They were in agreement that it was Alaska's longest river and North America's fifth largest river. The river has been called the "Mason-Dixon Line" splitting Alaska into two very distinct halves, arctic and subarctic, with the Brooks Mountain Range to the north and the Alaska Mountain Range to the south.

From Eagle to the Dalton Highway, the Yukon is a Class I (no rapids) area. I knew hypothermia would likely claim our lives if storms or whirlpools, or any wrong moves, dumped us in the middle of the often mile-wide, frigid (35° - 38° F) river. I knew grizzlies were a danger, bugs would be annoying, and if either of us became incapacitated in any way, we were isolated. I didn't realize how much trouble I was in until Bill announced, "We'll have to average about 40 miles a day." Without batting an eye (because my body paralyzed with the thought), I still managed a resounding "Yessss!" May 31 was the big day.

I had given a great deal of thought over the last four years to what the experience would be like. I studied topo maps (which didn't mean a heck of a lot to me), read canoeing books, books on the Yukon River and the Indian villages along the way. I devoured books about anyone who actually canoed the Yukon. With all the studying and canoeing and kayaking I had done over the years, nothing prepared me for how tiny the 17' canoe looked compared to the fast-moving Yukon River. It passes Eagle at 1.4 million gallons/second, with an average current of five to eight miles per hour.

Only my faith in God, Bill's expertise as a guide, and my sense of the ultimate adventure, forced me into that canoe. I had goosebumps the size of cannonballs.

I don't know if Bill was aware of how inadequate I felt at that moment, but then again, I knew absolutely, that I could do it. I had lived other dreams and I would live this one too.

He gave me a running commentary as we passed the Riverside Cafe, the Customs House Museum, Mission Creek, and Eagle Bluff. The town is named after the bald eagles that nest on the greenstone bluff that rises 1,000' above the town. It dates back 600 million years. It took a while before my eyes zeroed in on the stark white bald eagle head in a treetop nest.

Eagle, Alaska, was soon behind us, and we wouldn't return, until we had canoed across the Arctic Circle

Our "bare bones" equipment included: two big boxes and two small coolers of food, one waterproof bag each for personal gear, a four-man tent, poles, sleeping bags, pads, tarp, maps, and freshwater jugs, packed between two lawn chairs in the middle of the canoe. The chairs were a stroke of genius on Bill's part. They served as sides to hold the equipment. We each had daypacks with binoculars, cameras, film, writing materials, and other *necessities* at our feet, plus lifejackets, and water sippers to stay hydrated in the wind and sun.

Ice chunks on the riverbanks had gathered enough dirt in their long journey from numerous tributaries, to become black. The ice snagged and piled up on sand and gravel bars. When it broke apart, it made a clunking noise, and resembled glass shards that were pristine sparkly. It made a tinkling sound when the river ran through the hollowed pieces.

Our first stop was to talk with a fellow who was living off the land in a log cabin tucked in the trees. He had a large dog that adopted me, but she was so friendly, she nearly knocked me off my pins. We looked out on Calico Bluff, a major landmark on the river. The black and white limestone twisted every which way but loose.

We hadn't gone far when a storm appeared frighteningly fast. We double-timed to shore and Bill had a tarp shelter across a log quicker than you could say supercalafragalisticexpialidocious. The storm passed as quickly as it had come. It was the first of many times I heard Bill mumble into his growing beard, "She wants to pit herself against nature."

For lunch, we stopped at McMullen's cabin at a sloughs edge. It was built on stilts. During spring breakup, the river rises and backs up. We went inside. Bill reached around and closed the door after me, cautioning me to always make sure the door was shut. "Bears may come in right behind you." We were both wet from the rainstorm. He started a fire. We dried ourselves while a dinner of Ramen noodles mixed with fresh-canned salmon, cooked. With hot tea, it was a feast fit for royalty.

Bill explained that outlying cabins are usually left unlocked. "If anyone gets caught in the wilderness and needs food or shelter, they are welcome to use them." This hospitality saves lives.

My excitement was beyond description...for the first 30 miles. We pulled into an open sunny area and stretched out on the ground. It was one of many breaks we would initiate over the next two weeks. I often curled up right on the dirt bank and went to sleep, something I would never do back in my native Michigan. There were few bugs and Alaska doesn't have snakes.

At 35 miles, my eyes glazed over. At 8:30 p.m. and 40 miles, we pulled in for the night. Since I had agreed with unbounded enthusiasm that we would share the work, Bill wound me up, and I automatically carried gear and supplies to the sandbar. I didn't feel tired; I couldn't feel. My arms had dropped off at 38 miles. Bill put the tent on dry sand in the bushes to keep out of the wind. He fastened a small attachment on the tent opening to keep wind and rain at bay. We soon discovered that was a nuisance and didn't use it again.

Mama and Baby moose tracks were alongside bear tracks. Bill said it

Calico Bluffs, Yukon River Ice

was a small bear, "But they are sometimes more curious and more dangerous."

A hot meal, hand-dipped into my mouth by a sympathetic, much younger guide, renewed my strength. If I had any doubts about his wilderness camping ability, they disappeared when he balanced a time-honored, and fire-blackened kettle on the burning logs to heat water.

It didn't get dark, only darker. By the time dinner and chores were done, it was already quite late. A sleeping bag never felt so good. My arms experienced Excedrin Headache #435. I took three Vanquish. After about four hours, the aches disappeared and I fell asleep.

During the night, we both heard wolves howling. There is nothing quite like wolves howling to make you realize you are in the wilderness. While I have no desire to challenge one face-to-face, I thrilled at hearing them. Morning brought a glorious paddling day on a smooth-as-glass river. By afternoon it was quite warm.

We hadn't much more than commented on our disappointment in the lack of animals, when I saw a grizzly on the riverbank, grubbing for food. We watched him as long as we could backpaddle. He sniffed the air a couple of times but didn't run away. Less than a mile farther, Mama Moose lent us a distant view of her wobbly new twins. Later, a mother and her yearling ran along the river's edge, their hooves clicking against the gravel.

Yukon Moose

We stopped at several National Park Service cabins. They were similar and usually sunken into the permafrost, except for the cabin restored to its original condition to the tune of $73,000 (pricey!). Doors were heavy and bear-proof (if anything is bear-proof). The interiors were dark with bunk beds, barrel stove, a few utensils, and table and chairs. Windows nailed shut, with the business end of the nails protruding, discouraged bears. A logbook recorded where visitors originated, river conditions, and animal sightings.

It was a 60-mile haul to Slaven's Roadhouse our second day on the river, and our only night under a roof. Slaven's is a restored roadhouse from the days when paddlewheelers plied the Yukon and a roadhouse existed every 20 miles. The roadhouse is on the National Register of Historic Places, named after Frank Slaven who discovered gold on Coal Creek. Two anterooms led into one big room downstairs. Two large rooms were upstairs with kitchen facilities. The two-holed bathroom was 30 running steps from the back door.

Eating dinner brought a spurt of energy for getting water from Coal Creek to boil and let cool, before we poured it into plastic containers. The parasite, Giardia, is a threat no matter where you are.

Bill slept in a bunk bed in one room, and I had the second room with a mattress on the floor. It was the most uncomfortable night I spent the entire trip. It was light enough all night that I could read.

We are both early risers so we were often up and out by 6 a.m. Our one foray inland took us two miles along a curlicue path worn into the permafrost and muskeg along Coal Creek, to see the gold dredge. The NPS is preserving the dredge. It was shipped in from California and utilized until the 1960s.

It was eerie climbing narrow stairs to the many levels and seeing miner's tools on benches or leaning against the wall, as if they had walked off the job two hours before. This huge piece of equipment was so far away from anywhere. The Yukon River is still a highway through Alaska's interior.

The creek was still carving its way through several feet of ice, but we managed to pan for gold in the few open gravel areas. Bill played his harmonica. I explored and took pictures. We left wealthy beyond measure, not in the few gold flakes we found, but in the surrounding beauty, and a perfect crisp, spring morning.

By the time we returned to the roadhouse, the wind was whipping the river into whitecaps and great turmoil. Sand blew across a downriver island. While we waited for calmer waters, Bill built a fire in the barrel stove. We read and slept all afternoon.

Bill at Rest

Neither of us wanted to spend another night in a building. We took off about 6 p.m. We paddled close to shore but didn't progress more than three miles. The wind nearly blew us over crossing a slough. It wasn't worth the fight. The sky looked like it could let go any minute. We had little cover and no choices. I found a spot on the side of a rise surrounded by bushes. Bill cut willow branches to make room for the tent. The bushes helped keep the wind off, but we had mighty slanty ground to sleep on.

After a mad dash to set up before the deluge fell, the wind calmed, the rain went away, and the sun came out. We had a great fire and Bill played his harmonica. We agreed the first one to awaken would check the river. If it were calm, we would leave, *no matter how early it was*. I awakened at 2:30 a.m. The river was smooth as pudding. With caution the better part of valor, I tapped Bill's sleeping bag with the 44 next to it. True to his word, we were on the river by 3 a.m. Although the sun had barely dipped to the horizon, we watched it pop back over snow-covered mountains, a magnificent day on the Yukon.

During a slack time, I noticed Bill scribbling furiously, rewording future contracts, "There will be no paddling before my time."

Enormous ice chunks imbedded in the riverbanks during breakup, had snapped trees like matchsticks and undercut the permafrost. The booming sound of trees and banks breaking away and falling into the river, startled us many times, and changed the contour of the land. Glacial silt from spring runoff made the river gritty. The canoe sounded like it was pushing through sandpaper.

The Yukon River can change from calm and peaceful, to windy with high waves, within minutes. We went through "riffles," where the water over the rocks was only inches deep. Two streams converging caused violent turbulence, depending on the speed and volume of the water. Choppy whirlpools were a danger, and the current itself sometimes boiled and swirled as it moved over an uneven bottom.

Home Sweet Home on the Yukon

Because of our early trip, we shared the river with debris. Full-sized trees floated by. Collections of natural rubble (strainers) often forced us away from the inside river bend. It was really amazing that only an infinitesimal amount of it was human litter.

Bill constantly observed the weather, and I learned to do it, too. Stormy clouds were fascinating to watch, but a precursor to danger. We often experienced dramatic weather changes, but the worst of the whole trip, were the last three choppy river miles into Circle, Alaska. They were a nightmare.

Though Bill was no doubt tired, his strength, endurance, and revivability, were far greater than mine. This was our longest paddling day at 63 miles. Exhausted, I can't remember another time on the trip, when I felt more like having, "Scotty beam me up." Given terrain that didn't lend itself to camping, we knew we had to keep going. Even with a map, Circle could have been missed. It is not on the main channel. When we could finally see the town, with the wind and waves against us, it seemed like we paddled forever before we finally hit shore. Even at that, we were fortunate. People coming into Circle from Fort Yukon, said the waves downriver were four feet high.

Circle has about a 100 residents now but it was the largest town on the Yukon before the Klondike Gold Rush. Looking at it in 1996, it took a lot to imagine what it was like. Early miners named Circle. They thought they were camped on the Arctic Circle. They missed it by 50 miles. Steese Highway, mostly gravel, leads to Circle from Fairbanks. It was my last chance to back out. No way, Jose!

Our first stop was in the Yukon Trading Post, a combination log saloon, store, and restaurant. Bill carried his backpack with him so he had a chance to clean up before eating. I was a total wreck, but nobody screamed, so I didn't think too much about it. A hamburger and French fries never tasted so good.

People were friendly and we felt quite safe leaving our belongings in the tent. Camping is free on the riverbank. The wind blew so hard we tied the tent to the picnic table. Bill retrieved a food replacement box he had sent ahead to Circle, and used it to anchor the other side of the tent.

The Circle laundry had hot showers that required quarters. The hot water felt so good on my weary bones, I used eight of them. It took the first quarter and a half to figure out how it worked. I didn't feel so bad when I discovered Bill had the same problem.

When I went in, the doors to the showers were open, so I didn't see the door labels. I walked into the first shower stall. Later Bill came in and saw only the woman's door open. He realized I had gone into the men's shower. They were the same. We later laughed about it. I had been saying, "I am **WOMAN**; I can do anything" to talk myself into ability. Now, I told him, *he* could be **WOMAN** as well.

After watching the wind and weather for four hours the next morning, we stayed in Circle another night. The air was frigid. It wouldn't have been a good paddling day even without the wind. Bill borrowed a truck to drive 40 miles to Circle Hot Springs, but then we heard the road was closed at Central because of a forest fire. We could see the smoke from it.

I sat in the warm restaurant catching up on my log, making notes and eating fresh pie and milk, at $2 a glass. The rest of the time I read in the tent, slept, or wandered around town. Most were log houses, with a few frame homes. Planes tethered in back yards, strained to go flying. Snowmobiles slept until winter rolled around again. Gasoline was $1.73/gallon.

In the wee hours, dogs barked, and shouting drunks made dirt-scattering trips through the campground with horns blasting. Mysterious bells clanged. Although we both looked at it through somewhat glazed eyes, the sunrise was spectacular. No more overnighting in villages or buildings!

Bill had never guided beyond Circle. On leaving town, we were *both* in strange territory. Since shortly after leaving Eagle, we had been paddling through the 128-mile, 2,500,000-acre Yukon-Charley Rivers National Preserve. Our next 300 miles were through the unconfined waters of the 8,630,000-acre Yukon Flats National Wildlife Refuge.

The Yukon waters became braided and oxbows nearly touched. The river was sometimes 20 miles wide, and filled with 40,000 lakes, ponds, and islands. Despite my topo maps, we couldn't judge where we were. The maps hadn't been updated since 1955. With several feet of shoreline falling into the river daily, landmarks had to have changed a great deal in 40 years.

Old fish camps and cabins were marked on the map, but what we actually saw, few and far between, were of newer vintage. Since the decline of the gold rush boomtowns, the river valley is less populated.

It was truly amazing that two strangers got on so well. We never argued. I considered him to have the ultimate word about all things (that in itself amazed my children). Bill always thought about my comfort, although I occasionally questioned his advice.

In the land of two million migrating ducks, geese, and great supply, he said,
"Use goose poop on your lips, so you aren't tempted to lick them and cause chapping."

I wanted to hit him over the head with a paddle once or twice, but since he was behind me, he had nothing to worry about. I don't even remember what prompted those feelings, probably being tired more than anything. I'm sure he felt the same way sometimes, but as a guide, it wouldn't have looked good to other clients.

We didn't see many flowers blooming, although Bill did find some wild roses, and we had scent of pine. We startled our share of waterfowl. The geese honked; the gulls screamed; the Arctic terns squawked; and the ducks quacked up. Another strange bird softly played, *When the Saints go Marching in* and *Oh Susanna*.

We spelled each other for taking pictures, writing, or when Bill checked the maps. I had no problem holding the canoe on course in calm water, but I couldn't control it from the front in choppy water.

In quieter times, when the water was calm, the sun was warm, and billowy white clouds floated through azure skies, we laid back and let the current turn the canoe in lazy circles. It was unbelievably peaceful. I wanted to bottle a bit of that peace to give to so many who would never know its joy.

It was like living a prayer. I know that God is everywhere but I feel His presence more in solitude. I often talk about "Moments in time." This is what they are all about.

One of the things I most appreciated about Bill was that he knew how to be quiet. Friends questioned my wanting to make the trip with only one other person. A group of people generates too much noise. I wanted to hear, and see, and taste, and smell, and feel everything around me, without interruption. I got it.

We exchanged stories from our experiences and backgrounds. Bill was as family-oriented as I am, and very proud of his four teenage sons. He spoke of his wife with great love and affection. We were quite comfortable with each other.

He mentioned several times around the campfire that he was really enjoying the trip, and said I was good company. One night he added, "At least you *want to be here*." He explained that his most frequent raft trips, from Dawson City to Eagle, usually last five days. About two days out, one or two people will realize this primitive, camping, canoeing "stuff" isn't at all what they thought it would be. The rest of the trip they are miserable and make sure everyone else is, too.

After water was heated for washing in the evenings, we took turns, with one being in the tent to clean up, while the other did the same outdoors. Early in the trip, mosquitoes were not a problem although washing outside was a bit chilling sometimes.

Because I don't like to be cold, washing outdoors required what I call the amazing Minshall "Remove your under layers and wash under the outer layers" trick. It was fast, thorough, mosquito and wind free, and effective, sort of.

One evening it was my turn to be outdoors. The weather was warmer than usual. I took everything off as I washed, and stood there naked. Except for Bill occupied inside the tent, there wasn't another soul for a 100 miles. I knew God and the animals wouldn't mind. I didn't walk around; I just stood there and let the air dry my skin, and hugged myself.

For all of you who are so brave as to backpack the world or live in the wilderness for months on end, or do other things that I will never do, you probably won't understand. This was a wilderness "Moment" of sheer joy for the Midwestern Presbyterian Widow Minshall. I can't explain it, and I won't try. Maybe it was the closest I will ever come to "being one with nature."

After one rest stop, Bill couldn't find the maps. We pulled ashore, and he still couldn't find them. Going back meant lining the canoe upriver, and fighting our way back across a large slough, then overland to where we had stopped. It never looked like the current was strong until you tried to cross it. It would probably have taken us two hours. He completely unloaded the canoe and found them folded into a chair.

Since the maps didn't give us a clue as to our location, we surprised ourselves by arriving at Fort Yukon, the northernmost point of the Yukon

River, in less than a day and a half.

About eight miles from town, we had paddled over the Arctic Circle with nary a bump for recognition or celebration.

Fort Yukon, at the confluence of the Yukon and Porcupine Rivers, was the largest village we visited. It has a population of about 700, a mixture of Athabascan Natives and Caucasians. Two years after the arrival of John Bell of the Hudson Bay Company in 1845, Fort Yukon was established, the first English-speaking community in Alaska.

We asked some kids if our gear would be safe left in the canoe. Clearly they thought not. They directed us to the Sourdough Inn. The waitress agreed, if we left our gear for long, it would be forever gone. Bill found a fellow who tied our canoe below his house. Nobody bothered it.

The Sourdough Inn was weathered outside, which wasn't unusual; everything looks weathered in such unforgiving country. It also looked like it would blow away in the first strong wind. I used the upstairs rest room and peeked in the open bedroom doors. They were sparse but clean...and unbelievably squeejawed.

I ran into another Bill downstairs, a big strapping fellow with a full beard, coveralls, a nice sense-of-humor, and a glint in his eye. He said the Sourdough had been a brothel, school, dance hall, barber and dental combination shop, and now, a hotel and restaurant. The building had been Officers' Quarters for Eagle's Fort Egbert. Five building parts were floated down the Yukon to Fort Yukon, in 1926. Three parts went on to the Bering Sea. Two parts were caught in Fort Yukon and put together in the current Sourdough Hotel. No wonder the building was squeejawed.

After breakfast (two eggs for $3, or a whole breakfast for $9), we walked downtown. It was never really hot on the river, but it was very hot and dusty in town. Bill looked for material to repair the canoe. It had a tiny hole in it. He had been paddling with wet feet.

Fort Yukon can only be reached by water or air. Three-and-four wheelers are a popular warm-weather transportation, ranked right up there with winter snowmobiles. Gasoline was $2.20/gallon.

Although everyone we met was friendly, neither of us wanted to camp in town. The bucking waves slapped against the canoe, flipping water inside. We fought the wind and waves until we crossed the Porcupine River outlet, then pulled in. We were within sight of the village. The choice of campsites wasn't too great, but it was late enough in the day, and we didn't want to continue fighting the elements.

With our proximity to the trees and dry tinder, the wind was too strong to have a fire. After Bill repaired the canoe, we sat where the wind kept the mosquitoes at bay, and snacked on tuna, crackers, fruit, and a sipper. We watched pilots risk their lives making treeline bombing runs. They dropped red fire retardant on a forest fire that started while we were in Fort Yukon (Honest, we didn't have anything to do with it).

Beyond a curve in the river the next morning, the wind blasted us again. After several tries, Bill put up the tent. We slept and read. At 3:30 p.m., the sun was shining and the wind seemed calmer. Ha! Around the curve it was waiting for us. We couldn't win. We paddled 400 miles that day, and progressed, 15. The good news was that the patch job worked. Bill had dry feet.

Afternoons were generally warm, but the rest of the time it was varying degrees of cool to cold, and a fire felt mighty good. Firewood was plentiful. Logs and wood floated into convenient stacks on sandbars, where we sought nightly or breaktime refuge. I maintained my One-Match Minshall Girl Scout status, and in defending man's reputation, Bill became One-Match Elmore. The ashes of our fires built on the river's edge would wash away in the next storm. No one would know we had passed that way.

We saw only four boats on the river. The fish weren't running yet. The fish camps near the four villages were empty. Fish-drying racks, benches, tables, and shelters were made of available material, with the added blue tarp. Tin cans, and any other trash the villagers had accumulated, rusted on the ground, but they did have great views.

Alaska residents have subsistence hunting and fishing rights by permit. This means they may hunt or fish for the necessities of life but cannot sell the bounty.

On one of our colder lunch breaks, we walked back into the sand dunes and willow bushes and sat in the warm sun, watching the river in the distance. It was a popular place for Mama and Baby moose with the usual bear tracks following. Baby moose is a favorite bear snack. Bill saw a wolf track. A fox trotted along beside us as we canoed away. When we crossed a slough, a beaver sitting on an outcropping surprised us almost as much as we surprised him. He flipped into the water posthaste and slapped his tail as a warning to his brothers and his sisters all over that land.

Seeing so few animals disappointed us both, but Bill had sworn to protect my life for two weeks in the wilderness. He said confrontation with a bear or moose was unlikely; but to his credit, he defended me against an extraordinary amount of tracks.

Bill followed "The high water" or main stream. Only once were we forced into a slough. We didn't start across in time and couldn't get out of its current. After several curves, it became apparent we might not be lucky enough for it to have adequate water to connect to the river again.

The canoe mired in mud. Bill said, "We may have to get out and push." I said, "What do we mean 'we,' hired guide?" Fortunately, Bill had a great sense-of-humor. We muscled the canoe out and into deeper water. We found the main channel five miles downstream.

After battling again with foot-and-a-half waves, we stopped near a high gravel outcropping on the tip of an island. The chunks of ice we had been seeing were no longer evident on this side of Fort Yukon, but there were huge boxlike gravel depressions where the ice had melted.

We sat in our chairs on the hill, surveying our kingdom. Suddenly, Bill jumped out of his chair and went pell-mell down the hill. He had put his backpack on top of the other gear while he hunted for something, and didn't put it down in the canoe again. A gust of wind flipped it into the water. He rescued it, but not before his binoculars were ruined.

Many food items had a really high fat content, and I wasn't used to it. Bill obviously wasn't either. Happy hours were less champagne and caviar, more Maalox and aspirin with H_2O chasers. To be fair, Bill had only five days to buy food, and that required a 400-mile round-trip flight to Fairbanks. He also had to tie up loose ends of his business and think out two weeks of canoe travel with an inexperienced partner. Come to think of it, he was pretty brave.

Sometimes it was a matter of getting tired of the same thing. He discovered the large assortment of bagels had molded before we could possibly have eaten them. Actually, I was used to eating pretty green things from my RV refrigerator. Rather than waste them, he put them to scientific use. He threw them off the hill to see which way the main current went. Hmmm. I trusted my life to this person.

**I very much appreciated Bill giving thanks to God
for our safety and good health before each meal. After several days
of our combined gourmet cooking, we both considered it in our best
interests for him to continue.
By the ninth day, I detected his prayers becoming more frequent,
more fervent, and
infinitely more grateful.**

Our days started early, and by 5 p.m., I really needed to get off the river. Bill usually put up the tent. One night I built a big fire around a tree stump and baked potatoes, made barbecue to go over them, and baked apples for dessert.

The storm in the distance was suddenly *upon* us. It is amazing how quickly two people can get inside a zipped tent when a full-blown storm descends. The tent was well staked, but even with us in it, we thought it was going to blow away. The sides were blowing in against us, causing the water to seep through. After the worst was over, he opened the flap and I snapped a fantastic rainbow picture.

Beaver was the smallest community we visited, with about 70 Eskimo and Indian residents. It had log cabins, a few businesses, and lots of snowmobiles, four-wheelers, and boats. Every village had a decided hum. Enormous diesel generators provide electricity 24 hours a day. Fuel comes in by barge once a year.

Since the passage of the Alaska Native Claims Settlement Act, all Native villages are privately owned. Although I did take pictures, I always asked permission before taking people pictures. I kept a low profile, insofar as a complete stranger and female Caucasian can keep a low profile in a village that can only be reached by river or sky.

When our canoe pulled in, it was instant news. A guide led us to the showers. You might expect facilities in an isolated bush community to be primitive at best. Not true. Each village had a combination Laundromat, bathroom, and shower building operated by the local Tribal Council. They were new, well maintained and heated.

Looking in a mirror was no picnic. My face was bright red and swollen from wind and sunburn. I had owl eyes from wearing dark glasses and my hair appeared to have been combed in a wind tunnel. My skin had more a leathery look than its usual magnificent look of fine porcelain. I doubled up on lotion and Vaseline.

Village people always told us, "The next village is really bad. You can't leave anything in your canoe." Before leaving Beaver, they too, warned us not to leave our gear unguarded at the next village. We never experienced any problem with anyone bothering our gear.

Each village had its own personality and Bill made friends immediately. He always made connections between a cousin, a friend, or another relative in the village and someone who lived in Eagle. When it became apparent he was not an "outsider," we were accepted.

In a roadless community, where everyone depends on everyone else for survival, it is probably the only place in the U.S. that would open a post office on Sunday so he could pick up a food box.

I talked with a family whose summer home was Beaver. They had come to fish. Their winter home was Barrow, 300 miles farther north. I had been to Barrow in 1987. The wind chill factor on June 30th was -30. Beaver was definitely warmer.

Since I was part of a Nalukataq (whale-kill celebration) in Barrow, and ate muktuk, I asked them about it. The fellow fairly drooled. He loved muktuk. She said they eat it with meat but he likes it by itself. I have to be honest; I prefer pizza to fermented whale blubber. That's what is so fascinating about life in the far North; it is so different. They told me that lots of people had died in the river due to dumb mistakes. She also mentioned a bad spot upriver, but we never saw it.

Old Bill, who had unlocked the shower building and showed me how everything worked, came down to say good-bye. He had retired from the railroad in Fairbanks, and now, "Just helps people whenever I can." Others were helping, too; eight people from Beaver were out fire fighting.

Next to the last evening was the only time I felt down on the whole trip. I took a long walk in the sunshine, curled up on a warm sand dune, and cried myself to sleep. I realized this fabulous adventure was nearly over, and I wasn't ready for it to end.

Everything I read while preparing for the Yukon River trip warned of mosquitoes, black flies, ticks, and no-see-ums. Except for the times when the tent was in the trees, mosquitoes were not a problem until our campsite after Beaver. Even then it was more of an onslaught when we first arrived like, "Hey gals, we've got blood!" The fire and smoke discouraged them. I fell asleep to the buzz of mosquitoes, but they were outside. Bill accepted them in his usual laid-back demeanor. He only used his 44 a couple of times.

On that pre-trip afternoon when we discussed the nitty-gritty details, he said he would need help with chores, since it was just the two of us. I fully agreed; in fact, I insisted I be part of the experience, not just watch it. He had the brunt of it. He often said I was pulling my weight but then he was also very kind, so I can only hope it was so.

We started on a smooth-as-glass river at 6:30 a.m. with beautiful weather. We were beginning to see snow-capped mountains in the distance again. For several days, the highest elevation was a 50' riverbank. Swirling storm clouds brought whitewater and sand-filled mini-tornadoes to the islands.

We scrambled to set up the tent far enough off the river for tree protection. It thundered and rained off and on the rest of the afternoon. In between rains, I followed moose tracks down the beach.

We had to keep going at a good pace because Bill's son was going to meet us at the Dalton Highway. We were maintaining a day ahead of schedule, but it was always a possibility that the wind would cause us to need that extra day. Bill regretted that he didn't get a GPS. It would have been fun seeing exactly where we were, but then again, it was kind of exciting not knowing. In my RVing world, I often don't know where I am.

We hadn't passed the Dalton Highway because we'd have noticed the bridge (since it is the only one crossing the Yukon River in Alaska). (Unless of course, we had passed under it, thinking it was a low cloud, and we were now well on our way to the Bering Sea. Hmmm)

Bill was up at 4:30 a.m. The weather was still pretty bad. The river was smooth but the clouds were dark and ominous. Bill wanted to stay but I wanted to go while the river was smooth and energy was high. I was tired of lying around. I felt we could deal with the rain if we didn't have the wind. He was restless, too. He built a long-poled teepee on the beach with scavenged wood.

We finally took off in a slight rain, then the wind hit again. As we had so many times, we paddled within 10' of shore and kept going. Paddling next to shore often let us see what we would have missed otherwise, like the two sandhill cranes. I had never seen them before. Where the river undercut the bank, grass and weeds caught in the roots and lay over the edge, like a great curled carpet. Underneath was the dark frozen permafrost.

We never saw a peregrine falcon, noted in the Yukon-Charley Rivers Preserve, but bald eagles were everywhere. Two gulls harassed an eagle. They would not give up and managed to chase him away by constantly diving at him.

The following morning the air was still and the river was smooth, but I didn't want to get up. I didn't want to get off the river early. I was comfortable and liked listening to nature sounds, and Bill rattling around with the fire. The perfect guide had coffee ready and breakfast made. We enjoyed a calm morning. The days began with excitement and bravado. I shouted into the sky, "Good Morning, God, Hello World" and a chorus of "*Oh What a Beautiful Morning.*" A quiet voice in the back recesses of the canoe said, "*Now you know why we aren't seeing many animals.*"

Stevens Village, our last one, numbered around 100 residents. As did the other villages, this one had a couple of churches, a grocery and supply store, a post office, and school.

While I stayed with the canoe, Bill wandered. Two men came along and told me the blue-tarped place we had seen upriver about 16 miles, was where they were logging poles for a large community building. For food and gasoline, anyone could go work.

When Bill came back, he had Oliver Ben with him, a sweet old gent, who opened the showers for us. Bill had talked with several villagers and made connections with their kith and kin. Satisfied nobody would bother our gear, we combined our few dirty clothes in the Laundromat and took showers.

Originally I envisioned taking enough clothes for the entire trip, and washing only a few light things when necessary. I never dreamed we would have Laundromats and showers; however, the villages were interesting and the facilities welcome.

Our last stop was just before going into a long canyon between the Ray and White Mountains. The steep bank wouldn't have lent itself well to a campsite. The wind wasn't too bad on the gravel bar, but that also meant we had nothing but smoke to keep the mosquitoes away. I learned something with the advent of mosquitoes. I leave you with this profound thought,

**"If you moon a mosquito, repellent is the 'bottom' line
for comfort."**

My female friends had asked, "How will you go to the bathroom?" I was concerned because I figured we would be in tundra country with no trees. It is obvious to me that a great number of people have no interest in the answer to that question. Books about wilderness camping *never* touch the subject. May I be so indelicate as to answer this way.

Going is not a problem. Nature has a way of making everything come out in the end. Privacy wasn't a problem. Since we were both adults with adult functions, it was no secret we would have to "go" sometime. Bill stopped adequately often for such functions because we needed to take "arm breaks" anyhow. He said, "Gentlemen to the left, ladies to the right," or I would simply announce, "I'm going to find a bush." Since we had six children between us, we even used the word, "potty," occasionally. Holes were dug, waste was buried, and any paper used, was burned in the fire. With two people of the opposite sex traveling together, we were great respecters of each other's privacy in dressing, bathing, and finding suitable willow bushes. I never felt the least bit uncomfortable with Bill.

By the same token, the question from friends after the trip was, "Did you use two tents?" Bill had asked if I minded sleeping in the same tent or if I preferred a tent by myself. Since it would have meant extra gear, I told him, "As long as your wife doesn't mind, one tent is fine with me. I assume you will be a gentleman at all times," and having even a few short conversations with him, I knew he would be.

Besides, he had the gun.

Carpal Tunnel Syndrome surfaced with so much paddling. Sometimes I let go of the paddle and vigorously shook the tingling out of my hands. Bill suggested if I pounded my hands with a rock, I would soon forget the Carpal Tunnel Syndrome. His advice was priceless.

We had canoed beside ice chunks, through mountain passes lined with spruce, poplar, and birch trees, to the Taiga, "Land of little sticks," denoting the sparse tree growth above the Arctic Circle. We returned again to the wooded mountains carpeted with sphagnum moss. In the meantime, Mother Nature had painted all the sprouting rushes and willow shrubs in spring green.

Birds bathed in the big puddle next to the tent all night. With constant daylight, they never seem to sleep. The last day dawned sunny and windless, but I hated getting up. It was the end of a super adventure. We didn't build a fire. We packed and loaded while the mosquitoes ate breakfast, us. Two miles into the canyon, we ate ours. The canyon was long and straight, a change from the huge snaking loops we had canoed. We took our time and drifted quietly, alone in our own thoughts, knowing our solitude would soon be assaulted by *the world*.

I am a writer and still I can't adequately express what that trip meant to me. It was peaceful, exciting, dramatic, inspiring. It left me even more in awe of God and the wilderness. Whenever I need peace in the midst of chaos, I close my eyes and remember floating in circles in the current (preferably when I'm not driving).

We rounded a bend, and there it was, the silver Trans-Alaska Pipeline perched along the Yukon River Bridge on the Dalton Highway.

We pulled out near the bridge, 500 miles and 14 days wiser.
My terrific guide gave me a big hug and said,
"We did it. I'm proud of you."

The Yukon River Bridge, completed in 1975, is impressive, the only permanent crossing over the Yukon River in Alaska. The "Haul Road," or Dalton Highway, opened to the public in 1994.

Bill's son, Mike, drove the 500-mile return trip to Eagle with one major stop in Tok for fantastic pizza at Fast Eddy's Restaurant. Yummy. At 1:30 a.m., we rode the crest of the world, witnessing a magnificent sunset. The skies immediately lightened in the purple and pink of an Alaskan dawn. After a few hours of restless sleep, we were both dragging, but excited and telling our stories to anyone who would listen.

Charlie, the Good Life

Terese, Bill's wife, said several people had asked her how she could let her husband go off with a woman for two weeks. She said, "Complete trust." Amen. I said my good-byes.

Perhaps I have forgotten to mention there is one drawback to full-time RVing. You meet super people, but good-byes are frequent, and they hurt. It is Bill's business to raft visitors from place to place, and he probably doesn't get too close to anyone. He provided me with the means to live a fantastic adventure. Over two weeks, I felt we built up a very good rapport, and I would miss that camaraderie.

The sun was high in the sky when I left Eagle at 6 p.m. I stopped to fill a gallon jug with fresh water coming out of a mountain spring.

At the Walker River BLM Campground on Taylor Highway, the volunteer camp hosts, Val and Connie York, told me, "We don't have a single mosquito. They are all married with children."

My next stop was even more fowl than that joke.

Chicken Tracks To Anchorage

1996

I passed the newer version of Chicken, the Goldpanner, as I drove Taylor Highway toward Tok. They offer free overnight RV parking, but I still prefer "old" Chicken up the hill. A rivalry exists between the two. They were having a gas war. I filled the Sprinter at $1.59/gallon. Maybe they are always in the middle of a gas war. In 1992, I filled at $1.61. The fellow who waited on me said, "You're kind of a little thing to be driving that big rig." Hmmm.

Beautiful Downtown Chicken, AK

This was my third visit to Chicken. The gift shop, saloon, and cafe are all fastened together, tiny and quaint. I am fascinated with this area and its gold rush history, or maybe it's that big "Welcome to Beautiful Downtown Chicken," printed on the end of the gas tanks, that always bids me stop. Chicken, population 37, is an unusual name for a town. The name was Ptarmigan originally, but the miners couldn't spell it (let alone pronounce it). They renamed it.

Susan Wiren owns Chicken. If you don't want to get dizzy, do not follow her around. She is a whirling dervish of activity. I caught her long enough to tell her she was in my last book, *RVing North America, Silver, Single, & Solo.* She asked to see it, proceeded to buy several copies, and asked if I would like to sell my books out front. I set up my book display in the good company of Anne "Tisha" Purdy's adopted daughter. It was Tisha's cabin I saw in Eagle.

It was interesting talking with RVers and bus tour people, finding out where they had been and where they were going. The Chicken Creek Cafe has good food, mostly made by Susan. I like their reindeer sausage and burgers. One tourist walked around eating homemade blueberry pie. He had a big grin on his face like he had discovered Chicken's greatest secret. Good advertising.

The people working there were all kind and fun to be around. Jim was building Chicken's new Salmon Bake building. He had a big smile that said he loved everybody. Otis, another worker, was tall, full-bearded and really sweet. I think he lived in one of the "Chicken" houses.

At the end of the afternoon, the fellow who had pumped fuel, asked if I wanted to see the "Real Chicken." He insisted I wear boots. I wondered why until I realized spring melt had created a mud bog. One of the buildings was the schoolhouse where Tisha taught, and several buildings are living quarters for those working at Chicken. Guided tours are available. I am assuming that eventually everything will be restored, but little has been done to them at this point.

It was suggested I spend Saturday evening at the Chicken Creek Saloon. Since I had a friendly escort, I decided to find out what Chicken was like after the tourists go home and the locals come out. Chicken is the only place for miles around for them to socialize.

My friend built a fire in the old wood stove to ward off the evening chill. I discovered that the present Chicken buildings, including the saloon, had been there less than 20 years. The bar was tiny, crowded, and smoky. Besides the stove, it had a pool table, a couple of round tables with chairs, and the corner bar with stools. Hats and business cards were tacked to the ceiling and walls.

I met people I never would have met on my own. Chuck was tall, slender, short-bearded, blue-eyed, and had been an Ace helicopter pilot in Vietnam. He said, "Vietnam was a long time ago, and I don't dwell on it." He mines for someone else, but finds gold on his own with a metal detector. We talked about Quartzsite (AZ). He sells gold there sometimes, and I go to browse for at least a week, most winters. (A fun place to visit if you are in the Southwest.)

Jessie was short, wiry, had very few teeth, and looked like he had lost his last dollar. Looks are deceiving. I would never have guessed he was a talented glass sculpturist. He spoke so enthusiastically about his creations, I stopped to see them at Northway Restaurant in Tok. They were tiny and exquisite. I loved the covered wagon pulled by a moose, but what would I do with delicate glass sculpture in a motorhome?

My escort and I danced, and he taught me to play pool (I actually hit the ball about three times). Mainly, we talked about what we had in common. We both had grown families, attended church (when he was home), loved to travel, and he had wanted to come to Alaska with all his heart. He was retired and worked in Chicken for the summer, doing odd jobs and loving every minute of it.

I planned to leave the next day, but my new acquaintance had the day off and asked if I would like to go exploring and gold panning. Of course I said, "Yes."

I'll take a second here to reiterate thoughts about opening my arms to adventure. When I write about my Alaska adventures to dear friends, Betty and George from North Carolina, she confesses I scare her to death. For instance, when I wrote about the Yukon River trip, she said,

"Sharlene, how can you go off into the wilderness for two weeks with a complete stranger?" My reply, "He is a hired guide. It wouldn't be good for business if he molested a silver-haired grandmother."

Despite what newspapers, magazines, and TV tell you, *most* people are trustworthy. I certainly would not take off with just anybody, nor would I advise anyone else to do that. This comes under the heading of using common sense. I'm also not saying I couldn't make a fatal judgment one day, but I refuse to let the darker side of humanity imprison me behind a wall of fear. I tell my children, if somebody ever "does me wrong," I will have lived the life that God gave me, with a passion.

When I meet strangers, I listen. How do they speak of their children, their past, their friends, their late or ex-spouse, their God? Do they blame everyone else for their troubles? Do they pet the dog or kick it?

Personally, I don't care if they have Mayflower relatives. My background is Heinz, 57 varieties. I enjoy people because they talk about interesting experiences, places they've visited, and they embrace adventure as I do. Now that you've had your morning sermon, I'll continue.

Our gold panning came to naught. We decided to drive to Eagle for lunch. People in this country think nothing of driving 95 miles to the nearest place to eat. I had just been over the road to Eagle twice in the last 48 hours, but you already know it was my kind of twisty, windy road, and this time I didn't have to drive.

I was introduced to yet another interesting person. As it turned out, I had passed this abode at least three times in the past month, and always wondered who lived there. Mark looked pretty grungy. When he was invited to go to lunch with us, he insisted on cleaning up. Mark lives in a brown bus surrounded by the necessities of northern life, barrels of gasoline and equipment. It takes a second glance to realize his home and hearth is not a junk heap. He obviously can't store all that stuff inside so it has its place outside, and it is close by for effective use.

Talk about a metamorphose. With a bath and clean clothes, this was one handsome dude! Now, here is where I had some fun writing to Betty. I was not only going to lunch with *two* tall, dark handsome strangers, but one had a 357 strapped to his hip and the other, a 44. I wasn't sure whether we were looking for bear, or whether they thought *I* was that dangerous!

Mark has made gold mining his life. He has eight gold claims in four different places, with teepees set up for a place to live when he isn't in his brown bus.

To my friend's urging, Mark told these stories. He once was making his way up a mountain road from his canoe when a grizzly confronted him. The bear rushed Mark, and then stopped when Mark didn't run away. The bear rushed him again, and Mark still didn't run. He had a gun, but knew it would be ineffective and make the bear mad if it wounded him. Mark stood his ground. "Either the bear would eat me or go away." The grizzly started eating berries so Mark did too. Eventually the bear wandered away (Some potential dinners just aren't any fun).

He ran into another grizzly on his continuation up the mountain. The bear ran when Mark became aggressive. It seems to me that it not only gets pretty dangerous out in that wild country, but it would take you forever to make it where you were going. Especially since he also said it took him six hours to canoe downstream to his claim, and 12 to come back upstream. Having seen the stream he was talking about, I couldn't believe anybody ever canoed *against* that current!

By then, we were in Eagle. Once again I was in the Riverside Cafe. As we ate, which probably wasn't the best time, Mark explained his dishwashing methods. He *doesn't!* Mark says the trick is to, "Let the liquid dry right away then it doesn't create bacteria. If you let it layer without drying, then you get bacteria." If something does start growing, he throws it away. I asked, "If I came for dinner, would I have to eat on a dish that you used for six months?" He replied, "I have plastic for visitors," and he admitted to using disposable cardboard part of the time.

After he referred to himself as the "Brown Bus Weirdo," I asked if he thought of himself as a hermit. He was taken aback, "No, I feel a hermit is anti-social, and I'm not. I like being around people sometimes."

He was enjoying lunch. He certainly was charming, and fascinated me totally. He had beautiful brown eyes, an infectious grin, and he didn't seem to mind my 1,001 questions. He was married once upon a time. Over and over again, I hear about wives who have returned to the lower 48 for a more gentle life. Living in Alaska is a hard life for women.

Then we got down to basics. He goes into town (Eagle) about four times a year, and into Fairbanks once a year *for a year's supply* of food. I know they used to do that a 100 years ago. After talking with more miners during the summer, I realize it isn't all that unusual in places only reached by canoe or by foot.

He mentioned buying a 36-pound bucket of peanut butter and a 60-pound container of honey. He says he gets the basics that he can fix quickly, because he doesn't like to cook. He said, "I don't get much fresh stuff, unless it's berries or something that grows near me." With that method of dishwashing (or non-method), he should have plenty of green.

Mark is self-taught, especially in geology, or "Anything that will help me find the gold." He talked about making a laboratory to test the stuff. He certainly sounded like he knew what he was talking about. He writes songs, and designed a recording studio into his dream cabin that he described down to the last two-by-four. It seemed rather an unlikely place to find that type of place where he intended to build it, but the dream was real, and at 41, he has a chance of making it come true.

By the time we dropped Mark off at his brown bus, I felt a real loss when I hugged him good-bye. I feel a certain affinity with anyone who is living his dream. I'll never know if he makes all his dreams come true or not, because it is unlikely I'll ever see him again. The memory of our conversation about his unusual lifestyle has brought a smile to my thoughts many times since.

I never thought I'd return to Alaska or that area again, but in 2001, I once again drove the road to Eagle. Much to my disappointment, Mark's brown bus home was gone. I could probably have found out what happened to him but I didn't want to impose. And also, I really wanted to think that in the five years since I had been there, that he really had built that dream cabin financed by his major gold vein, and was living happily ever after.

By the time my friend and I returned to Chicken and said our quick good-byes, it was already evening. Another new friend, another goodbye. Given the time of year, it was still daylight, so I fired up the Sprinter and took off.

I hadn't gone far when a fifth wheel came toward me on the narrow dirt road. About then I hit soft dirt and thought I was going over. The Sprinter tilted and ran along the ditch at a miserable angle, hitting brush and dragging dirt. If I didn't keep moving, I would be there permanently. About 30 yards later, I angled it back up over the shoulder onto the road. When I reached a pullout, I accessed the damage. The generator exhaust pipe needed straightening, and the step was forever creamed. I pulled weeds and dirt out of a few places, but nothing appeared permanently damaged. Even the surface marks rubbed out. I was quite happy this happened where land lived, and not near a 1000' drop.

The inside was a lot like it would be if a mad bear got loose within the Sprinter's confines. The silverware drawer had upchucked. Everything on the counter made a spectacular dive for the floor. Fortunately, the office equipment and everything else was tethered.

This story is also to emphasize the need for safe driving practices. I consider myself a good driver, but the unexpected happened.

I love early mornings views, especially on a ridge. It was 4:30 a.m. I purposely moved early to avoid the construction workers. The road was a mess the last 40 miles to the Alaska Highway.   A month had passed since I left Dawson City. I could hardly believe the adventures I had experienced in four weeks.

Tok would normally be a decision time between driving the loop toward Fairbanks or toward Anchorage. I didn't have a choice. It was June 18 and I was flying out of Anchorage on the 20th.

Tok 2001

Bill Elmore, my Yukon River guide, no longer had his rafting business. He went back to work on the North Slope at Prudhoe Bay. He and

Teresa were living near Tok and leaving shortly to go on their own RV summer adventures in the "lower 48." I had lunch with Teresa at Fast Eddy's and caught up on news of their family, including the fact they had just become new grandparents.

A local recommendation took me to newly-opened Tok RV and Repair. Bill checked the exhaust system that threatened to asphyxiate me each time I stopped for a few minutes. He said I needed a donut. I said I had already eaten breakfast. (Just kidding.) I asked when he could fix it and he said, "How about right now?" It is amazing how often that happens in Alaska.

With a SKP discount, the gas at the Tesoro station on the north end of town was $1.84. I bought propane and took advantage of their free dumping, water, and RV wash with fuel fill-up. The Hyder-forwarded mail hadn't arrived at Tok so I forwarded it on to Hope.

I had been hearing a strange clunking noise since morning. I went back to Tok RV and requested a test drive. Bill said the universal joint was sloppy and not to worry about it. I told him I always worry when I hear a "new" noise. It was almost 5 p.m. but he took it apart and worked on it until it was fixed. He showed me the inside of the end piece that was supposed to have a ring of bearings in it. Nothing was there.

One of his helpers picked up the part and said, "This is cracked. It is a good thing Bill caught it because it could have caused a lot of trouble if it had fallen apart." Bill said, "I didn't catch it, she did!" Since it was so late, he allowed me to park for the night.

With a load of groceries and everything else full or emptied, the Sprinter and I departed on the Tok Cut-off, a beautiful route but so far it has never been a beautiful road.

Whether you would call them Kodak Moments or Fuji Dramas, is debatable, but when Mount Sanford (16,237'), Mount Drum (12,010'), and Mount Wrangell (14,163') come out to play, it is a breathtaking panoramic sight. These always snow-covered Wrangell–St. Elias National Park and Preserve Mountains stretch all the way to Glennallen. It was the first time I saw them without fog. The 42-mile Nabesna Road side trip into the park was new territory.

The Nabesna Gold Mine is at the road's end. The mine closed in the 1940s. A few people still live there, as they do in a few places along the road. I drove through relatively flat country surrounded by somewhat stunted forest and that stupendous continuing scenery.

Thirty miles took me through iffy soft road in some sections and very rocky in others, until I found myself contemplating the freshening Lost Creek Crossing. The stream flowed through bits and pieces of winter's leftover snow, growing swiftly with the rain that gave the Sprinter another bath. The Milepost said the road beyond Lost Creek deteriorated and crossed several more streams in its last 15 miles. With its advice and my own common sense (Yes, have some), and a fair number of boondocking spots, I turned around and parked above Rock Lake for the night.

Nabesna Road Boondocking

It was May 31, and as the sun rose, I climbed on top of the Sprinter for a good panoramic view. I was rewarded on all sides. Dark clouds filled the northern sky. Within a couple of hours they had moved out of sight and blue skies prevailed. Rock Lake was still covered by mushy ice. A trip down a muddy trail revealed moose tracks with an impressive amount of moose poop jewelry possiblities indicating he was a big hummer.

Breakfast was a half-cup of cholesterol-free oatmeal with almonds, raisins, a half banana with milk and just a smidgen of fat-free French-vanilla creamer. Hardy and delicious would last me well into the day. RVers have it rough don't ya know.

I turned off the heat and opened the window to hear the birds heralding spring even though it wasn't evident in anything but the new pussy willows near the lake. I pulled my covers over me, sliding back into a light sleep once more after breakfast and a walk, relishing the peace and quiet. The fresh, clean, cool air felt good on my face. When I say cool, I'm talking about the frigid kind that sweeps down off all that snow, a good deal of which would be there until winter returned. In fact, winter may not have made its last gasp. The mountains were powdered again with fresh snow in the night.

It was wonderful. I had no place to be. No one knew where I was. E-mail informed my kids that I had arrived in Alaska but they didn't know where I was going next and I didn't either. I finally got up and it was still only 7:30. The sun warmed on my back. I sat at the computer and recorded my thoughts with the magic help of solar panels and an inverter.

One of these days I will be able to afford a satellite telephone and e-mail access so I only have to go into town once a summer. Perhaps I should take lessons in bringing down a moose or a few of those cottontails, then I would be more independent and not need that land line to town. I suppose I'm not that hardy and I'd no doubt shoot myself in the foot with a gun.

After four days of sleeping, reading, working, and not spending any money, I drove toward the Tok Cut-Off another six miles and parked.

A couple in a mini motorhome the same size and vintage as the

Sprinter, stopped for the night also. Norm and Mary from Minnesota had driven to the Panama Canal and did they have the stories! No, it didn't make me want to go; it made me want to have gone. They were also interested in my comparatively dull stories. We spent most of the afternoon, and with their dinner invitation, the evening together. I ran into them three more times over the next few weeks and we always exchanged interesting tidbits.

After collecting information at the Copper River Valley Visitor Center (Corner of Glenn and Richardson Highways in Glennallen) and a great hamburger at The Hitchin' Post, I continued on the Glenn Highway. I found the Paper Shack Office Supply where the Milepost advertised a "book exchange." They also sold groceries and "Basic liquors"

The owner was a very exuberant lady who called everybody Sweetheart and Love and affectionately hugged all comers. "I was a teacher for 400 years," she said and how her students must have loved her. I put a couple of bucks in the big "change jar," and exchanged seven novels. I left with a hug and a lot of joy.

Little Nelchina State Recreation Site on the Glenn Highway had 11 campsites and no fee. Couldn't beat the price. Normally I would have grabbed a river site to be as close as possible to the rushing water sound. It was rushing a bit too madly for my taste and seemingly on the rise. I took the ridge site, with a safe distance between us, closed my front curtains, turned on the propane ceramic heater, curled up on my bed and read. The rain had no time schedule nor did I. Life was good.

1996

Information on road conditions is available at the visitor center in Glenallen. State Recreation and private campgrounds are frequent. At the junction of Glenn and Richardson Highways, the people at the Copper River Valley Visitor Center were friendly and helpful. Always stop at visitor centers. They are a wealth of information about accommodations, tours, and "What's happenin" locally.

We'll hit Valdez and McCarthy later in the trip. Now, we'll continue toward Anchorage. Look in your rear view mirror for more spectacular views of the Wrangell Mountains.

Have I said "spectacular" too many times already? Too bad. I have seen it green and I've seen it white. From Glennallen to Palmer is spectacular. You'll be driving between the Talkeetna and Chugach Mountains with many places to pull off. Please stop. Absorb the beauty; don't just fly by it, you might miss the two moose munching along the green strip between the highway and the trees.

Don't fail to stop at the Matanuska Glacier overlooks. It flows out of the Chugach Mountains. This is one of the glaciers you can get to, but entrance is through a private campground, and there is a fee. It might be worth it because they have a trail leading right up to the glacier.

In 2001, I was enjoying the same scenery when someone said, "Charlie?" Jack and Joan Rumohr are fellow Escapees and fellow (originally) Michiganders who had flown up for 10 days via some free air miles and were soon to be on their way home. Again, the small world.

I have stayed in the Matanuska Glacier State Recreation Site and hiked their ridge trail. Great views of the glacier and I also saw a mother moose with twins. One of them lost his footing and rolled down the steep mountain, got up, and scrambled after his mother.

You'll find plenty of activities in and around Palmer. One of my favorite stops is the Musk Ox Farm. I've always said moose are so ugly, they're cute. By the same token, musk oxen also have faces only their mothers could love.

If you want a pet but can't take it with you, these shaggy beasts are available for adoption. A couple of noted surrogate fathers are Alex Trebek and Garth Brooks. The Musk Ox Farm is a domestication project started in 1954. The musk ox is considered a "Unique prehistoric remnant of the last great Ice Age." It was spring, and the babies had just arrived from Musk Ox Heaven.

Musk Ox, Palmer, AK

If you want to own something that is "softer than smoke," buy an item made from "qiviut." As a protection from the frigid weather, musk oxen grow layers of soft underwool called "qiviut." I have never held anything so soft in my life. An ounce of qiviut is eight times warmer than an equal amount of sheep wool. They shed this in warm weather, but it is also combed out with a regular pick comb and spun into yarn. The Native Alaskan Knitters Cooperative knits it into clothing. It is a working farm run by volunteers. Tours are available.

The Palmer Visitor Center has a showcase garden to walk through. It is only a few blocks from the Visitor Center to the United Protestant "Church of a Thousand Trees."

The Mat-Su Valley has an interesting agricultural history. In 1935, the Matanuska Valley Project brought more than 200 families from the Midwest Dust Bowl, to the Palmer's rich valley land to build a farming colony supported by the federal government. While the project wasn't totally successful, the Mat-Su Valley is now a thriving agricultural region.

Palmer is a decision point, but since you wouldn't want to miss the

Kenai Peninsula, let's head down toward Anchorage. We'll go to Fairbanks later in the summer.

In 2001, the library across from the visitor center, had a long list of Internet users ahead of me so I stayed overnight in Palmer's The Homestead RV Park where I had Internet Access for $2, and a laundry. Nice park. It was too early for their summer evening musical.

If you have an interest in Native culture, stop at the Eklutna Historical Park. More than 80 "spirit houses" are in a sacred burial ground of Dena'ina Athabascans. We listened to a talk about 350 years of culture and traditions, by a knowledgeable host. We then toured the spirit houses, the prayer chapel, and the 100-year-old hand-hewn log St. Nicholas Russian Orthodox Church, on our own.

Originally Native people were cremated and the spirit houses were built as a home for the ashes and personal effects. Natives began burying their dead during the last half of the 19th Century, but spirit houses are still built on top of the burial site. The spirit house also shelters the departing spirit of the deceased and provides a cherished place where the Great Spirit can visit.

When an Indian is buried, the family places a new blanket over the grave instead of flowers, as is our tradition. A cross is immediately placed at the foot of the grave signifying the deceased was Orthodox Christian. On the 40th day, the family erects a spirit house atop the grave, painting it in traditional colors unique to each family. The shape and design are at the discretion of family members.

Close by is Thunderbird Falls. It is an easy two-mile round-trip hike back to the 200' falls. The path follows Eklutna Canyon through a birch forest to a boardwalk and viewing platform. In the same area, drive out to the Eagle River Visitor Center in the Chugach State Park.

Anchorage has a lot to offer. I was caught up in Alaska's aviation history at the Alaska Aviation Heritage Museum near Anchorage International Airport. They have details of the Wiley Post-Will Rogers plane crash at Barrow. Other legends of Alaska history were Carl Ben Eielson, who flew Alaska's first airmail run in 1924. Many of the bush planes rescued from ravines, mine tailings, and other obscure places, are being restored. They have over 30 vintage aircraft and exhibits.

Nearby Lake Hood Seaplane Base is the busiest, and largest, floatplane base in the world. I love to watch them take off and land. Alaska is noted for its plane population. Alaska has nearly six times the pilots, and 16 times the aircraft, per capita, as the "lower 48." You'll probably see more planes tied down in back yards than RVs! It is not all that unusual to see signs on Alaskan roads warning of their use as emergency landing strips.

A Michigander runs a lesser known, but extremely busy airport to the south of Anchorage International. It is restricted to tourist season and accommodates only 747 flights. Their business is transporting blood. Stop in and tell him Charlie sent you. His name is Moss Quido.

While I was in downtown Anchorage picking up mail, I wandered over to the Log Cabin Visitor Information Center at 4th and F Street. They have current information on activities, nightlife, museums, and tours. Next door, Bandstand Park has shade trees and benches to sit on and listen to free summer concerts. Food and souvenirs are for sale at nearby stands. The Anchorage City Trolley Tour is only $10. RV parking is $5 for all day on Third Avenue across from the post office.

If you want to see all of Alaska in less than an hour, see "Alaska the Greatland" on the Omnivision screen at the Alaska Experience Center. I really enjoyed that. The Alaska Earthquake Exhibit is there also. That was especially interesting after visiting so many of the places affected. While you watch the quake story unfold in the theatre, you actually feel the rumbling and shaking of a simulated earthquake through your seat.

I stayed at Centennial Park just outside of Anchorage. Some pleasant big campgrounds, with all the amenities plus, exist within the city limits, but their prices are not as pleasant as Centennial Park. It is a dry camp park for $13/night. They have showers, dump station, and telephone. I like it because it is in a wooded area, and convenient.

Leaving my precious tin tent in the airport parking lot, I flew from Anchorage to Wenatchee, Washington. I picked up my car in Leavenworth, and drove to the University of Idaho at Moscow for the Life on Wheels Conference. In writing my plans to a good friend, I realized how often we skim, rather than read, letters. Her reply was thus, "I had no idea the Russians were so interested in RVing."

I was an instructor for the Life on Wheels Conference for five days. RVers or "Wannabes" numbering 430, came to listen to 41 charged up instructors from varied backgrounds and expertise.

I had two basic messages.
One, life is short; live it to the fullest.
Two, if I can live this lifestyle, anyone can.

The Life on Wheels Conferences are the brainchild of Gaylord Maxwell. From 6:30 a.m. "doughnut hours," to late afternoon "meet the author" sessions, people from all walks of life listened, learned, and asked questions. They were an enthusiastic group.

After being in my Adventure on Alaska and Canada class, students Jim and Linda Schrankel, surprised me with a copy of Alaska by James A. Michener.

Three times in my four trips to Alaska, I have invited friends to visit. The first of these was Jane.

Down on the Kenai

1996

When I returned to Alaska, I kept a low profile and stayed in the airport parking lot. I had paid for two weeks of long-term parking so I took advantage of it. Without interruptions, other than constant airplanes, it was time to pay the piper. I caught up on columns, wrote about the conference, answered mail, and mailed books.

Dall Sheep, Turnagain Arm

My Fourth of July was uneventful until evening, when the lady whom I call my "surrogate mother," arrived from Florida for a two-week visit. I lived with Jane and Orville Parker during the time I studied to become a Medical Secretary, more years ago than I care to mention. We remained friends through the years. She is now a widow and occasionally visits me in my travels. This was Jane's first trip to Alaska. Our first direction took us to the Kenai Peninsula.

The Seward Highway is a designated National Forest Scenic Byway and rightly so. It is one of the prettiest routes you will be on. It has everything. Seward Highway follows the shoreline of Turnagain Arm. If the fog takes a hike, you can see down and across the Arm to glaciated snow-covered mountains.

Stop at one of the many turnouts and look above or around you. I can almost guarantee you'll see Dall sheep posing on the cliffs or whales swimming in the Arm. Your clues of their presence are visitors craning their necks, looking through binoculars, or scanning the water. The sheep look like they are posing. It is great fun to watch these unbelievably agile creatures.

Sunken Dreams, Turnagain Arm

Of great curiosity to me, are the mud flats. When the tide is out (tide table books are available nearly everywhere), all the water in Turnagain Arm returns to Cook Inlet and ultimately to the sea. It looks like a great, irregular bowl, filled with lumpy, dark, chocolate pudding.

Do not walk anywhere on the mud flats.
Some of it is quick sand and
extremely dangerous.

Dead, naked trees (ghost forests) and sunken buildings rest in the marshes along this section of the Seward Highway. It shows firsthand the destruction of the 1964 9.2 earthquake. The Arm dropped 6-12', allowing the lowlands to be inundated with saltwater and killing the trees.

Alyeska Ski Resort had grown drastically since I was there in 1987. The Kobuk Valley Jade Company, and The Bake Shop with its great cinnamon rolls, are still there. This is crowded both summer and winter. I have never yet ridden the Alyeska Tramway to the 2,300' level of Mt. Alyeska. Seven Glaciers Restaurant, and the view, are open year around. Many exciting activities begin at Alyeska, flightseeing trips, gold panning, etc. (*In 2001, the parking was still a disaster for RVs but they are working on a solution.*)

26 Glacier Tour, Whittier

A ticket office for the Alaska Railroad is on the Seward Highway. The Alaska Railroad was once the only way to reach Denali National Park. The Denali Highway opened in 1957 and the George Parks Highway opened in 1972. I talked with homesteaders on the 1987 trip. The husband moved to Alaska to build bridges in Denali National Park in 1937. There were no roads. They brought in a trailer by train and lived in it until they skidded a cabin to their property.

Tours on this scenic railroad go from Seward to Anchorage and from Anchorage to Fairbanks with stops at Denali National Park and a motor coach return. Tour arrangements are made through The Alaska Railroad or the tour companies.

A friend and I signed up for a Twenty-six-Glacier Tour on the M/V Klondike high-speed catamaran. The Alaska Railroad took us from the ticket office on Seward Highway (at Portage), through two tunnels, one 13,090' long, and the other, 4,910'. The trip is nearly 25 miles round-trip and connects with the Alaska Marine Highway.

In 2001, the tunnel through the mountain had been altered to accommodate a highway alongside the railroad. This eliminated the adventure for me. The toll was $40 for RVs which I thought was excessive and definitely not adventurous!

With a population of roughly 250, Whittier is a fishing community. It is a great jumping-off place for seeing Prince William Sound; and besides, it's named after one of my favorite poets, John Greenleaf Whittier. They have a RV park for self-contained RVs who come in via ferryboat or train.

Some trips are shrouded in fog; but that day, it was as clear as a bell with unbelievable sunshine and warmth. Our smooth-sailing catamaran took us up College Fjord to see Harvard and Yale Glaciers. They began at the top of the Chugach Mountains and the great Columbia Glacier. We passed Wellesley, Vassar, Bryn Mawr, and Smith Glaciers. In Harriman Fiord, we visited Harriman Glacier, named for Edward Henry Harriman, father of Averell. The glaciers on the left were named after women's colleges and on the right were the men's colleges.

Dozens of sea otters with babies resting on their bellies, floated on their backs. Their bellies are also used as tables to crack clamshells open. If we went too close, they dove. They are able to dive to depths of 120 feet. I'm not sure what happens to Junior when they dive.

We saw an American bald eagle's nest and several eagles, as well as a noisy kittiwake rookery.

We returned to Passage Canal where the captain said if we could see 40 miles down Wells Passage, we would see, "At four minutes past midnight on Good Friday, March 24, 1989, the tanker, Exxon Valdez, slamming into Bligh Reef, spilling over 10.8 million gallons of crude oil into the Sound." The brochure assured us, "These areas are now a dynamic wilderness laboratory for recording the progression of natural changes, and the re-establishment of ecological equilibrium."

They now believe the epicenter for the 1964 Alaska Earthquake, was on the peninsula between College Fiord (where we were) and Unakwik Inlet. You are unlikely to remember the names of 26 glaciers, and one glacier will look like any other by the end of the day; but it is worth the $120 (1992) ticket. It is a narrated 110-mile cruise with a great crew. It would be fun even if you weren't seeing some of the world's most spectacular scenery.

When a tidewater glacier sheds icebergs off its face into the sea, it is called "calving." To actually hear the loud boom of a glacier calving is amazing. The ice crashes into the water, leaving pristine ice so blue you won't believe your eyes. Back to the Seward Highway, and Jane, and continuing down Turnagain Arm.

We spent the night overlooking the river and mountains in Ptarmigan Creek USFS campground for $9/night *($10 in 2001)*. I think Jane didn't realize how different it was going to be. She wanted to phone her son to tell him she had arrived safely. Remember, folks, you will not find telephones hanging on spruce trees. Plan ahead if you'll need a phone.

The Exit Glacier Road was paved for about four miles, but the rest of the nine-mile trip was miserable washboard under construction. I have discovered that driving faster over washboard is less miserable than inching my way along. Perhaps I am just hitting the peaks that way! (*In 2001, Exit Glacier Road was completely paved.*)

Exit Glacier, part of Kenai Fjords National Park, is one of the few places you can drive to, and have an easy quarter-mile walk right up to a living glacier. A paved, wheelchair accessible trail leads to a glacier view. From there, you can walk across the gravel to the glacier base.

It is not wise to climb on the glacier.
There is a longer trail to an overlook.

A good-sized stream comes from under the glacier and warning signs advise you not to stand too close to the ice. You can't see it move, but it is living and moving. Ice chunks and rocks fall. I mean, how much more "up close and personal" do you have to be with a glacier?

Seward is part of the Alaska Marine Highway System and has RV hook-ups and dry camping all along the harbor. We paid $8/night for dry camping and watched the comings and goings of kayaks, ferryboats, and cruise ships on Resurrection Bay. *(Camping was $10 in 2001)*

Sidewalk traffic brought humanity in all its varied forms and dress, ambling, in-line skating, or biking. Harbor seals swam along next to shore.

If you have reasonably good walking skills, RV camping is close enough to walk to the many galleries, shops and the bayfront activities. This is another jumping-off place for flightseeing, kayaking trips, day cruises, fishing charters, sled dog rides, and the Alaska Railroad. July 4th, which we missed by two days, is a blast.

They have a footrace up Mount Marathon. It is a 1.5-mile trail climb to a 3,000' elevation. The return is a fast slip and slide down a gravelly decline. Anyone can get in on this, "One of the oldest foot races in the U.S." by registering. Do I see a mass exodus as all of you register? Well, it might be fun to watch anyway.

Previously, I enjoyed driving out to Lowell's Point. The hike to Caines Head State Recreation Area begins there. I'd like to do that hike, but not alone. Early in WWII, the territory of Alaska was attacked and occupied by Imperial Japanese ground forces. Fort McGilvray was established at Caines Head, one of the strategic spots for defending the Port of Seward. Seward was the southern terminus of the Alaska Railroad and a critical supply line for the war effort.

The remains of the bunkers and gun emplacements built to guard the entrance to Resurrection Bay, are still there. Three miles of the 4.5-mile trail must be hiked during low tide.

Miller's Landing at Lowell's Point, has a campground, interesting store, and charter services. Coffee is free, and five-cent fishing advice is guaranteed. It doesn't get much better than that.

Seward has a memorial to Benny Benson, a 13-year-old orphan from Seward, who designed Alaska's deep violet-blue flag with the golden stars. He explained, "The blue field is for the Alaska sky and the forget-me-not, an Alaska flower. The North Star is the future state of Alaska, the most northerly of the Union. The Big Dipper is for the Great Bear, symbolizing strength."

St. Peter's Episcopal Church has a unique mural, "The

Resurrection." Resurrection Bay is used as a background and Seward residents are models. Dutch artist, Jan Van Empel, painted it in 1925.

The Seward waterfront (Hoben Park) is the official Milepost 0 of the Historic Iditarod Trail. The Iditarod Trail Sled Dog Race begins in Anchorage now, but the trail started here in 1908 and went 1,200 miles to Nome.

2001

An Auburn, Indiana, friend, Linda Bassett, visited me for 10 days. We go back to age 17 when she became a lab technician and I became a medical secretary. Somewhere between then and now, we raised families, she became the owner of Bassett Office Supply, I became a writer, and we both became widows. As you know, RVers have to be adaptable and flexible. She was the perfect RVing companion.

As Linda and I pulled into our city campsite along Resurrection Bay, the people next door were barbecuing salmon. A small world again. We both got hugs from Judy and Nick Santamaria. I had met them at North Ranch the winter before. We hadn't had dinner yet so they offered us half of their salmon. We took it! Delicious.

Godwin Glacier Dog Mushing

The Alaska SeaLife Center next to the University of Alaska Institute of Marine Science near the ferry dock, had opened. Unfortunately, with a limited time schedule, we spent only two hours in the Alaska SeaLife Center. A visit really needs to be at least four hours long, and a whole day would be better. This beautiful waterfront building houses research and creature rehabilitation funded by private donations and the Exxon Valdez Oil Spill Restoration fund.

Depending on the floor you are on, you have an aboveground or underwater habitat view of everything from a seal to a puffin gliding right past your nose. They have outdoor exhibits and "hands on" as well. This place is fascinating for kids as well as adults.

Linda was brave enough to leave the entire trip planning to me. Even I had a surprise coming when we flew via helicopter from Alaska's version of summer, to a winter day on Godwin Glacier above Seward to put our mushing knowledge to a test. We landed in a big snow bowl with a 100 barking sled dogs. We had two rules to follow. Rule #1 was to hang on tight and Rule #2 was to follow Rule #1. We were each given an opportunity (?) to "mush" the dogs. Uh huh!

The front sled held a sitting visitor and a standing "real" musher on runners behind the barking power. Held by ropes, the tandem sled carried a visitor and a "pseudo" musher following rules #1 and #2 fervently. If our feet slid off the runners, perhaps as we were applying brakes at "the" Mushers instruction, we would merely fall back in the snow (At 490 miles an hour!). I was still a bit apprehensive til I "mushed" a couple of miles around the valley in the blowing snow. I couldn't let Linda outdo me and she was a natural.

Linda smuggled a couple of squirming sled dog puppies-in-training aboard the helicopter but they noticed. She reluctantly gave them up. The pilot flew us over more glaciers before our return to the airport over the numerous RVs parked along Resurrection Bay shoreline.

At first glance, this adventure is pricey at $299.25. Since we paid individually, it wasn't as bad as for a couple. However, if you break it down, I still think it is worth it. You get a helicopter tour over the glaciers, Seward, and Resurrection Bay. The dog sled ride is so much more than you will experience anywhere else. The atmosphere and the ride itself on a "real" dogsled, surpasses what I have seen anywhere else. Sled dog rides usually consist of either a big sleigh affair or a regular version on wheels. You have a chance to be on top of a glacier and actually see how the dogs live (and the people who care for them).

Linda's 10 days ended with a Chiswell Islands Glacier Tour, more goldpanning at Crow Creek National Historic Site, and major shopping for her grandchildren. Linda went home a happy woman despite the weather. Although we were disappointed when Dusty Sourdough's nightly program didn't materialize, we enjoyed our last dinner together at the Sourdough Mining Company in Anchorage.

Between the Sprinter's usual problems, boondocking beside isolated streams, and some unusual activities, Linda gave me a tiny Eskimo angel pin. She said I needed another among the legion already on my shoulder. I wonder what she meant by that.

In the fall after I returned from Alaska, I contacted Editor Dave Kurtz of Auburn, Indiana's Evening Star and he printed a story and photograph on Linda's Alaskan trip. She wasn't aware of it until the morning it hit the streets. Great fun!

1996

But back to 1996 and Jane's visit. The Seward Visitor Center hands out a card that you don't get just anywhere. This one lists the Tsunami Safety Rules. The strongest earthquake ever recorded in North America, 9.2 on the Richter scale, shook Alaska in 1964. Seward had an estimated $22 million in damage. The waterfront fell into the water, bridges collapsed, and oil storage tanks exploded. If that wasn't enough, the tsunami came with 30' sea waves that continuously pummeled the town until the next morning. An earthquake movie is shown at the community library, and the Resurrection Bay Historical Society Museum has a quake display.

Jane and I opted for boarding the Kenai Star for a full-day Kenai Fjords Wildlife and Glacier Cruise, for $99. Seward is the gateway to the Kenai Fjords National Park. A National Park Ranger gave a running narration of the sights.

He explained that a fur coat, which they constantly groom, protects the sea otters. They are called "old men of the sea." "The only part that isn't covered by fur, is their feet. That's why you see them swimming on their backs with their feet out of the cold water." Made sense to me.

They promised we would see cormorants, kittiwakes, and puffins. We did. They didn't promise Humpback whales. Sometimes finding whales is a fluke, but we found several in a cove. The engines shut down and we drifted in their bath water.

Dall sheep posed on the mountain. A new mother nursed her baby on a precarious cliff to protect it from predators. We saw bald eagles, porpoises, and a raucous colony of reddish-colored Stellar's sea lions.

At Holgate Glacier, we enjoyed our delicious all-you-can-eat salmon buffet, and the narrator explained "Burger Burps." "After the glaciers calve, the little ice burgers burp, like popping champagne." Unfortunately, since our beautiful sunny weather had turned into "swell" weather, we weren't sure all the burps were coming from the ice burgers.

By the time we started back into the continued swells, an alarming number of visitors had turned a deep shade of puce. The helpful and sympathetic attendants handed out barf bags and ginger candy.

Our cruise was to include a run through the Chiswell Islands National Wildlife Refuge. Since the bow aimed directly into the water, then directly into the sky, the captain used good sense in turning back. Nobody objected. Funny how rough seas brought a Gordon Lightfoot song to mind, "The Wreck of the Edmund Fitzgerald."

We returned along the Seward Highway, following a section overlooking Kenai Lake, to Tern Lake Junction, turning left on Sterling Highway toward Homer. The big pullout at Tern Lake has a boardwalk and viewing platforms with informational signs.

Because of its fame as a fishing Paradise, campgrounds are abundant on the Kenai Peninsula. I don't give a whit for fishing, but the scenery is worth the trip. The extraordinary color of Kenai Lake is from glacial melt. We stayed overnight high above the Russian River in a USFS paved RV parking lot for $5. The Kenai River kept us company. It is very scenic along there and heavily fished, to the point of fishermen being almost shoulder to shoulder. I once saw a mother moose and her baby swimming across the river.

Soldotna has a huge Fred Meyer Store. They encourage RVers to stay overnight in designated areas of their lot, and offer a dump station and water fill. During season, it is always jammed. The store has everything. It is a good place to replenish and refresh.

The Interpretive Center for the Kenai National Wildlife Refuge is near Soldotna. It covers a good bit of that side of the peninsula. It is the largest moose range in North America, and usually I see a lot of them.

On one trip or another, I have stopped at most of the beaches along the Sterling Highway, such as Clam Gulch. It lived up to its name with lots of clamdiggers there. Scenic pullouts on the cliff high above Cook Inlet allow overnights for zip. You will have company if you park on any of the scenic gravel pullouts overlooking Cook Inlet. The facilities are zip. The cost is zip. The scenery is zippy.

I'll mention here that the camping has changed in the last several years. Dry camping isn't encouraged anywhere, but until this last trip, many pullouts were available for free overnights. A lot of these places have disappeared into formal campgrounds. Signs denying RV overnight parking are proliferating.

In 2001, except for rest areas, I found no open boondocking overlooking the Inlet. The land had either been built upon or just closed off. This may have happened for several reasons, the number one reason being,

It takes only a few rotten RVers in the boondock barrel to spoil privileges for all of us.

We can't blame the State of Alaska (or anyone else) for disallowing the privilege of boondocking if idiots dump sewers or leave trashy messes behind. I would like to think that 99.9% of RVers live by the Girl Scout rule (probably boys, too),

"Leave it better than you found it."

While I'm on the soapbox, I was at a stoplight incline behind a RV. Liquid was pouring out of a sewer tank. It wasn't water runoff from filling too much. That happens to me, too, and it always embarrasses me because I'm afraid people assume it is the sewer. Without a desire to get in a fight with anybody, I tried raising the RVer by CB. It was either turned off or he was ignoring me. I was going to ask if he was aware that his sewer was pouring all over the street.

A number of people feel it is OK to let gray water leak out because it is only bath or dish water.
Think again!
I don't advise it anywhere.
People other than RVers look at it and think the worst.

It takes just a bit of planning ahead to find places to empty your sewers. In Canada and Alaska, sewer dumps are listed as service station perks, offered with a fill-up. The Milepost advertisements are great places to find relief from that full feeling.

2001

On a bluff above Cook Inlet, a historic Russian Orthodox Church overlooks the original Ninilchik Village whose curlicue paths wind through the old log buildings. The still-active church sits among the wildflowers, mostly purple fireweed, with the cemetery cuddled by a white picket fence. A lot of people zoom right by Old Ninilchik. You can't drive into the town but there are parking areas. Abandoned boats are near the beach, and camping is down there too.

Fish Dinner

A mile or so beyond, down a steep paved hill from the Sterling Highway 40 miles from Homer, Alaska, I found for $10 a night, all that I required, a dry-camping spot with a magnificent view and a public phone.

All tent styles, and all sizes and vintage of travel trailers, truck campers, motorhomes, and fifth wheels settled into life at the Deep Creek State Recreation Area. Across Cook Inlet, Mts. Iliamna (10,016') and Redoubt (10,197') gleamed in the sunlit silence of their snow and glacier-covered majesty. It was June 21, the longest day of the year. Approximately 500 miles below the Arctic Circle, this was as close as I was going to get to 24 hours of sunshine.

California visitors were behind the Sprinter watching bald eagles. Our conversation ran to recent Alaskan adventures and questions. She asked, "Are you traveling alone or are you waiting for a fisherman?"

"I've been traveling alone. What did you have in mind?"

Early mornings found gulls raucously dining on whatever delectable fare arrived with the last tide. Hundreds of American bald eagles dotted the cliffs and trees. From grandpas and grandmas to small children, people in a variety of boots and hip-waders hunted for telltale sand dimples. Quickly down on their knees, they dug furiously to grab the

Church with a View

razor clam, keeping an ever-watchful eye to the incoming tide.

I accompanied Delores and Bill Schneller from Bend, Oregon, on a clamming excursion. Bill said, "Yesterday I almost lost Delores. She went after a clam clear up to her shoulder. She hung on to that clam for dear life but he wouldn't give up." She said, "I thought I had hold of a rubber band. A man came over and dug parallel to my spot and helped me get him. I felt like I was stuffed in first and pulled out backward!"

Personally, I couldn't see expressing that much energy going after something that was bent on reaching China. They rinsed the clams, putting them in seawater and a handful of cornmeal for a couple of hours to initiate self-cleaning.

Delores put a few clams in a bucket of boiling hot water. After a couple of minutes, the shells peeled right off, then she put them directly into cold water. She cut out the stomach with kitchen scissors and snipped off the sandy neck tip. She opened the neck and pounded it to tenderize it. "The 'digger' has the fat and that's really what's delicious. I dip them into beaten egg after patting the moisture out. They go into corn meal or Panco (a flaky commercial breading). I put them in egg again and with a little oil in my big old iron skillet, I cook them about five minutes until they're golden brown."

Digging Dinner

While the Schnellers cleaned their bounty, two brothers who were clamming and halibut fishing, and I, sat with them, hopefully making their job go faster with all the stories. David Jones, a retired construction worker from Molalla, Oregon, told this on his brother. "Clinton went to bed. When he woke up, he brushed his teeth, took his pills and inquired whether I was going to sleep all day. Then he realized he had been in bed only an hour and had been fooled by the bright sunshine." Clinton, a California retired fireman, got his licks in later. It was fun to see their warm brotherly relationship at work.

An interesting beach feature was the huge tractors with oversized balloon tires that backed boats and trailers into the water, almost up to their diesel engines, until the boats floated clear. When the boats came in, they came full tilt on to the trailer. Somebody in arm-pit-high booties hooked the boat to the trailer and they were hauled in. The boat and trailer were hooked to a pull truck or RV and they were on their way.

Visitors from Washington to Florida to Maine were going on charters to catch that halibut of a lifetime. A gang waiting for their charter boat: "Hi, I'm Jack." He shook hands with everybody, each giving his name. Another arrived. "Hi, I'm Jim, this is my brother, Todd," going through the same get-acquainted procedure.

A little girl was very excited. Once her daddy swung her into their smaller private boat, she planted a kiss on Mommy and Daddy and Grandpa, even though they were all going with her. When that was over, she puckered up for another round. Get 'em while you can.

I noticed a neighbor's license plate. "Where in Michigan are you from?

"Niles."

"You're kidding! That's where I raised my kids and lived until I started full-time RVing." A small world. Jerome and Leona Young were on their eighth Alaskan trip.

I heard a shout from outside, "Are you guys SKPs?"

"Yes." Larry Leonard checks out the local campgrounds about once a week to see if fellow Escapees are nearby. He and wife, Peggy, spend summers in Alaska. He gave me SKP hugs and invited me to their Fourth of July picnic. Eventually I visited their neat nest on Deep Creek. I couldn't stay because I had to fly from Anchorage for a Life on Wheels Conference in Idaho.

One morning I awakened and saw no mountains. I could have been parked next to Lake Michigan. As the morning progressed and the fog disappeared, the two white mountain peaks reappeared.

The Postmaster directed me to the Senior Center. They generously allowed me to retrieve my e-mail while we watched two Sandhill cranes dancing wildly in the field just outside their window.

1996

It's a nice drive along Anchor River Road off the Sterling Highway. It leads to several river and beach campgrounds, but I took Jane out there just to prove she had been there. A sign declares

Kachemak Bay

Anchor Point, Alaska "North America's most westerly Highway Point."

On a clear day, the Kachemak Bay view from Bluff Hill, just before you descend the hill into Homer, is a Kodak/Fuji Moment. Don't miss it. Homer has a population of about 4,500 and has most anything you might need.

We took advantage of Homer's sewer dump and water fill for $2, before going out on the spit. On Homer Spit, I drove Jane around the loop to see the private campgrounds that have all the amenities. We spent the night in a city-run campsite for $7.

Homer Spit, extending five miles into Kachemak Bay, dropped several feet during the earthquake. Rebuilt mostly on stilts, restaurants, shops, charters, and campgrounds dominate the side opposite the huge marina that floats up and down with the tide.

We had halibut, shrimp, and scallops at the Boardwalk Fish and Chips. Food is reasonable, fast, clean, and the small restaurant sits right on the water. Actually, on Homer Spit, it's almost impossible to sit anywhere else. I had my first clam chowder on the boardwalk in 1987, during a cold, miserable, foggy day. I don't know if it was the weather or the good cooking that made me fall in love with clam chowder.

On that same trip, I had my first halibut and haven't gotten over that yet either. Fred Cushman, one of our group of five in 1987, went on a charter-fishing trip and brought back a 50-pounder. His wife, Madelaine, baked it for all of us. He figured with all his expenses, the fish cost about $3 a pound. Not bad, considering the memory he made.

Evening is a fun time to watch people at the fishing hole. The term "Combat fishing" could describe the people standing shoulder-to-shoulder. There might be as many as a dozen fish jumping high in the air at one time. At that point in their lives (or deaths), they aren't interested in eating. They mostly react out of instinct when lures pass in front of them. Three seals swam and fished within the hole, too.

2001

Linda breathed a sigh of relief when the fog cancelled her first kayaking excursion. Instead, since it was a five-foot minus-tide, we taxied across Kachemak Bay for a Natural History Tour. Our guide, Mare, led us through the wilderness identifying plants, mushrooms, flowers, and berries. Reaching China Poot Bay, she instructed us, "Be careful. Every step may kill something. If you pick up a rock or a creature, put it back in exactly the same place."

Mare gingerly pulled a four-foot-long, slimy-looking, bright red ribbon worm from its rocky bed to let us touch it. In unadulterated passion for her work, she exclaimed, "This is staggering! What a beauty! An honest eight-year-old's comment, "It looks like what comes out when I have a

Bear with Me

bloody nose." To two Midwesterners, everything from something that "throws its guts out" to ward off an enemy and then grows them back again, to the enormous colorful starfish, was fascinating.

Our afternoon walk to Lost and Found Lake was straight up and straight down with constant tree roots to trip over, the difficulty exacerbated by rain. After both falling twice, we were green and brown stained and so wet our corpuscles were soggy. Hot showers and The Boardwalk's chowder-filled sourdough bread bowls revived us.

There are numerable side trips leading to fantastic places from Homer Spit. Keep turning the pages. I'll tell you about them in the next chapter.

The Bear Facts

1996

Seldovia

Three times I have visited Seldovia, a community reached only by air or sea. Unless you stay overnight, the tours aren't quite long enough to see everything. I like more time to inhale the fragrance of a new place. In 1987, I took the Alaska Ferry System.

Seldovia is one of the oldest communities on Cook Inlet. St. Nicholas Russian Orthodox Church, built in 1891, dominates the scene overlooking the harbor. If you do nothing else, walk to the top of the hill. I love boardwalks, flowers, small villages, and boat harbors. Seldovia fits the bill. Sod grows its own garden on old log cabin roofs. It has art galleries, shops, and cafes, or you can sit and contemplate bright orange Arctic poppies pushing between rocks on the harbor wall. They say Seldovia is, "Just beyond the end of the road." Places like that appeal to me – or have you noticed?

Most tours include a look at Gull Island. I saw my first puffins there. The captain told us, "They burrow into the dirt on the rock tops, lay one egg, and abandon the hatchling as soon as possible. It is forced by starvation to come out and find its own food." So what's new, my kids were forced by starvation to cook for themselves. (Maybe it wasn't quite that bad but don't check with them.)

He also said that since the 1964 earthquake and the 1989 Exxon oil spill both happened on Good Friday, "I've decided not to get out of bed on Good Friday any more."

The Saltry, Halibut Cove

Halibut Cove

The Kachemak Bay Ferry is the Danny J, a small "classic" wooden boat, leaving from Homer Spit. We rode outside in the mist. The mountains were fogged in. We did a slow turn around Gull Island to see puffins, a few sea otters wrapped in seaweed, kittiwakes and cormorants. The stench was bad on a cool day and I can't imagine what it would be like on a hot one.

Halibut Cove is on Ismailof Island. A tiny post office floated on its own dock. One of our all-women crew, said it had many post office boxes as a requirement of the government, "The keys hang in them because nobody bought any. This aversion to buying unnecessary boxes was known before the building was put up, but it didn't matter." She added, "No one needs them in a place where people seldom lock their homes."

After landing, we were instructed where to find the bathrooms, the most important part of the tour. A barn-type building on the boardwalk had a rounded bottom that made me wonder if the Ark had been greatly misplaced. The guide explained the boat was floated to its dock and made stationary right there with the barn on it.

It was a pleasant walk to the restaurant. Starfish clung to rocks and poles under the boardwalk. Houses on stilts lined the upper boardwalk. Curious horses lived in a pasture across from an art gallery. The gallery lady pointed out three island galleries. The whole island is a picturesque gallery. During the peak of the herring-fishery days in the early 1900s, 36 saltrys operated in Halibut Cove. The island also lays claim to a colorful prohibition history with bootleggers, stills, and revenuers.

It is a private island. The Danny J runs ferry service twice a day for residents, bed and breakfast guests, and the Saltry Restaurant. Private boats can come in, but their only landing places are the restaurant and the post office unless they live on the island.

The Saltry, the island's only restaurant, was at the end of 12 boardwalk blocks. They bake their own bread. I couldn't resist the nut-raisin bread with butter, a hot mug of coffee, and potato-broccoli soup, at $7.15, especially with the unique setting. Reservations are required.

It was pleasantly cool sitting outside overlooking the harbor. Raucous seagulls added their two-cents worth to the soft music and quiet conversation of my fellow travelers. Huge modern houses didn't seem to fit in. The older ones were charming, their windowboxes overflowing with poppies, bachelor's buttons, sweet peas, pansies, and daisies.

A mother shouted to her children who were fishing off the boardwalk, "I'll be right back." She left in a fishing boat from the dock below. Floating stairways descended from the buildings, accommodating whatever the tide level. It was low tide at that moment but they have the third highest tides in the world.

The sign on a picket fence surrounding a six-foot-square garden just before going through the gate to the top of the hill, said, "Please don't pick my flowers." I didn't.

The "Phenomenal Tree" trail to the natural stone arch was steep. I was accompanied by chattering red squirrels through a dense, towering Sitka spruce forest, Devil's Club plants with bright red berries, and lots of red elderberry and fern. The path ended behind a split rail fence, above the arch on the backside of the island. A gentle breeze blew in my face. I leaned on the fence and saw Homer Spit in the distance and a black beach below me.

I found a child's lonely grave hidden in the forest. Birds sang and bees buzzed. Water lapped at the shore below. Tall ferns rustled in a slight breeze. Perhaps it wasn't a lonely grave after all. An islander later told me the two-year-old girl had died in a fire. "All the cove felt her loss keenly. She was the only child here at the time and we lavished her with our love."

The same talkative native explained that the other grave at the top of the hill belonged to "Ham-handed Larsen." "He was so strong, they gave him jobs that were big enough for two Swedes and one Norwegian. He was a great storyteller and a terrific dancer. He taught all the woman on the island to dance."

At Tillion's Art Gallery, they featured octopus-ink artwork. One of the "washes" was of a woman walking naked along the shoreline of a lake. I wasn't the only one wanting to be "one with nature."

A number of sculptures were of island people. One was a mother nursing a baby. When the sculpture was finished, the artist realized that the mother's head was falling off. It stopped toppling in time to make it look like the mother had fallen asleep nursing her baby. The sculpturist firmed it in that position. Take it from one who knows, the sculpture is a natural.

Couch Potato Extraordinaire

Halibut Cove was too charming to absorb in only two-and-a-half hours. If you go, take raingear and dress in layers. Take binoculars, cameras, and wear good walking shoes or boots.

Katmai National Park

My next adventure was definitely weather oriented for safety and pleasure. If the fog is too thick and doesn't show any signs of lifting, you wait or cancel out.

Three planeloads of cameras and film flew from Homer's Beluga Lake with a few photographers aboard as well. A sign over the pilot's door said, "Bear Facts: Never run! Speak to the bear in a calm voice. Wave your arms slowly or clap your hands. Retreat slowly. Always give bears the right of way. Pilot Facts: Never run! Speak to them in a calm, loud voice. Tip generously or retreat slowly and clap your hands." Hmmm.

Our pilot circled over the water whenever there was something to see below us, like the "Fin whales." Bald Mountain Air Service flew us into a Shelikof Strait bay at the edge of Katmai National Park with its lush green islands and great beaches. We were shuttled from the seaplane to a base boat where we ate whatever food we brought. We weren't returning for lunch and couldn't take food with us.

It was difficult negotiating in and out of the skiff wearing thigh high boots, but it soon became apparent why we needed them. Gary, our guide, instructed us to stay together at all times. "Don't let the bears get between us. They get confused. Groups intimidate bears. If we all stand up, we will look like a whole herd of bears." He also said, "These are coastal brown bears, grizzlies, just like at Denali, but they get a whole lot bigger. They eat lots of fish and berries after a hard winter."

According to the Katmai National Park Service brochure, that huge brown bear is "Earth's largest terrestrial carnivore." I wasn't sure I liked the sound of that.

Fearless Leader at Katmai

We went over the side and into the water through the mud and seaweed. We were to kneel, bend over, or sit at all times, so there was no chance we would intimidate the bears (who were they kidding?). The kneeling was dryer with the long boots. The skiffs returned to the base boat. We were there for the duration. A good thing we didn't drink a lot, because there was no place to get rid of it, and the guide wouldn't allow us to go any-where.

The bears shuffled along peering into the water then suddenly heaved themselves into the waves. It looked like they tried to land on the fish. They don't catch their fish every time either.

Gary said the two young bears near us were probably four-or-five-years old. "They stay with the mother until she kicks them out about their third year." They looked like they were going to fight, then settled into playing, standing, biting, rolling on the ground, and chasing each other.

It is illegal for guides to carry guns. Gary said he had never needed one. Beyond the stream, a big furry couch potato bear watched us for a long time. Gary said "The Couch" was pushing a I,000 pounds.

Despite strict orders not to bring food, one fellow started eating a sand-wich. Everybody noticed. Gary immediately told him to get rid of it. He stuffed it into his mouth all at once, and looked awful for a few minutes until he could get it down, sort of like a pelican gorging on an oversized fish.

After a few minutes, bears surrounded us. The guide was always very aware of what was happening. We could look in any direction and see bears. He said there were 13 or 14 different bears, "We get to know them by their scars, color, or actions."

Bearly Surrounded

The other visitors were from Switzerland, Italy, Australia, Germany, and Canada. The husband of a vivacious, sparkly Australian lady, was watching their small children so she could come on this bear trip. His planned $17,000 moose and bear hunting trip alleviated her guilt. Made sense to me.

The fog moved in slightly and we had a steady light rain. It enhanced the scene, rather than causing a hardship or discomfort. We were asked if we wanted to leave, but nobody was interested. The bugs wanted to stay because of the fresh blood. When Gary handed me the repellent, he said, "These are ENT bugs. They go for the eyes, nose, and throat."

I hoped nothing chased me in those boots.
I couldn't have run if my life depended on it; but, of course,
I would have given it a bloody good try.

We were on an elongated island with a stream passing on either side of our small group. We sat fairly close to each other. We were each engrossed in bear activity, photographing, and conversing quietly. The closest bears were probably 15 feet from us. The bears ignored us. Only occasionally would one lift his head, sniff the air and come toward us. Gary expected us to move when he said move, then he stood up waved his arms and yelled. The bear always ran away.

We left following a circuitous route around the bears that took us through swift streams, and over slippery rocks and shells that would have cut bare feet to shreds. I waited for the last skiff. I didn't want to leave. I rather envied the German couple who were staying overnight on the ship to go bear-watching during the evening. The privilege would cost them a $1,000. Though it was worth every penny, $450 for the day was steep enough for me.

On board the base boat, the crew served fresh deep-fried halibut.

That wasn't hard to take. It was late when we shuttled back to the sea-plane and flew over the seals, puffins, lush green islands, and deep blue water, a perfect place for kayaking.

During the return trip, the clouds lifted enough to allow us views of glaciers and mountaintops sculpted in rock and mounded with snow. We saw more whales. The three-hour, round-trip plane ride was certainly a major part of the adventure.

It is difficult for them to have boot sizes for everyone, so if you have the opportunity, take your own thigh-high waders. Take other necessities like cameras, film, bug repellent, raingear, lunch, and something to sit on. It is a fantastic experience.

As exciting as it was, the four-million-acre Katmai National Park across from Kodiak Island, is much more than bears and scenery. It is volcanoes and history. I want to visit The Valley of Ten Thousand Smokes and -- did I say I was going back?

On our way up the peninsula, Jane saw her first moose grazing beside the road. By the time I turned around and went slowly back, we could see she had a baby with her. We didn't do anything overly exciting on the way to Anchorage, so I'll describe a couple of things from later in the season.

I drove the Skilak Loop off Sterling Highway and stayed at Upper Skilak Campground on the lake. The sites were level and paved. The paths were gravel and paved. Picnic tables had extensions for wheelchair use. I couldn't believe so few people were using the campground.

Summit Lodge is one of my favorite stops. It is on the Seward Highway after the turn toward Anchorage. Huge doors have leaded glass win-

Begich-Boggs Visitor Center

dows with bear and moose carved on them. I've eaten breakfast or lunch there several times with friends. Even if the food wasn't good (and it is), the view of Summit Lake surrounded by trees and mountains, would make up for it.

Portage Glacier

At the Begich-Boggs Visitor Center at Portage Glacier in Chugach National Forest, Jane and I watched the movie, "Voices from the Ice," and walked through the simulated ice cave. *In 2001, other exhibits had re-*

placed the ice cave. I was disappointed in its demise but the new exhibits were great. Iceworms were in a dish on the counter this time.

If you don't believe iceworms live between ice crystals near glacier surfaces, a Forest Service interpreter will take you on an "Iceworm Safari." The wiggly wildlife isn't nearly as intimidating as the bears.

The glacier is receding at the rate of approximately 350' per year. Since I was there in 1987, it had disappeared around the bend. The narrated tour to the glacier face aboard the MV Ptarmigan, is the only way you can see Portage Glacier. It usually costs $21 per person, but we were told the last tour of the day is half price.

The boat stayed close enough to the glacier front to see the little bit that calved. It was crumbling over a huge rock formation so it was not as dramatic as calving usually is.

Williwaw USFS Campground has nice campsites. From the observation deck, you can watch salmon fight their way upstream. It is interesting but sort of sad. The Williwaw Natural Trail hike led to beaver dams and to the falls coming from Middle Glacier.

Wasilla

Jane's time was passing quickly. We saw a full view of Mt. McKinley (roughly 170 miles away) as we drove through Anchorage. We made a beeline for Denali National Park on the Glenn and George Parks Highways (Alaska Hwy #3).

I am fascinated with Iditarod racing, mushing, and dogsledding. At Wasilla, it is almost 14 miles along Knik Road to the Knik Museum and Sled Dog Mushers' Hall of Fame. This museum has all the information on Knik, a gold rush village from 1898. They have race history, musher and winner portraits, and dog-mushing equipment. It isn't open every day. Check before making the trip. They used to use adhesive tape or electrical tape to fasten booties on sled dogs. Now they use Velcro. Have we progressed or what? You can also stop at the Iditarod Trail Sled Dog Race Headquarters to see sled dog puppies, dog racing memorabilia and watch a film.

Another trip off the Parks Highway will take you to Talkeetna, a small but mighty town. This is one of many places you can get Mt. McKinley flightseeing tours. There are other kinds of tours and museums, but what really interested me, was their annual Moose Dropping Festival. I had every intention of going, but Jane and I made a decision after Denali, that we would either head for Fairbanks or return to Talkeetna. We couldn't do both. Fairbanks and the paddlewheel trip won out. One of these days! (*In 2001, Linda and I missed the festival, also, but enjoyed walking through all their gift shops.*)

Denali National Park and Preserve

A "Subarctic Sanctuary"

Mother Love

In four trips into Denali National Park, I have five times driven the 14.8 miles of paved highway to Savage River. Private vehicles may not go beyond that point without a camping or special permit. My favorite time is at dawn or sunset. I've never failed to see animals. I have taken the bus tour through Denali six times. Each trip has been memorable and different.

I've seen dozens of grizzlies, sometimes right next to the bus, and sometimes so far away I had to use binoculars. During other trips, Dall sheep posed on the mountain above the bus. Moose and babies are often all over the place, but nary a one stepped out for Jane to see.

On a short hike at Eielson Visitor Center, I once sat quietly on the trail and caribou grazed close enough to touch. A dozen people watched a fluffy-tailed fox being outsmarted by an Arctic ground squirrel. I've seen eagles, wolves, marmots, and ptarmigan.

The High One

The bus makes several scheduled comfort and leg-stretching stops. The driver also stops whenever anyone sees an animal. They pull over allowing enough time for everyone to rush to the side of the bus where "somebody sees something," to take pictures or ooh and ah over the sights. You may not get off the bus except during scheduled stops, unless you are a hiker.

In 1987, I didn't see Mt. McKinley, even though I was within sight of it for at least five days. In 1992, I saw it from every direction but under it, from Anchorage, Fairbanks, flying over it to Kotzebue, in the park, and from the Old Denali Highway.

In 1996, Jane and I saw it from many places, but only bits and pieces as the clouds would allow. There are never any guarantees. The 20,320' mountain, the tallest in North America, is big enough to make its own weather. If you are lucky, it will come out to play. It is a thrill you can't imagine.

Regardless of The High One's temperament, the scenery has never been a disappointment. It is so varied with mountains, braided glacier-born rivers, and glaciers. Out of June, July, and September visits, my favorite was seeing it dressed in autumn splendor. Golden aspen trees stood against green pines with red and orange ground cover in the foreground, and a background of mountains freshened with new snow. It was almost hard on the eyes.

The roads are gravel and well maintained. When buses meet in exceptionally narrow areas, one bus stops and the other sidles by. The drivers are excellent and have a great sense of humor and fun.

You pack your own food and drink. Food is not available on the trip. The round-trip to Eielson is approximately eight hours (66 miles), give or take a few minutes for exceptional animal sightings. The Wonder Lake trip is 11 hours (84 miles). A shorter version goes to Polychrome/Toklat. Time goes quickly, and most people sleep all the way back.

Climbing "The High One" is extremely popular because of the challenge. Mount McKinley has a vertical relief of 18,000', greater than that of Mount Everest. According to geologists, it is still rising.

Take binoculars, cameras (with long lens), extra film, insect repellent, raingear, lunch, and drink. Wear layered clothing and sensible shoes,

Shuttle buses cost $12 to $30, depending on your destination. This does not include the $3 entrance fee. Sign up at the Visitor Center. You can make reservations or if you aren't too fussy when you go, you can take a chance with a walk-in reservation. I've never had a problem getting on a shuttle even during high season, but that doesn't mean you mightn't have to wait a day or two. Narrated bus tours are available for various prices. Multiple or season shuttle bus tickets are cheaper if you intend to go more than once.

During Fourth of July week, we were able to get on a bus at 6 a.m. the day after we arrived. I prefer early trips but many people like later in the day. It doesn't make a lot of difference as far as seeing animals. We took the Eielson Visitor Center trip for $20 each. *($23 in 2001)*

Denali has seven campgrounds, three accommodate RVs. There are no amenities except water. Riley Creek Campground near the Visitor Center has a dump station. The campground fee is $12 a night, with a minimum of three nights at Teklanika, 29 miles into the park. At Teklanika, you are allowed to drive in and out once. You must use a ticket for the camper bus. Towed vehicles must be left at the Riley Creek overflow parking lot. *(Still $12/night in 2001)* Without reservations, Jane and I stayed in Riley Creek our second night at Denali.

If you are waiting for a campsite, or a ticket on the shuttle bus, guided hikes or hiking trails might fill your time. (*In 2001, Linda and I took a guided nature hike up the mountain with a very knowledgeable ranger. I encourage you to do this if you are physically able to hike. You'll learn a great deal about the area.*)

A free bus is provided from the Visitor Center to the dogsled demonstration. The ranger in charge did an excellent job explaining how the dogs are trained. "They are bred for specific characteristics, friendliness and good work ethic. These dogs actually like 60,000 visitors! They have a two-layer coat with insulating hollow hair. They wrap their bushy tails around their noses in the cold. We have exercise contracts with people who work here, to walk the dogs 3-4 times a week."

The dogs were hooked to a sled and pulled it around the loop. The dogs get extremely excited about running and go lickety split. (Do not take your own animals with you.) Denali is the only National Park that maintains a dog kennel operation with working sled dogs. This is a chance to see the kennels up close and see how the dogs live and work. Dogsleds are still used for ranger patrols to contact backcountry winter visitors, deter illegal hunter and trapper activities, and haul maintenance and emergency supplies to remote patrol cabins.

Denali Caribou

If you still need something to do, go outside the park for river rafting, flightseeing, or horseback riding. If you want an afternoon's ride with experienced professional guides, rafting the Nenana River is a good trip just outside the park. Guided rafting, when they do all the paddling, is not quite as exciting as when you are part of the paddling team, but not everyone needs that thrill. I enjoyed it thoroughly.

I was disappointed to learn that the gravel spit in the Nenana River bend, about two miles toward Fairbanks, had been taken over as a private RV park. It used to fill with boondocking RVers, all waiting to get into Denali. The private park had a closed sign on it at 5 p.m. The park Jane and I paid $10 to stay in was crowded, noisy and not level. All the places where I had previously parked overnight along the river had been signed for no RV parking.

I don't know their reasons for taking this privilege away. It surely wasn't because the campgrounds were empty, or that we didn't spend enough money in the area. I guess I'll never know.

In 2001, I made my fifth trip to Denali and my seventh bus tour through the park, this time with Linda. She saw only the bottom half of the mountain but we did see lots of animals including one you rarely see, a wolf.

There are now tours that will take you to backcountry mountain lodges at the park road's end, and really beautiful tour company lodges just outside the park. Although boondocking close to the park seems to have disappeared, we found plenty of boondock places within 20 miles of the park entrance.

Ester

Jane and I continued on to Ester Gold Camp, 10 miles out of Fairbanks. A lot of people flit right on by, but I love the place. Don't expect fancy. It's a miner's camp.

We paid $10 for dry camping. They had a dump station and water. Reservations for dinner at the Bunkhouse Buffet were $14.95 each. The menu featured good simple food like baked halibut, reindeer stew, and

Ester Gift Shop

country fried chicken. This was my third time to overfeast. The house specialty is Alaska Dungeness Crab and costs about $4 more.

If you've never seen the Aurora Borealis, go to the Northern Lights Show at the Firehouse Theatre. It is a photosymphony melding of classical music and shimmering lights on a 30' screen. According to Leroy Zimmerman, who puts the show together, "The feelings are beyond understanding when you see the Aurora Borealis. You don't know whether to cry or get down on your knees and pray." Almost to the night, two months later, I saw them. He knew of which he spoke.

Ester is the home of the "World Famous Malamute Saloon," swinging doors and all. If your table isn't full, other visitors will be seated with you. They squeeze in as many as possible. It is a happy atmosphere. You throw your peanut shells into the sawdust on the floor. Alaskan history hangs on the wall, a hangman's noose, gold pans, washboards, picks, and axes. The bar was barged downriver from Dawson City

The performers are bundles of energy and entertainment. Anyone would agree with the song assessment in "Dad Gum, Dad Gum, Dad Gum Govn'mint Woes." Their scientific name for all true Alaskans is "Alaskan Basicus." "They are all crested, wear a baseball cap, and eat only stream-caught salmon, ice cream, and beer."

By the time your trip is over, you will be well acquainted with, and I hope, a fan of Robert Service. At the Malamute, they call it "Service with a Smile." You could have heard a pin drop as performers recited poetry that brought the North Country to life. You could feel the cold in your very bones, and the loneliness was palpable. Oh yesss!!

Their drinks are as potent as an "Ice Worm Cocktail" or as mild as a "Prunella Pinfeather." Just don't ask the waiter if he has a "Fuzzy Navel" as I did in 1992. He said that was a dangerous question! Hmmm. They mentioned having their special Alaskan flag, "As a reminder of the hardships we had before we became a state." As a political statement, he added under his breath, "We don't need no special reminder to remember the hardships we've had since we became a state." Hmmm again.

(*I stopped here again in 2001 and it was just as entertaining although the patter hadn't changed much. Show $14 and camping $15.*)

Fairbanks

In Fairbanks, Jane and I visited the Tanana Valley Farmer's Market. This is fun to do in almost any Alaskan community. It was small, but had great fresh fruit, yummy baked goods, and crafts.

The University of Alaska Museum is a must stop. Their answer to Michigan's Babe the Blue Ox, is "Blue Babe," the World's only restored Ice Age bison mummy. (I'll get a lot of flack claiming Michigan's right to Babe the Blue Ox, but one of her footsteps did make Lake Michigan.)

An interesting display in 1996 was, "Forced to Leave," about the WWII internment of Alaskans. This is a good place to get a thorough explanation of the Aurora Borealis via video.

Lynn at Barrow

In the Aurora Dome, we sat for a program presented by the World Eskimo-Indian Olympics. We saw athletes of the Northern Inua perform traditional games, songs, and dance. It was informative and humorous. Trying the "One-foot-high-kick" would injure me for life. They jump straight up with one foot coming off the ground, and the other kicking straight up to hit the ball. It is like doing vertical splits. The world record leap is over seven feet.

This is a good place to encourage you to fly to at least one of the outlying villages. In 1987, I flew from Fairbanks to Barrow, an Inupiat Eskimo Village of around 4,000, the northernmost point of the North American Continent. It is called, Top of the World, and who would argue that, being 330 miles north of the Arctic Circle, 1,500 miles from the North Pole, and surrounded by frozen tundra. Dress warmly.

I visited a former Girl Scout of mine who lived up there for two years.

I was able to see and do more than perhaps the average tourist, but tours cover a lot of territory.

Lynn explained the Eskimo philosophy, "Whether it is a whale kill, paycheck, or anything else, they share what they have. They believe if they are ever in need, their friends will share with them also." I asked Lynn how living among the Eskimos had affected her life. She said, "It helps you set priorities. You don't worry about having a Chemlawn truck in your yard. It gives you perspective in your life after viewing someone else's culture."

Lahka, Dances with Burgs

I joined Lynn's Eskimo friends at a Nalukataq, a successful whale-kill celebration. We sat in a semi-circle. Men carrying big buckets and wearing plastic gloves, placed a handful of "Muktuk" in each of our containers. The fermented whale blubber resembled bloody, uncooked liver; chewed like bubble gum; and with no disrespect to my hosts, tasted like Lynn's description, "slime." I really do prefer pizza.

Children were tossed high in the air from a sealskin blanket. Lynn commented, "When the adults get in on this, an ambulance is kept on hand. Adults tend to get overly enthusiastic with their tossing."

Near the airport, is a memorial to Wiley Post and Will Rogers, who died in a plane crash 15 miles south of Barrow in 1935.

Kotzebue

In 1992, I took a two-day tour from Anchorage to Kotzebue, with a Nome overnight. Kotzebue is 26 miles beyond the Arctic Circle, and I thought it was the most charming of the "far-out" villages I visited. Perhaps some of that was due to the terrific brother-sister tour-guide combo. It is one of the oldest communities on the North American Continent and only 200 miles from Cape Dezhnev, Russia.

I learned that calling my RV a "Rolling igloo" is correct. Lahka said the word "Igloo" means, "Place to stay." A regular two-story house costs between $65,000 and $250,000.

The guides pointed with pride to the one "real" tree in town. I puzzled at all the beach driftwood in that treeless tundra country. Lahka explained, "It is transported by floods from the wooded mountains."

All the distant villages have freezing and permafrost problems. Pumps within the pipes keep water and sewage moving so it doesn't freeze.

Our guides took us on a "tundra walk" and dug down into the permafrost so we could see what it was like. They pointed out the Alaska cotton plant; blueberry, cranberry, salmonberry plants; and the plants they use for smoking food, and dying colors. I'm happy to report that dandelions are alive and well in Kotzebue.

At the Inupiat Culture Camp, the Inupiat culture and lifestyle were explained. They demonstrated how to skin and tan animal hides to make mukluks and parkas. We shared lunch and conversation with our charming guides. The reindeer stew was delicious.

The highlight of our Kotzebue visit, was the NANA (The Great Hunter) Museum of the Arctic, with animal and sealife exhibits and Arctic environment dioramas. After the slide show on Eskimo culture, three elders, one an 88-year-old man, played drums and sang for dancers who told of their traditions and history. We participated in a blanket toss and danced the native dances.

Kotzebue's first mile of paved road was due in 1996. Residents were concerned about the four-wheelers and the new "strip."

Nome

I stayed overnight in Nome's Nugget Inn and ate dinner at Fat Freddies, only 130 miles from Siberia. At dinner I experienced one of those "Moments in Time" I have talked about. It is as though I am mentally backing off and assessing what I am doing, and I can't quite believe my good fortune in being where I am. Fresh flowers were on the table but outside the window, only a few feet from me, icebergs floated on the Bering Sea in mid-June.

The one thing I didn't realize until the tour the next day, was that the beachfront property is public domain and open for anyone to pan gold. I wasted the evening wandering. Hmmm. I could have paid for the whole trip. Well, maybe not, but it would have been fun.

Lest you think that is an impossibility, the guide said, "They took $37,000 of placer flour (finer than dust) gold from the beach last year." She also added, "But we all know how miners tell tall tales." She mentioned the red garnets sprinkled on the beach. "If you find red garnets, you'll usually find gold nearby." I blew it.

If I had had extra room in my suitcase, I might have brought back a tiny, furry creature that will grow up to be a sled dog. This little guy was only a month old and a wiggling bundle of joy. Our tour had taken us to visit Howard Farley, a musher in the first Iditarod Race. He now raises dogs and promotes what he calls, "The Last Great Race."

He gave us the history of the race; "The Iditarod Trail Sled Dog Race started in 1973. Ancient hunters used the Iditarod Trail previously. Later it was a supply and mail route to and from the gold-mining camps in bush Alaska. The seed for this race and its legends was planted in 1925, when a diphtheria epidemic struck Nome. Vital serum was relayed from Nenana to this tiny Eskimo Village by dog team. Planes in those days were grounded in winter due to harsh weather conditions. Twenty volunteer mushers carried the serum 674 miles in 127 1/2 hours, saving the people of Nome."

He also said, "Women winners not only dominated the scene for a while, but put the Iditarod Race on the map." The first woman to win the race was Libby Riddles in 1985. Susan Butcher became a four-time Iditarod champion in 1990, and set a new speed record for the second time.

He explained that, "The term 'Husky,' usually means any dog pulling a sled." He raises Siberian Huskies and trains them, running them in the sand when he doesn't have snow. The dogs were eager to demonstrate.

Our tour included gold panning at the Alaska Gold Company, a Historic Mine Site and still an active operation. A 108-ounce gold nugget mined there is now in the Smithsonian Institution in Washington, D. C.

The population of Nome is around 4,500. They have just about every kind of store you might need. The guide said, "Nome is a pretty jazzy town with three roads leading to small outlying communities, as far as 87 miles. We have an Arts Council, a theatre group, and lots of kids. We have long winters, you know."

Tours give a good taste of the outlying communities. Overnight isn't enough time to soak in the native culture, history, or the local stories but I definitely recommend a flight to any of the bush villages.

Alaskaland Salmon Bake

Determined by whether you leave from Anchorage or Fairbanks, whether it is one day or overnight, etc., tours include airfares will run between roughly $350 and $500. It is a lot of money, but maybe you'll never have the opportunity again. The nice thing about flying to Kotzebue is having a great aerial view of Mt. McKinley, depending on whether the weather is turned on or off.

Fairbanks Continued

Fairbanks offers many activities. At the Alaskaland Salmon Bake, they have a big semicircle cooking area where salmon and halibut are prepared. Meals include salad, sourdough rolls, baked beans, and blueberry cake. I have waddled out of there four times now. Making reservations is a smart move. The RV caravans eat there.

While you're waiting, you can wander around their gold mining exhibit and see the equipment they used during gold rush days. The authentic renovated 29 log cabins that house the shops on the boardwalk were donated by pioneer family descendants. You can write postcards, eat ice cream at outdoor tables, or just soak in this historic stampede theme park. The Visitor Information Center is in the Sternwheeler Nenana, the second largest wooden vessel in existence, permanently docked only a few yards from the Chena River.

Walk through the Alaska Native Village and see the workings of a mine or a fish wheel, visit the Pioneer Museum, or ride the Crooked Creek and Whiskey Island Railroad.

Stay for at least one Alaskaland evening. The Farthest North Square and Round Dance Center offers some form of dancing each evening during the season. You can watch or join in.

I must have been a dance hall girl in a former life. When I watch the performers at The Palace Theatre and Saloon, I am right up there doing the can-can in the Golden Heart Revue. They always have good advice for tourists, "No matter what the locals tell you, moose droppings do not taste like pine nuts."

In 2001, I stayed overnight in the parking lot for $5 but it was extremely noisy. In 1992, I attended a Sunday service in a tiny log Presbyterian Church in Fairbanks. Susie and Claude Swaim introduced me around and invited me to a family gathering in their tiny log home that evening. Nine years after our continued exchange of Christmas notes and pictures, I joined them again for church, this time it was their yearly Sunday morning Jazz concert at the University of Alaska. Wow! Talk about food for the soul!

They met on a hospital ship. "When the war was over, I asked her, 'What are you going to do now?'"

"Go to Alaska."

"Can I go with you?"

"We'll have to get married first."

"I almost backed out," he added with a grin.

They told me wonderful tales of visiting Hawaii and cruising Alaska's Inland Passage within the past year. Claude was 99 in November 2001, and Susie trails behind. What an inspiration they are.

Alternate Activities

It used to take two or three weeks by stagecoach to reach Chena Hot Springs from Fairbanks. Now you can drive the 75 miles in a day. I rode up there with a friend in 1992, but neither of us was prepared to stay and soak. Chena Hot Springs Road is paved and follows the Chena River through, what else, the Chena River Recreation Area. There are many campgrounds along the way, and RV parking with electrical hook-ups is available at the hot springs.

Gold miners discovered the spring in 1905, and used it to alleviate rheumatism. The springs come from the center of a 40-square-mile geothermal area at 156°. They cool it first, so your goose won't be cooked.

The Springs are 129 miles from Fairbanks, and you can go on up to Circle as well, two adventures for the price of one.

The Riverboat Discovery

I thought I had been on as many riverboat trips in my lifetime as I needed, but Jane and I both really enjoyed the day trip on the stern-wheeler Riverboat Discovery. The commentator's narration was interesting, informative, and broken up by activities on the shore. A Piper Cub took off and landed along the shore for our benefit. "They really deliver. Recently, a pilot delivered a baby while he was flying the mother to the hospital. The bush communities live and die by the sound of the mail and medical planes flying in and out." How a pilot could deliver a baby while he is flying, remains a mystery to me. Either the mother did all the work, unaided but encouraged, or someone else was in the plane. A taxi driver I might believe.

Fish Wheel

Four generations of the Binkley family have owned and operated the riverboat for a 100 years. The river history of this family dates back to prospectors, fur traders, and Native people. They all relied on the rivers as their only link to the outside world. "The old paddlewheelers used one cord of wood every hour 24 hours a day. Now we use diesel engines."

We went from the Chena River into the Tanana River, the largest glacier-fed river in the world. "The glacier rock is ground into glacier flour that causes the silt and the water's gray color." He said it was a completely uncontrolled river with no navigational aids.

The river supports salmon. "The silt goes right through the gills, but because of the silt, the fish cannot see and are easily caught." There you go, those of you who like to fish.

We stopped for an over-the-side visit with Susan Butcher. She talked about her dogs and showed us the puppies she was training. She said, "It takes one and a half weeks to teach them to go, and two and a half years, to teach them to whoa."

Later on, we stopped to talk with "Dixie," a full-blooded Athabascan Indian. She demonstrated cutting up salmon and drying it in the smoke-house. Salmon is stored in cache houses after it is dried. Cache houses are the tiny cabins you see at the top of four long poles. Tin cans are placed near the top of the poles to keep animals from robbing the cache.

We watched a dog-mushing demonstration by Susan Butcher's assistant and long-distance racing team at the Old Chena Indian Village, and then we exited the riverboat for a guided tour.

They showed us how the Indians might have lived before they had contact with the outside world. They were constantly on the move follow-

following the animal herds. Their houses were made of skin, and snow was packed around the outside for insulation. A cabin, with insulation and windows, was used after contact with the outside world.

A pregnant guide explained that diapers were made of moss or rabbit fur, "The first earth-friendly, bio-degradable, disposable diaper. After it was used, it was buried, and more moss or fur applied."

Several girls modeled clothes. "Each person had their own design, and it was always good for a husband to know his wife's design. It gets very dark here in Alaska in the winter."

All parts of hunted animals were used. Eating tools were made of bone. Moose antlers were scrapped against a tree to summon another moose. "The moose would hear it and think another moose was invading his territory." She held up a long narrow tube and said, "If you are very quiet, I'll call a moose. I have to be very careful, one might come." She held it to her lips and whispered into it, "Here, moosey, moosey."

Suddenly, as we were all getting into the hang of the ancient arts, a telephone rang in somebody's pocket. It was incongruous there in a wilderness Indian village.

At the turn-around, we enjoyed complimentary coffee and donuts, and later, had canned salmon and crackers. The salmon is canned by the family company and sold only on the riverboat. It was delicious, and deliciously expensive, but worth it.

(*In 2001, I did an El Dorado Gold Mine tour just outside of Fairbanks. This gold mining history tour is also owned by the Binkley family and is well done. It involves a train ride into a permafrost tunnel and gold panning. ($27.95 for about a two-hour tour)*

Twelve days, 1,300 miles, and a lot of Alaska later, I said good-bye to Jane Parker at the Anchorage International Airport. By the time she flew back to Stuart, Florida, she had traveled over 12,000 miles. Jane is young at heart and I'm proud that she (and her four kids) lets me tell everyone she is my surrogate Mom. (*In 2002, this eighty-something lady is living with a son and daughter in New Orleans but still talks about her 1996 Alaskan adventure.*)

As for me, I wanted to land in one place and stay there for a while. I didn't know where. As a full-time RVer, I tossed a coin and headed back down the Kenai Peninsula.

The Hope of My Universe

1996
Hope, Alaska

The 17.7-mile road to Hope is paved. From the Seward Highway, it passes the site of Sunrise City, a ghost town from gold rush days. Coming from the apple-tree country of Michigan, I appreciated Hope's claim that the first apple tree in Alaska was planted in its bosom.

Hope is 88 miles almost directly south of Anchorage on the backside of Turnagain Arm. As the crow flies, the mileage is considerably less. Although I hesitate to say that anything is beyond Hope, Porcupine USFS campground is. It is at the end of the Hope Highway, just beyond Hope. It is perched on the side of the mountain with great views over the Arm. It is beyond Hope's only gas station, owned by an 83-year-old lady. The pump read $1.73 a gallon. *(In 2001, she was still there and presumably five years older.)*

Before Anchorage existed, and before the gold rushes happened at Dawson City or Nome, "A man named King" gave Hope the distinction of becoming Alaska's first gold rush town. He discovered gold in Resurrection Creek. It flows past Hope into Turnagain Arm. The town was named after Percy Hope, the youngest gold rusher to get off the boat. As with all boomtowns, the gold gave out and miners pushed on to other gold rushes. It is hard to imagine Hope as a rowdy town of 3,000. It has dwindled to the 250 who live there now.

The food is good at the Discovery Cafe, a tiny one-room restaurant. If you are lucky, as I was, you can listen to Tito, the owner, telling local stories to the cheechakos. The cafe serves another purpose. Several bookshelves are filled with mysteries, love stories, stories of the North Country, or whatever your interest. They are for trading and I did.

I stayed around Hope for the next five weeks, sometimes on the Old Hope Townsite campground just beyond the Seaview Cafe. It had electricity for $10, or less for boondocking. The best spot was at the far end with unobstructed views of the mud flats and Turnagain Arm. Henry's One Stop provided a sewer dump for a reasonable $5 fee. Henry's also had a Laundromat, small store, and a full hook-up campground in the trees, but he didn't have the view I needed for inspiration.

Early mornings or evenings, I walked the path above the mud ravines that reached out toward the Arm. It paralleled the pasture where three curious horses lived. They came to greet me until they discovered I didn't carry treats.

The mud flats and the tides fascinated me. The outgoing tide left interesting indentations and mud rivulets. It was usually quite windy out near the Arm. I wore my hair down because I loved feeling the wind in it. Once again, for some reason, I felt free and uplifted and joyful.

Hope was a victim of the 1964 earthquake. Many of the historical buildings collapsed or floated away on the tide. Apple tree roots dropped into the salt water and died. During the winter months now, the water actually laps at the Seaview Bar.

Upper Cook Inlet has the second greatest tide range in North America (in the world, I heard) at 38.9'. (I had seen the highest at the Bay of Fundy in Nova Scotia.) I didn't see it, but they sometimes get "bore tides," steep, foaming walls of water up to six feet high, that go down Turnagain Arm at speeds up to 10 knots.

The second highest tide of the season was expected in Hope on August 1. The water came into the campground, all over the pasture, and the horses were driven back against the fence. It stopped at 33'. Fishermen and campers moved to higher ground.

Linda, the Postmaster, said that once a year her family puts on old clothes, and spends a day playing in the mud, choosing their tide time and place very carefully. "It ruins your clothes. You can't wear shoes because if you get stuck, you can't pull your foot out of the mud." Playing in the mud was one thing I wanted to do before I left, but I needed to have someone pull me out, if necessary. I never found quite the right conditions. Linda cautioned, as everyone locally did, that the mud flats were extremely dangerous. Rising or falling water tables under the surface, can suddenly change the solid surface to quicksand.

In my full-time travels, I have learned, "It's a small world." Chuck Anderson was a motorhomer who parked at the Seaview Campground for many summers. On the day we met, he drove me to Henry's One Stop for milk, and then wanted to visit friends who had been coming to Hope for 13 summers. He hadn't any more than introduced me, when the lady asked, "Do you know Miriam and Bob Johnson?" I went into shock. The Johnsons were friends of mine from New Carlisle, Indiana. Fran and Bodie Bodemiller had been neighbors of the Johnsons at one time. Miriam had sent Fran my books and told them to watch for me in Alaska. It was really amazing that we crossed paths. Alaska is a big place.

Actually our paths more than crossed, Chuck was kind enough to take me to the Hope Christian Church each Sunday and we always sat with Fran and Bodie. Services didn't start until 3 p.m. At first I thought this was because the place needed to warm up in the winter; but then I realized the minister and his wife, Charles and Clara, drove from his morning service in Seward, approximately 75 miles away.

Through the three of them I met and heard about very interesting people, including Billie and Ann. Billie built the little church from logs he dragged down from the high country, and Ann was Postmaster for many years. Ann also volunteered at the Historical Mining Museum, an intriguing place to spend a few hours. Billie worked on an outdoor cabin exhibit. Everything he touches has to turn out "just so," probably better than the original building.

Everything about Hope was appealing. I took different routes to the post office when I was tempted to "reboot" the computer via my foot. I liked the dust smell I kicked up. Picturesque cabins hid in yards high with natural growth. Wild pink roses decorated gray unpainted fences, and old squeejawed birdhouses perched on posts. After a rain, everything was reflected in the puddles, and the trees hung over the road and dripped. Even the mud had a fresh smell to it.

Everything was green and lush. Purple fireweed grew taller than my head and waved in the breeze. Devil's Club was thick with leaves and bright red berries. The cow parsnip that looked like an enormous Queen Anne's lace from the Midwest, was rampant.

Hope Sunrise Library was built in 1938, and used as a one-room schoolhouse. Volunteers keep it open. It was a cozy place to go on a summer day and look through old clippings, newspapers, and books.

The Seaview Cafe had a warm, friendly atmosphere, and the fragrances were heavenly. The shelves held Hope memorabilia and another trading library. The wood walls were gray-weathered, and bouquets of plastic flowers lived on the few yellow oil-cloth-covered tables. Robert was a chef from Anchorage, working on his degree. His cooking did absolutely nothing for my waistline. With camping nearly on the doorstep, it was pleasant to go there for friendly conversation, hear local stories, meet people, and eat pancakes, pies, and burgers that were out of this world. Occasionally, I restrained myself and just had coffee.

We all teased Robert. He was an accident waiting to happen, and it usually did. One day he had a black and bruised eye, walked with a strange limp, and the rest of him didn't look too good either. He and his friend, Paul, had a wreck, "We went airborne, end over end both directions, and smashed up both ends of the car. Ended up in the ditch." Chuck and I saw it later. It was completely and irrevocably totaled. I told Robert they must have something pretty special to accomplish on this earth for them to have survived that accident. He began to refer to himself as, "The chef who refused to die."

What a place to raise kids. They had the whole summer for fishing, exploring, and playing. Two little girls, about eight-years-old, walked up the street past the cafe. As they chattered, the white horse from the pasture plodded between them. He didn't even have a rope around his neck. He reached down and nuzzled one girl's hand. Rewarded, he then nuzzled the other girl's hand. He was more dog than horse.

The first foray into the cafe was to have the halibut dinner. My mouth still waters. The next day, I went back for their weekend BBQ special. I had in the meantime become acquainted with the Williams' from Iowa.

When they came in, the place was jammed. They joined me. During our conversation, I didn't notice that the husband had gone up and paid my bill, as well as theirs. When they left Hope, I was the proud recipient of a big hunk of fresh filleted salmon that Howard had caught in the creek. People are kind.

Postmaster Linda said there were nine bears poking around town when I arrived. She and her husband had set a bear trap with moose meat. The trap was metal, strong, and supposedly bears couldn't hurt it. That night they watched a bear pick it up, spring it, and mangle it. He shredded a duck decoy from their pond to the point they couldn't find it. That was one upset bear.

Another lady told me she had watched the horses chase a grizzly out of the pasture a few days before. A fisherman claimed a bear had interrupted his fishing. I asked if the bear chased him. He said, "No, I just backed away slowly." I didn't see any of the bears but over the next few weeks, I saw a moose once in a while.

A Day in Hope

All the bear brochures tell people to make noise to warn them you are in their territory. Although I've never met one nose to nose, it is always a possibility. Fran came out of their fifth wheel to take a shower one morning. A bear was by the telephone booth (waiting for a call?). Apparently neither one of them had brushed their teeth yet because they split without conversing.

The salmon were running. The place was packed with people fishing. I had no interest, but just in case any fishing nuts are reading this, I did hear this comment, "I get so tired catching fish; my wrists are sore."

On the third Sunday in July, Hope sponsors a 5K Run and Bazaar. It started at the Hope Social Hall with a book sale and art exhibit. The Social Hall was built in 1902 and is still used for meetings and weddings.

The event brought runners and supporters in from quite a distance. They milled around greeting old friends and doing warm-ups. Others were taking pictures, eating, and enjoying the sunshine and camaraderie. After instructions via a bullhorn, and warnings that bears were in the area, they were off, old ones, young ones, hotshots, and little kids. Encouragement flowed, a pat on the backside, or shouts, "Yeah, John, way to go, good job, you're almost there." What a great summer day.

On my way through the campground one evening, I saw Gordon Bort playing a saw for a group of admirers. He made different sounds by bending the saw as he drew the bow across it. That particular saw was made especially for playing, but he said you could also build a house with it. Gordon doesn't read music. He had learned to play the saw through a correspondence course. A buddy he had grown up with in Syracuse, New York had come to Anchorage to surprise Gordon, and the two families were camped at Hope for their reunion. When they left, they gave me two "Conies," white hotdogs made with veal.

Next to the Seaview Cafe is the Seaview Bar. Joyce and Don own both of them, as well as the motel and gift shop. Joyce ran the saloon in the evening. It was a gathering place for leftover tourists, locals, and occasionally, nosy writers like me. Chuck helped Joyce for a couple of hours most evenings. If nobody came, they played cribbage.

One night the Sweet Adelines, who were weekending with their leader who lived in Hope, ran a karaoke in the bar. The next day, Fran, Bodie, Chuck, and I went to the Social Hall to hear their fun program.

The railing in the front of the cafe, was a good place to enjoy the sunshine while waiting for the phone. If you looked up on the grassy mountain meadows, you could sometimes see sheep grazing. I wanted to twitch my nose and go up there.

One afternoon Robert sent a young lady from Anchorage over to my RV to go hiking. Gull Rock Trailhead is at the far end of the USFS campground. It goes through a forest cathedral, across a rockslide, and down through an avalanche gully, hugging the flower-bedecked cliffs above Turnagain Arm.

Donna was 37 and in the process of getting her second Bachelor's Degree. She told me about working on a fishing boat the summer before, with three guys she didn't know. She had even more adventurous bones than I did. She did the cooking (naturally) and helped bring in the nets. I asked how she liked the experience. She said there were only a few instances when she questioned what on earth she was doing there, but "We saw so many animals and such incredible scenery, I realized that other people spend thousands of dollars to see what I saw."

Although I made many trips into town, most of my five weeks were parked in a USFS campground on Resurrection Creek. I hadn't shut off the engine before a fisherman gave me salmon that wouldn't fit into his freezer chest.

I parked six feet from the water. My solar purred and my computer hummed. The hosts were SKPs, and Chuck (another one) often brought other campers or visitors to my door to say hello. I think he was trying to marry me off.

Chuck always had interesting stories about campers. Two couples, each with babies less than three months old, were going backpacking over the mountains. He asked if they were aware of the bears. They told

Man and Moose

him about a fellow in Fairbanks who had written a book about bears. He said that bears had never been known to attack a group of more than two people. Chuck said, "Good, you take the book and throw it at the bear in case he hasn't read it."

The only other camper was Mike. He was from California and came to pan for gold. The campground was alongside a recreational gold panning area. He claimed he found more gold in a day there, than in all the years he had panned in California. He panned dirt by the bucketful instead of standing in the cold creek for hours at a time, and said he never failed to find something. One night he knocked on my door to show me his treasures of the day. He had found quite a few nuggets, just smaller than peas, and wanted to share his excitement.

I tried my luck at gold panning. The water was frigid. After I couldn't feel the cold any more, I figured my feet were frozen. A champion gold panning couple from Austria was in the park a couple of days. They panned really fast. I did it their way, not knowing whether I was whisking away a wealth of gold or not.

My equipment was rudimentary at best. I had a gold pan. Along with it, I used a steamer basket and a Tupperware dish. They helped to weed out the bigger rocks (or nuggets!). After four hours of getting my hiking boots, socks, and feet soaked in icy water and mud up to wherever, I had about 10 gold flakes to show for it. That was nothing compared to the silver flake who was doing it. That gold panning proved one thing beyond a reasonable doubt: I would earn more at writing than gold mining, which also meant I was destined to be poor. I found enough gold dust and flakes to see a glint in my tiny vial (if I held it in the right light and in the right position).

If you are interested in serious gold panning, write or visit the Alaska Public Lands Information for a list of recreational panning places where you may legally pan. Don't pan just anywhere because you will likely cross paths with an irate miner. They get pretty touchy about anybody panning on their claims. You are allowed only hand tools and light equipment for recreational panning. Check it out before you do it.

A few people came in to camp or pan for gold; but it stayed quite peaceful. No matter how cool it was at night, my window toward the stream was open. With the cool air and that lulling stream, it was great for sleeping.

The pinks and king salmon fought their way upstream to spawn. Fishermen were elbow to elbow down on the inlet at Hope. Up on the creek, the fish that made it through the gauntlet of inlet fishlines, fought only their battles against time.

The mountains were covered with wildflowers. As I walked around on one of my writing breaks, I was startled to see autumn's first tinges. It was only the last day of July! That night, I saw something I had never seen in Alaska. I opened the curtains, and a full moon shown in all its glory. I had never been up there late enough to see it before.

Chuck Anderson knew I was working, but I could count on his bringing my mail up from Hope. Bodie, an older version of Christopher Reeve, was a retired engineer who spoke in engineereze. Most of the time I understood him. Fran and I had many good conversations. They all had terrific senses-of-humor, and their stories of life and characters in Hope, were priceless.

They warned me about the miner who was always looking for a new bride. He had married several times. Many years ago he advertised nationwide for brides for his whole mining crew, as Bodie put it, "To take care of their biological needs." Only one came. The wedding was quite elaborate with a period setting and a horse and buggy. Alas, the marriage collapsed, and he was alone once more.

One of many things I didn't find the time to do when I was in Hope, was rafting the Six-mile River. It is described as, "Tranquillity, interspersed with moments of high drama." It is a guided trip and dry suits are required, but I will do it...sometime.

I drove Chuck's car into town behind his motorhome, instead of having his kids come out for it. We had dinner at Ole's with his daughter and came right back. Everything was closed up the cafe, the gift shop, and the bar. It was a Monday, August 19. Nobody came to visit so they closed the doors early. I was the only one left in the campground. Chuck and I said our good-byes, and he drove back to Anchorage.

I felt pretty lonely. I left. I stopped at the post office to say goodbye to Linda, and saw Fran and Bodie at the Museum. They invited me to dinner at the Discovery Cafe. It was fun, but sad. My time in Hope had come to an end. Summer visitors were fast disappearing, and the air had a definite feel of fall.

As with all communities, Hope had people from all aspects of life. In every village where I stayed for a while, I eventually discovered the (some) town secrets. One village wasn't so different from another; only the names were changed to protect the innocent and the not so innocent. Everyone has a story to tell. As with everywhere else, some were sad, some poignant, some brutal, some comical, and a few, joyful.

I parked overlooking a scenic spot tightly held by mountains. I closed the drapes and read the evening away.

2001

Hope doesn't have a lot of what travelers think they need. It doesn't have ATM machines or a bank, but most cafes and gift shops take credit cards. Hope doesn't have a movie theatre but the tiny Seaview Bar has live entertainment weekends and jam sessions on Thursday nights where everyone is invited to "Bring your musical instruments, singing voices, and dancing shoes." A new outside raised sundeck stretches between the bar and the café. Hookups were $15, drycamping $10.

Once again I salivated over the Seaview Café's Fish and Chips. It is halibut breaded lightly with something that has dill in it, and served with a homemade secret-recipe tartar sauce. The personnel had changed but they were still exceedingly friendly types. Beth, the waitress, and budding sommelier, sat down and chatted when there were no other customers. She and Matt, who worked the bar and cafe, were both from Michigan. So far from our native state, we felt like kin. Matt was to return to a Michigan medical school in August. I discovered later that he couldn't tear himself away from Alaska. It has that kind of affect.

Tito's Discovery Café burned down in 1999, but he was back in business with a spiffy new building. He said it was rebuilt totally by volunteers with donated materials so he wouldn't have a mortgage. He was so amazed and appreciative that people would do that for him. I told him that anything could be accomplished in the name of love. He was still telling stories to customers.

Hope had two public telephones. Now it has only one, at Henry's One Stop. The Hope-Sunrise Library is still run by volunteers, as is the gift shop next door. Marion was so cheerful and upbeat I left the area with many books from their summer sale. I later visited Marion at her cabin and met her husband, Mark. It started as a small old building but little by little, they are redoing and adding and making a beautiful wilderness nest.

Fayrene and Marion both helped me with Internet problems on the computer. Fayrene, and her husband, Scott, own the GoldRush Bed and Breakfast down the street. It is a historic pioneer log cabin built in 1916.

Linda is still the Postmaster. With sending books and receiving my forwarded mail, I saw her a lot. She was a wealth of information and I always had a wealth of questions. We made a great team.

My friend, Chuck, died a few years ago, as did a couple of other people I had met. Robert, the chef, had disappeared into the world. The population had dwindled to less than 150. Ann and Billie are continually active in the community and in attending the Hope Christian Church. The same minister and his wife still drive in from Seward each Sunday to give a 3 p.m. service. I didn't see the white horse and I'm sure I wouldn't have recognized the two little girls any more.

The Resurrection Creek Recreational Goldpanning Area five miles away continued to call to me. I took Indiana friend Linda Bassett up there prospecting. She was born to it. She hunkered down beside Resurrection Creek and swirled that dirt until all that was left was enough of that engaging yellow metal to have it encased in a necklace at Sourdough Dru's Gift Shop. I had to drag her away.

I returned to Hope several times over the summer and spent a lot of that time up on the creek. I would not have been brave enough to survive what goldrush women endured but in remembrance, I gathered buckets of glacier meltwater and added a bit of the world's greatest Tide. I washed Jeans, sweatshirts, socks, and unmentionables. I rinsed them in more freezing water, rung them out, and hung them to dry for three days. Yup, that was Minshall's contribution to honoring pioneer women.

Peaceful solar ran my computer. I watched the wild spring snowmelt carefully. When it spread over the road and a few inches up the Sprinter's front wheels, I left.

On my way out of Hope, I stopped at the museum. The Sprinter's ignition clicked at me when I tried to get underway again. I inquired if anyone mechanically inclined might be in the vicinity. Within 15 minutes, "Carney Joe" appeared in a vintage brown pick-up truck. As soon as Joe sat behind the steering wheel, I knew the problem was a "guy thing." On the first try, the Sprinter's engine roared to life. It was a faulty starter solenoid. In case it failed to start again before it was replaced, Joe showed me how to strategically place plier handles to create a spark and start the engine, thus bypassing the starter.

Carney Joe is 44 and got his name from working Alaska carnival games for five years. He is constantly busy doing odd jobs in and around Hope, plus keeping up his own property. He lives "up the road" a ways and says, "I didn't have electricity until recently but I still don't use it all the time." He obviously is a self-sufficient man.

He said if I came back through Hope he would gladly "go through the Sprinter, give it good look and see if it needs anything in particular." Then he gave me a hug and said, "God Bless you in your travels." That was a first, and he wouldn't accept any remuneration for his expertise.

A few weeks later I returned and left a message on his door. He found me in the campground, installed the new solenoid, wandered through the Sprinter adding power and brake fluid, airing the tires and perusing the exhaust system, generally with a critical eye to the Sprinter's welfare. We again had an interesting conversation about North Country life, his girl friend that I met later, and witnessing his faith to people who wanted to listen. Although I did get another hug and he again wished me "God's Blessings" before he left, I had to twist his arm to get him to accept $20.

After several visits to Hope and Resurrection Creek, I left for the last time on August 1. It was sad. I again felt like I was leaving home.

But you know, it didn't end there. I still get e-mail from Fran and

Bodie who have even more fond memories of Hope than I do. Several people I met in Hope last summer who went there because they read about it in the 1997 version of this book, have written or e-mailed. I have heard from Beth (Seaview) twice. Linda (and Chuck) Graham, the Postmaster, sent me a fall picture of Hope taken from up on the mountain. She said, "We enjoy your visits, so don't take so long to come back and see us!" And who knows – I just might make it back one day.

View toward Chugach State Park near Anchorage

As always, it is the people you meet along the way who make full-time (or part-time) RVing such a wonderful life.

After leaving Hope and visiting Homer one more time, it finally happened. My sons-in-law always knew it would. Their mother-in-law was living under a bridge. At the Hope Road junction and the Seward Highway, I boondocked under Canyon Creek Bridge. The road was so high above and the stream music so loud, the traffic sounds were inconsequential and the nights peaceful.

It was a good place to make a decision. Should I drive to Fairbanks and at last do the Dalton Highway? This might be my last Alaska trip. You guessed it, the Dalton won. Goodbying my way along, I passed through Anchorage, Palmer, Denali National Park, Ester, and finally...

"Build a Road and She Will Come"

2001

I had flown over the Dalton Highway on my way to Barrow in 1987, but when I debated whether to drive the Dalton Highway in 2001, my craving inner soul whispered, "Travel the gravel of **all** Far North Country roads." The last great challenge, the North Slope Haul Road, better known since public opening in December 1994 as the Dalton Highway, still crawled 414 miles north to Prudhoe Bay, unexplored by the Sprinter and me. Alaska and Canada Highway moguls spread rumors, "Build a road and she will come."

At the beginning of this 996-mile round-trip from Fairbanks, the Sprinter's odometer read 207,000 miles. In readiness, groceries, gasoline, propane, and fresh water were loaded. Sewer tanks were emptied. The Sprinter was outfitted with six new tires, plus maps and other info from the Office of Public Lands, to keep us on the straight and narrow, sort of.

The fireweed plant that Alaskans use as a gauge for winter arriving, was on its last petals, not a good sign when driving 299 miles beyond the Arctic Circle, the farthest north anyone can contiguously drive in North America. I could have taken advantage of a "fly-drive" package, driving a rental unit one way and flying back, but then the Sprinter wouldn't have had that notch on his various traveling belts.

The 11-mile Steese Expressway out of Fairbanks was a tease. Thirty miles into the next 73 miles on the Elliott Highway, the pavement ran out. Small trees were stuck in major road holes. The first sign on the official Dalton Highway stated, "50 mph next 418 miles." Who were they kidding? I already knew I wouldn't be traveling 50 mph. Twenty miles later, I pulled into a wide panoramic viewpoint. It was August 12 at 11 p.m. The rain stopped. The sun briefly exposed infinite blue mountain layers as it slid over the horizon. The wind howled and rocked my cradle. By dawn five semis shared my space. I never heard them.

In 1996, the Yukon River transported me 500 wilderness miles from Eagle to the Dalton Highway by canoe. It was exciting to once again look down on the giant oxbows of North America's fifth largest river. Alaska's only Yukon River bridge, the 2,290' wooden-decked E. L. Patton Bridge, carries both the Dalton Highway and the Trans-Alaska Pipeline across its six- percent grade. Nine, ten, and twelve-percent grades are not uncommon on the Dalton.

The Hot Spot Café opened at 10 a.m. The waitress said, "We don't serve breakfasts." I sipped my coffee and she soon came back, "As long as I'm making breakfast for him," indicating a trucker, "would you like what he's having?" I quickly said yes. The trucker was mostly amiable, answering questions and pouring me coffee. "The road isn't all that bad, but it's better in the winter when the potholes are filled with snow." He let me know in a hurry that he didn't cotton to RVer driving habits. I countered, "And I don't appreciate tailgating truckers when I'm driving the speed limit." After he discovered we were both quick-draw, we agreed that bad drivers live on both sides of the fence, and settled into a nice conversation.

Hot Spot Cafe, Yukon River

Beyond the Yukon was new territory. The $8 billion, specially coated steel pipeline is often visible in its 800-mile journey from the Arctic Ocean to Valdez. During the entire course, it crosses 34 major and 800 minor rivers and streams while crude oil courses six-mph through its 48" pipes. It snakes up a rise, then zigzags a good distance to the right or left. It emerges next to the road or crosses beneath a bridge and climbs the mountain, only to return beneath another bridge going the opposite direction. It burrows into a hill or under a river and materializes on the other side. A little less than half its length is underground. In the aboveground permafrost areas, the pipe is insulated and jacketed.

Because the pipe flexes during expansion and earthquakes, it is not fastened to its supports. It sets on Teflon pads to control its harmonic vibration. In the state that has the largest number of earthquakes, this is good planning. The same reason explains the pipeline meandering. Arch-shaped concrete saddle weights keep the pipeline from popping up in flood-prone areas. Giant "headache bars" prevent large vehicles, such as the Sprinter, from ramming the pipeline on the frequent private access roads. They were not on every access road; however, so I wondered at their effectiveness.

Blueberries and lowbush cranberries were in full juice along Finger Mountain's half-mile BLM wayside interpretive trail. Finger Rock, one jutting "tor" or granite rock pinnacle, of many in the area, was used as an early aviation landmark

It is always thrilling to cross the Arctic Circle whether by plane, canoe, or RV. I duly collected a code word from the sign's backside to earn an Arctic Circle Trading Post certificate. A third of Alaska is beyond the Arctic Circle where the sun neither sets on the summer solstice, nor rises on the winter solstice. I hit the first of several construction areas and muscled the Sprinter through it and on up the muddy mountain.

The Sprinter is used to bad road, but I admit this was the ultimate in bad. Exacerbated by rain, conditions prompted driving no more than 10 potholes per minute. It is, after all, a haul road. I expected to meet trucks, and kept my eye to the mirrors alerting me to what was coming up behind me as well. I slowed (Not easy when you're only going 15 miles an hour or less) and pulled to the right as far as possible, flipped the turn light on, and allowed all trucks a fast right-of-way. They appreciated it with a wave or a CB comment.

A pickup driver's remark to a trucker said it all, "You got the load; you got the road." I kept CB Channel 19 and my lights on at all times.

Gobbler's Knob at 1500', should have allowed my first glimpse of the Brooks Range. It was encased in fog.

Much to my surprise and relief, the first of three chipped-seal highway sections lasted until the former mining town of Coldfoot. This is the only place between the Yukon River and Deadhorse to refuel. Gasoline was $2.35/gallon as opposed to Fairbanks' $1.59 and $2.15 at Prudhoe Bay. Services included a restaurant, motel, post office, dump station, tire repair, and RV hookups.

I asked a fellow pumping gas what the road ahead was like. "I just drove all the way from Prudhoe in a four-wheel Jeep. What are you driving?" When I told him, he said, "No way. Turn back now." Another chimed in, "There was one area of really bad stuff where it was deep rock and they had just filled it in. Considering what you've already come through, you can probably make it. If you don't, they'll have to pull you out just to get you out of the way." As I headed out, I wondered if I felt comforted.

Alyeska Pipeline

The setting sun appeared long enough to light up Sukakpak Mountain and give me a fickle promise of good weather at sunrise. This limestone deposit was transformed into a massive 4,459' marble tower by heat and pressure. Ice mounds, called palsas, around its base are pushing up through the soil and vegetation. Go figure.

This major landmark may have been used as a border between the Inupiat Eskimo and Athabascan Indians. These first inhabitants still depend on the land for sustenance. The land along the Dalton belongs to BLM, State of Alaska, or the Native Corporation.

In the shadow of marble estimated to be 375 million years old, I opened the window and slept to the soothing sounds of the Middle Fork Koyukuk River. It rained.

A tour group stopped for a break the next morning. I was waiting for the fog to lift. I asked her, "How is the road? I have gotten 10 different opinions from 10 different people."

"Welcome to Alaska. Road conditions change by the minute."

I had been traveling through the Boreal Forest with its tiny ragged spruce trees that easily could have been a 100 years old. I was now

Atigun Pass

headed into the Brooks Range, the northernmost extension of the Rocky Mountains. The tree line at this latitude is roughly 2,250' as compared to southern Colorado's 12,000' tree line.

A grader pushed mud on the long 10% grade. I stopped far enough back to get a run for it when the road cleared. From the CB I heard, "Come on Motorhome." I tried to forget the "slippery in wet weather" warning as with a good head of steam and on around him, the Sprinter chugged his way up Chandalar Shelf, ever grateful I wasn't sharing that narrow space with the semi I met at the top. I guess you could say I was semi-frightened. The wide-open alpine tundra was purple, yellow, red, and orange, so brilliant that with sunshine, it would have been too much for the eyes.

The 12% grade toward 4,800' Atigun Pass was completely fogged in. I could see less than two Sprinter lengths. I had the road to myself. Signs announcing each avalanche path zone did nothing for my confidence. I saw only the road's narrowness as the Sprinter negotiated tight, steep curves, crossing the continental divide on Alaska's highest road system pass. Waters to the north empty into the Arctic Ocean; to the south, they empty into the Bering Sea.

The architects and builders of this road and pipeline are quite amazing. I am fascinated with our country's roads anywhere, but as with the Alaska Highway when it was new, the Dalton Highway leads through the middle of nowhere. Not only did they build it across four major natural zones, each with its own geologic and weather problems, but it was begun in April of 1974 and finished five months later!

The pipeline was completed in 1977. Going over Atigun Pass, it was buried in insulated concrete cribbing as a protection from avalanches, rock slides, and to maintain the frozen ground.

During the North Slope descent, the fog disappeared and the world opened to extraordinary scenery as I drove between the Gates of the Arctic National Preserve and the Arctic National Wildlife Refuge. Small caribou herds stood majestically against the horizon or blended into the colorful tundra. They were quite magnificent holding their massive antlers high, perhaps to their own detriment. Bow hunting is allowed within five miles of either side of the highway.

Along with hunters whose tents and truck campers proliferated wherever a few feet of solid ground prevailed, I watched a grizzly bear rooting near a tree a few feet from the road. He was oblivious to his fascinated audience. For all the many sightings of rock and stump bears, I also saw real grizzlies grubbing their fill under and near the pipeline.

The highway and pipeline are within a BLM corridor from the Yukon

River to Slope Mountain at Milepost 301. Marion Creek BLM campground is near Coldfoot, with occasional undeveloped campsites along the way. Private campgrounds are at the Yukon River and Coldfoot. There are innumerable turnouts and informal camping areas for self-contained RVs along the entire route. Dump stations are only at the Yukon River and Coldfoot.

Just below the Ice Cut, a steep, rocky grade, I stopped for the night. With constant pothole dodging, except for the few miles of chipped seal paving, and wrestling through deep mud and rock construction areas, by nightfall I was exhausted. I still had 89 miles to go. Each night I debated whether the end justified the means, but with eternal optimism, by morning I convinced myself the road would be better.

Twenty miles later a sign warned, "Road work next 27 miles, 35 mph." I went over a hill and into an unbelievable construction mess. The flag lady stopped me in mud and rocks eight to ten inches deep, while a huge backhoe did its thing. At her instruction of, "Just kind of wiggle through the machines," I rolled the rest of the way down and eased "into" a section about two feet deeper than the rest. I gingerly drove about two Sprinter lengths and crawled up the other side in first gear, and on up the next hill with a minimum of fishtailing.

Until my small computer went belly up, I had been e-mailing my kids but after starting on the Dalton, I sent them a couple of long letters that went to the whole family. This was part of one letter.

So that's my world, kids. As always, I wish I could zap you all here so I could talk to you, find out about your world, and have you each enjoy this marvelous spot, and see the life I lead. I am so blessed, especially that everyone, including me, is so healthy, but the Lord looks after me in His mysterious ways. Before I started on that last 100 miles north, I did a lot of debating and praying because what I had heard wasn't good.

The caribou bow hunters were out in force and two bunches of them were camped at the Ice Cut as I was (a boondocking gravel area off the road). In the morning I went over and ask these two fellows about the road conditions. "In that? By yourself? We used our four-wheel drive several times to get through. I don't think I'd try it." The other, "Ah, you can make it if you don't stop, just gun it and go for it." Of course I took the second one's advice.

Right after I had gone through the worst of it about 20 miles up the road, these same two guys passed me, waved, immediately turned around and went back whence they came. They had followed me to make sure I got through!!!! They are part of my story but they'll never know it because I have no idea who they are.

Flaggers get lonely on this road, and quite chatty. One fellow told me, "I work in Coldfoot for a few weeks and about eight weeks here, then I don't have to work for the rest of the winter." It didn't sound too bad. "Twenty-five years ago I lived in Michigan. I came up here for a visit and loved it. I thought to myself, 'I can live here or I can live in Detroit, let me see...'" I could see his reasoning.

He also told me that the previous week the road had been dry and smooth (smooth being relative) but the rains had made it bad. "There are two other really bad places ahead of you. Just consider it an adventure." He was the second one who told me that. My one consolation was that I wasn't experiencing the major dust clouds usually associated with traveling the Dalton. I was almost convinced that was a good thing.

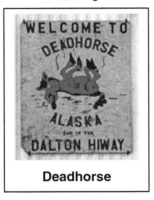

Deadhorse

Lakes, large and small, were abundant and beautiful, but not necessarily reachable. The University of Alaska's Arctic Biology facility on the banks of Toolik Lake has no public access. A three-mile side road reached glacially formed Galbraith Lake and an undeveloped public campground. Closer to Prudhoe, I drove on the Coastal Plains, paralleling the Sagavanirktok River that runs into the Arctic Ocean.

The flatness was broken up by the occasional pingo, formed by the freezing bed of a spring-fed lake that is covered by vegetation. The sprinter was driving over a possible 2,000' of permafrost, sometimes on the wrong side of the road for a smoother surface. The permanently frozen soil is a barrier to drainage, creating moist tundra dotted with tiny lakes and ponds and surrounded by an amazing wildflower display.

On the eastern side of the Sagavanirktok River, the Franklin Bluffs rose in colorful yellow, tan, and orange. Great chunks of last winter's ice were still jumbled along the banks. The bluffs are named after Sir John Franklin who disappeared in 1847 searching for the Northwest Passage. It was cloudy but even partial sun was welcome after all the rain. Storms dotted the vast horizon.

Deadhorse, Prudhoe Bay industrial area's support community, has the Arctic Caribou Inn and Arctic Oilfield Hotel, where oil field employees and tourists can buy the amenities. Don't expect fancy. This is a prefabricated-construction oil drilling camp, not a tourist town. Repairs, fuel, telephones, airport service, and tours are available, but there are no banks or ATM machines.

At the Prudhoe Bay General Store and U. S. Post Office, I asked the clerk if it was o.k. to park the Sprinter in their lot while I looked around. "It's definitely o.k. All rules are reversed here. You can park anywhere." They had everything from A to Z including a V for vest and a certificate declaring I was a survivor of the Dalton Highway. I overheard the postmaster say, "The rain was so bad they cancelled roadwork for two days." Now they tell me. I parked with well-used North Country pick-up trucks. Block heater cords dangled from every radiator.

After a picture-taking session with the famous "Welcome to Deadhorse" sign featuring, what else, a dead horse, I read the bear warning sign that added, "Be careful; we aren't kidding!" I signed up for a combination $50 oilfield and Arctic Ocean toe-dipping tours. I thought the price a little steep but the Dalton Highway and local roads all end at Prudhoe Bay security gates with no public access. "What do I need to bring?" I asked."

'That depends on whether you are going swimming in the Arctic."

"Bathing suits required, right?"

"Definitely not," he said, "Just bring a towel."

A young couple buying tickets asked, "Did you see the two musk ox about a 100 yards off the highway?"

"No, I must have been concentrating on the road." Although I have seen them at the Palmer Musk ox Farm, I was very disappointed not to see them in the wild.

Several places offered dry camp RV parking but I chose to overnight next to the Sagavanirktok River after I topped off the Sprinter's tank at a self-serve fuel station. Scooting a shallow pan under the fill spout was required when refueling. With potholes slowing me to less than 20 mph, my gas mileage was a sliver better than the usual six mpg.

Movin' Day the Prudhoe Way

I awakened warm and cozy on August 16 but my nose was very cold. Making a mad dash to turn on the propane ceramic heater, I jumped back under a pile of covers. I was thrilled with the clear skies and sunshine but the wind was rocking the Sprinter and the temperature was 30 degrees! As I entered the tour lot, the Sprinter coughed and died three times before I could get it parked. When I got back, it worked just fine, no doubt the result of fervent prayer and the Sprinter's realization I was taking him seriously about heading back immediately after the tours.

Our guide was Orion, as in the stars. Someone commented on the unusual name. "I was born in Alaska. A lot of guys have that name. I think it's because the nights are so long." He works at other jobs when he isn't guiding. "The bears have gotten on to the fact that we burn all waste. It is stored briefly in big bins waiting to be burned. The bears come for the kitchen grease. You can't run them off with a truck. They just look at you. They are a little more scared of a 'digger.' Even then they just go and sit for a while then come right back."

Prudhoe's population is 90% men with 2,500 people living there in the summer and 7,000 in the winter. Workers live in hotels or in the camps either in Deadhorse or along the pipeline, working rotation of two weeks on and two weeks off. I asked how they got fresh water. He explained, "It is a precious commodity. We use recycled wastewater and salt water processed from the ocean."

He pointed out big machines called "Rollagons" "These are used for winter exploration, new drilling, building, and repairing. They can go anywhere and do anything, utilizing ice roads. When winter is over and the ice melts, there is no evidence they have been out on the tundra.

"Changes in technology have helped in oil production. In the past, they needed 60 to 70-acre pads to drill for oil. With new technology, now only a 15-acre pad is required." An Emergency Response station is staffed 24 hours a day, 365 days a year.

Humor is evident. The Haliburton Company owns Prudhoe National Forest, lock, stock, and barrel. It is five plywood pine trees painted green, the only ones this side of Chandalar Shelf. Referring to a nearby pingo, Orion said, "That is 20' tall Logan Peak, our highest point." A Figures of Eight sculpture honored the first major oil find in 1968.

We passed through a security checkpoint, then waited while a huge building rumbled past us. Orion said, "They are moving an entire camp to another spot. The original building was probably barged in as one piece. Buildings are often moved." Pointing across the compound, he added, "That building was not there four days ago. They may be setting up to re-drill an old well now that technology has improved. They lay plywood down and move the buildings across them on tires that cost $30,000 each." Suddenly the cost of the new Sprinter tires didn't seem so bad.

He indicated pipeline control tower and pump stations, and a meter station, "It's like a big cash register where they see how much oil is pumping. We pump 20% of the nation's oil."

We stopped long enough to examine the pipeline and view a cut-a-way showing how a "pig" works. A "dumb" pig is a scraper made of blades and/or brushes that cleans the accumulated wax from the inside walls. "Smart" pigs monitor the pipeline to recognize problems.

Orion pointed out small sand dunes on the way to the ocean toe dipping, which didn't last long. The blowing snow added to the ambience. "It can snow anytime. We had several inches on the Fourth of July this year. When winter comes, you can't see where the ocean begins and the land leaves off. Everything is white. It gets down to -20 to -60 degrees January through March."

With that thought in mind, I said goodbye to Deadhorse and Prudhoe Bay and headed into blowing snow, determined to make it through the worst construction and Atigun Pass before I stopped. Seeing the gaggles of geese headed south in a V for victory sign, I knew I had made the right decision.

In the middle of the worst construction mess, a motorhome was stuck. After much worker shoveling, and attempts by a four-wheel drive truck and a dump truck, the backhoe hooked up and they were pulled free. In the meantime, huge machinery and big trucks lined up on either side of the hole, waiting to get through. I was second in line. I waited until the truck ahead of me was on its way up the hill, then I put it in first, gunned and wrestled the Sprinter through it and on up the hill with smiles and thumbs up from the guys.

Excedrin Headache #445

Cool temperatures, dark clouds, and the threat of possible snow on Atigun Pass spurred me on. I stopped to let several truckers go by, "Make a path over those mountains for me."

"Looks like we might need one." But this time the mountaintop provided marvelous views. Mama and Baby Dall sheep ran beside me.

I woke up beside the braided Dietrich River and a magnificent crisp, clear day. I heard a trucker say the road was washed out near Livengood so I decided to stay and enjoy the sunshine. The dark brown pound-cake mountains wore a powdered sugar dusting. Some of the pound cake had more rugged peaks than the others. I walked, bundled against the cold, ever mindful of juicy blueberries and the grizzlies that love them.

Late the second day, I drove through the pleasant long twilight evening and parked at the Jim River Bridge. As I was reading about 11 p.m., the motorhome suddenly moved violently. Quite sure of what I would see, I jumped up and looked in the right rear view mirror. A black bear stood on his hind legs with his front paws up on the Sprinter. I remembered succinctly why I advise all boondockers to keep the keys in the ignition for any emergency get-a-way. I turned the key and it clicked. "Oh, no, please, Lord, don't test me now!" I prayed. I tried again and the Sprinter's engine roared to life. I moved the Sprinter back and forth a couple of times and the bear ran off.

Shortly, he was back again, trying to get into the bear-proof garbage container. This time I got a good look. He was a big hummer. He ambled toward the Sprinter. I started the engine again. He ran off.

Three things I was especially grateful for in my prayers that night; #1, that he didn't put his paws on the window where and while I was reading; #2, that he didn't put his paws on the screen when I was sleeping with the window open; and #3, that he didn't have a can opener. The next morning I found his paw prints embedded in the Sprinter's mud on both back corners. The prints on the left side were on the window right where I would have had it opened and he would have pushed through the screen.

On the way back, with at least partial sunshine, gravel "belly dump" trucks and construction workers were out in full force. Discussing my night marauder at the Arctic Circle with a fellow who checks fiberoptic cable lines along the Dalton, he said, "If the bear had wanted in, nothing could have stopped him." He also said communication with Prudhoe Bay that morning revealed, "It's all white up here this morning." I had escaped at the right time.

A mini motorhome that had flown around me toward Prudhoe, flew around me again as I leisurely made my way around the potholes. Later I saw it parked at the road's edge, surrounded with orange pylons. Nobody was home. It looked like a broken axle.

Nine days and a magnificent journey later, I promised the Sprinter no more rough roads. He looked at me haggardly, with droopy-lidded Sealbeams and said, "Yeah, yeah, I've heard it all before."

"Well, maybe the Mackenzie Route to Yellowknife." Hmmm.

After that major rough Dalton Highway, I expected a relatively uncomplicated drive from Fairbanks to Tok, to decide then whether I would turn left to Dawson City or go straight back on the Alaska Highway. That wasn't to be.

All problems are not major. A small truck twice pulled up beside the Sprinter and the driver signaled me to pull over. A big dog in the front seat grinned at me. I guessed the guy couldn't be all bad. Pointing to the Sprinter's backside, the Good Samaritan indicated that my spare tire was about to jump the bumper in a spectacular suicide attempt. Having experienced that disaster previously in West Virginia, I wasn't anxious for a reoccurrence. I was extra conscious of bumps as I continued.

I was driving later than usual, hoping to reach the outskirts of Tok before stopping. That wasn't to be either. Suddenly smelly smoke was welling up around me. The CB clicked off. The engine quit. The power steering shut down. I wrestled the Sprinter off the road gingerly so I wouldn't go in the ditch but quickly before it stopped rolling. I worked my way along a steep slope through thigh-high weeds to open the hood. The smoke cleared but I couldn't see anything.

The electrical system completely shut down. Nothing worked. The engine wouldn't start. The frig was out. The RV lights were out. The only thing working was my solar. I could use the computer! The generator would start but it wouldn't run anything.

By the time I checked everything to no avail, it was dark. What was the point in stewing all night? I went to bed. At dawn my subconscious remembered the serviceless cell phone. The solar inverter worked so I charged the phone. One of those "mini-miracles" provided full bars. Three hours following my 911 call, twice transferred, a tow truck collected the Sprinter and took me to Tok RV. After checking for a short, a melted house battery post and a solenoid (a different one) were replaced.

Judy and Nick Santamaria were there having a problem fixed too. We commiserated. Theirs was fixed by mid afternoon and they left after giving me some chocolate kisses and encouragement.

In the meantime, back to 1996 and a chapter of adventures before we do the "other" major North Country highway, the Dempster. Below is an advance peek of Crow Creek.

The Fair and the Fireweed

1996

Ken, a good friend from California, was flying in for a sea-kayaking trip in Prince William Sound. I had only done river and lake kayaking. I was excited about trying something new. It was late August and tourists had dwindled. After Ken's plane reservations were already set, the company canceled. When he arrived, we made other plans.

At Girdwood (south of Anchorage), Crow Creek Mine has a campground for self-contained RVs. It is an 1898 mining camp, a National Historic Site, with eight original buildings and mining equipment. It is easy to wander for hours looking at equipment and reading the history.

Many places offer gold panning. They hand you a bucket of salted dirt and you pan in a hokey sluice box. You always get something. Crow Creek allows you to hike along the creek and pan wherever and whatever. If you don't know how, someone will show you. We found one large flake and some dust. *($5 in 2001)*

After panning, we went through all the Crow Creek buildings including the Blacksmith's Shop, Mess Hall, and Barn. Barney and Cynthia Toohey, owners of Crow Creek Mine, have lived there for 20 years. None of the buildings, including their personal beautiful cabin, have electricity or running water. They love it. They no longer endure Alaskan winters; however, they visit Mexico or the Caribbean.

We drove beyond Crow Creek to the Crow Pass Trailhead and went hiking. Crow Pass is a steep three-mile hike following the Historic Iditarod Trail. We left at 3:15 and didn't get to the mine and falls until six. It was hard to believe this steep trail was the original Iditarod.

The views above tree line were incredible. Bright fall colors were coming on strong but the summer flowers were hanging in there. Dark wispy clouds took turns shadowing the mountains and glaciers, and fresh snow dusted the surrounding peaks.

We examined the mining equipment and ruins and sat for a while, surveying our momentary kingdom. The climb in the sun forced us to shed extra shirts, but with the sun going behind the mountains and a frigid breeze blowing through the pass, it didn't take us long to put them back on again.

One activity I didn't want to miss was the Alaska State Fair's Diamond Jubilee at Palmer. Animals exhibited were different than at the Van Buren County Fair back home in Michigan. There were llamas, alpacas, musk ox, and reindeer. In the heart of the famous agricultural Matanuska Valley, oversized cabbages weighed in at more than 80 pounds. The Diamond Jubilee Giant Cabbage Weigh-off prize was $4,000.

We ate everything that wasn't nailed down, deep-fried halibut, ice cream in homemade cones, cheesy popcorn, pizza, and elephant ears, but junk food is what an evening at the fair is all about.

Entertainment featured Alaska Racing Pigs, Scheer's Lumberjack Show, and Bud Bog, among others. The Guess Who came (I guessed and I still didn't know who). The Blessid Union of Souls came (and I didn't know who they were either). The Alaska Native Dancers performed and Alaska wasn't too far away to attract the rave of Nashville, LeAnn Rimes. Homesteader Events included wood splitting, ax throwing, crosscut and bow sawing and other activities most of us rarely see.

A grandmother danced to the music with a tiny tot. Kids had their faces made up with hair pulled into different styles and spray painted with sparklies. One little tyke, painted like a cat, was quite patient with the whole business. When she looked into the mirror, however, the reaction was priceless. She couldn't quite believe it. She looked away and back quickly, as if the image would change. She was a wee bit awed with her feline image. I loved being caught up in fair excitement and it was fun having someone with whom to share it. We wanted to return for the next day's activities but morning brought heavy rain with it.

If you are ever near Palmer, Alaska, the last week of August, or first week of September, go to the Alaska State Fair.

We headed toward Hatcher Pass on Fishhook-Willow Road. The rain stopped, the clouds lifted, and the sun came out. We passed the Motherlode Lodge where I had eaten on a previous trip. I was in new territory. We continued up a pothole-filled road at 15 mph. The Sprinter zigged and zagged, and slowly ascended through the scenery to the Independence Mine.

Independence Mine

The Independence Mine is a State Historical Park at Hatcher Pass, elevation 3,886'. Gold was discovered in this area as early as 1886. It was years before independent mining claims were brought together under one company. In 1941, a peak year, 34,416 ounces of gold was mined. Today that would be worth $17,208,000.

Immediately surrounding the mine, Boomtown grew to 22 families. Now the mine and buildings are silent save for visitor conversation while walking the trails and looking into shafts, tunnels, and buildings. Interpretive signs explain the history.

The manager's family house was renovated for the Park Headquarters and Visitor Center. It was a neat building with pictures of bygone days. Even though it was warm outside, they had a fire going. I asked about the road over Hatcher Pass. They said it wasn't too bad. They brought out a map, and said it was another 30 miles of what we had just come through, potholes, with a couple of bad hairpin curves. When they discovered I had a motorhome, they said I probably shouldn't. When they saw the size, they said, "We don't recommend it."

Despite knowing how bad the road was ahead, I hated to go back over the same territory. I decided to forge ahead. I hadn't yet seen a hairpin curve that couldn't be negotiated with a little backing up. The first quarter mile was narrow, washed out and potholed. Then it improved to potholes and boulder tops sticking out of the ground that I had to weave around. Traveling was slow, but the scenery was worth it. We looked down on lakes, waterfalls, glaciers, and streams wending their way through the valley. Aspen groves were golden. Low cranberry and blueberry plants were bright red and orange.

The hairpin curves were wide enough for a wide turn with no problem. Only a few impatient souls flew around me. I let them. We stopped several times along Willow Creek to admire beaver engineering. Active beaver houses with four, five, and six-foot dams corralled large expanses of water. Not one beaver came out to say hello. Ken had never seen a wild beaver.

Along a narrower, puddle-filled road through the bushes, we found a campsite on Willow Creek. It took some maneuvering to get in place. Someone had left a note on the tree, "Anyone is welcome to camp in this site, but we are coming to use it over the weekend." It was the perfect spot with the stream rushing along just outside our windows. The next morning we reached the George Parks Highway.

At Cantwell, before turning onto the old Denali Highway toward Paxson and the Richardson Highway, I filled with gas and asked about road conditions. I don't know why I ever ask. I know you can't take the word of a tourist, who will usually say, "They're terrible;" and the locals who *always* say, "Not bad."

The Denali Highway is the original road that led to Denali National Park and Preserve before the George Parks Highway was built. It has impressive views and remote camping places, but it was September, and I hadn't counted on hunting season. Trucks, four-wheelers, tents and hunting camps were everywhere. The scenery was impressive but the road was much worse than previously. Along with a lot of washboard, each pothole did its best to outdo the previous one.

I have learned that driving faster on washboard is smoother than going too slowly, but it was a challenge to fly over the washboard, and slow down quickly enough to avoid the potholes. I pulled over often to let others by, and then swallowed their dust. Gravel roads don't bother me; a certain amount of washboard and potholes don't bother me; but 114 miles of driving an average of 15 mph, got to me. The last 21 miles into Paxson were paved.

For quite a distance after leaving the George Parks Highway, Mt. McKinley played in and out of the clouds. We stopped and walked back along the one-lane multi-span Suisitna River Bridge, 1,036' long, to take pictures, and eventually camped in a pullout beside Clearwater Creek. The sun shown, but fall chill was in the air.

Denali Highway has everything, glaciers, archeological sites in the Tangle Lakes District, and kettle lakes left behind by blocks of glacier ice melt. Some of the road is built along "eskers," great ridges of gravel formed by streams flowing under glaciers. It has Alaska's second highest highway pass at Maclaren Summit, 4,086'. I'll tell you about the highest later.

While Mt. McKinley is outstanding, the Alaska Range is no slouch. We could see Mt. Deborah (12,339'), Hess Mountain (11,940'), and Mt. Hayes (13,832'), and their accompanying glaciers, all mounded in snow, some of it fresh. On our other side were the Talkeetna Mountains. As we approached Richardson Highway, every curve brought a more beautiful sight with the fall colors against the stark white snow.

Would I drive it a third time? Of course, but I would go during a quieter time than hunting season, and take several days to explore the side roads into the trailheads. In addition to the hunters, blueberry pickers were out in force. We saw trumpeter swans and beaver but no large animals. They were hiding from all the hunters.

Let's fast forward left to Delta Junction. When we arrived at Paxson on the Richardson Highway, we turned right toward Glennallen, but I want to mention the Richardson from Delta Junction to Paxson. Unless you are in Alaska a long time, and deliberately seek this highway, it is probably one of the roads you'll miss. It is quite a beautiful route, a bumpy one either time I've been on it, with the usual good and bad areas.

Delta Junction, at the junction of the Alaska Highway and the Richardson Highway, is the official end of the Alaska Highway. I had driven from Delta Junction to Paxson in 1992, and experienced views of the same mountains I saw on Denali Highway; Hayes, Deborah and Hess. It is an opportunity for excellent views of the oil pipeline.

In the summer, Richardson Highway was decorated with purple fireweed and in September, it was dressed in fall colors. Along with the mountains, were Black Rapids and Gulkana Glaciers; plus Summit, Paxson, and Willow Lakes. The road follows the Delta and Gulkana Rivers part of the way.

Leaving the Paxson area, the Chugach Mountains were in the distance one direction, and Mounts Sanford, Drum, and Wrangell, the other. Their lower reaches were draped in fall colors with more than a bit of new snow dusting their tops. I stopped at the junction of Glenn and Richardson Highways at Glennallen to get current information on McCarthy.

McCarthy

We made reservations. I had driven the motorhome to McCarthy in 1992, and vowed to go back because it was such a neat trip and place. I wanted to stay at least two weeks. As good weather and Ken's time were running out, and I wanted to stay longer if I ever drove that miserable road again, we took the $60-per-person round-trip van tour.

Leaving the Richardson Highway, I drove the paved Edgerton Highway to Liberty Falls State Recreation Site for the night. Continuing the 33-mile stretch into Chitina the next day, we passed Three-mile Lake, Two-mile Lake, and One-mile Lake (Does this show a lack of imagination, or am I being picky?).

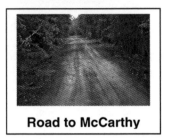

Road to McCarthy

The driver of the van, Wen, and his wife, were missionaries from Siberia, 150 miles above the Arctic Ocean. They were home for the summer and he had interesting tales to tell about their unusual life. The best part of taking the van was that I could relax and enjoy the scenery without worrying about the Sprinter's undercarriage or a flat tire. (Plane trips are also available)

Everything about the road to McCarthy fascinated me from the first time I heard about it from the volunteer hosts at Chilkat State Park, the Keitels. They had traveled it many years prior to the "improvements." The word improvement should be taken with several grains of salt; although from the stories they told me about their first trip, improvements really had been made. If you're driving, a National Park Service ranger station is in Chitina and they can tell you about current conditions. The ranger station was closed both times I was there. I asked other people, and took the advice of the worst out of three. The Sprinter wasn't thrilled with that decision but I was.

The McCarthy Road begins just outside Chitina at the Copper River. After approximately 60 miles of dusty, narrow, and washboard road, it ends at the Kennicott River. It follows the roadbed of the Copper River and Northwestern Railway. The CR & NW was referred to as the "Can't Run and Never Will" Railroad. This was used from 1911 to 1938 and transported 200 million dollars worth of copper ore from the Kennecott Mine. The McCarthy Road is an "improved railroad bed."

Although the rails and ties have been removed, sometimes old railroad spikes surface. For that matter, I've seen some of those "removed" ties underneath the dirt that got scrapped to the surface. At any rate, it is a dirt road, narrow enough in spots to require waiting at iffy turnouts for vehicles to pass. On my two trips, I never saw a great deal of traffic on it.

The twelve-million-acre Wrangell-St. Elias National Park and Preserve surrounds the McCarthy Road. Alaska owns the road but it is well to remember that most of the land near the road is privately owned.

One of my favorite spots is the one-lane Kuskulana Bridge at Mile 16. It was built in 1910 to cross the 385' deep, Kuskulana gorge. New decking and metal guardrails were added in 1988. When I drove it with the Sprinter, bungee-jumpers were diving off the bridge. If I ever take leave of my senses enough to go bungee-jumping, I want to go off the Kuskulana Bridge. At the very least, I will have magnificent scenery on the way to meet my Maker. None of this fair jumping stuff off a derrick!

We stopped at the crinkled railroad trestle over the Gilahina River. It is part of the original railroad bed. Our rest stop included a long enough period to go water a bush (I was used to that after the Yukon River trip). The van dealt with the washboard road better than the Sprinter. We passed still lakes and beaver dams with early-morning scenery reflected in them.

Wen said that many of the McCarthy residents were attracted to this

Tramming

secluded place to get away from the world. When tourism began to take hold, they changed their thinking and joined in.

When I drove the Sprinter to McCarthy, I parked in an upper, roughly-dozed parking space. Signs warned that floods might come swooshing through if the lake ice up above gave way. I pulled my dangling self hand-over-hand across the wild rushing river in two places via an open-sided, two-seated tram. Except for a few people in tents, truck campers, and small RVs, no one else was around. After I trammed across one river section, I walked a quarter-mile and trammed across the other. I walked another quarter-mile into town and paid a $5 fee for a narrated shuttle ride to the Kennecott Mine and the Kennicott Lodge.

In 1996, things had changed drastically. The Kennicott River area had been turned into a rough-cut campground with a fee. I'm not sure whether the combination information-ticket building was makeshift, or just built that way to blend in. If you were going to ride to the mine from McCarthy ($8), you had to buy your tickets there. It

McCarthy Lodge

was after Labor Day so there wasn't a choice of times. They didn't charge for using the tram. A telephone booth lived in the parking lot -- amazing. Previously, they used only radiophones.

Ken and I crossed on the tram, then went by mini-bus for the five-mile ride to Kennicott Glacier Lodge and the Kennecott Mine. The second tram was no longer necessary because the river changed its course and the bed was reasonably dry.

Nothing had changed at Kennicott Glacier Lodge. It has a long porch with bright hanging flowerpots and views of the mine, glacier, and mountains. Food and lodging are expensive. Everything has to be trammed across the river once the ice has broken. I've seen gasoline drums, plywood, bikes, and other items brought across on the trams.

After the discovery of copper in the early 1900s, the Kennecott Mine grew into a community with a general store. Miner's families purchased items using corporation scrip. A dairy barn and refrigeration plant also

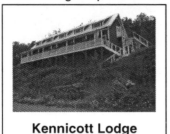

Kennicott Lodge

existed. The hospital had one doctor and several nurses. Pneumonia and head injuries were the most frequent cause of death. They had a school, and a recreation hall for dances, basketball games, and art shows. It was a company town with strict conduct rules. The cottages used by the foremen and their families are being renovated for rentals and private use.

The spellings of Kennecott and Kennicott are different. The glacier was named after Robert Kennicott, an Alaskan explorer. Due to an error, the mine was spelled Kennecott, and it was left that way.

McCarthy sprang up to provide the miners with what Kennecott didn't, newspapers, restaurants, hotels, pool halls, saloons and a red-light district. The combined area now has about 35 year-around residents.

When the mine closed in 1938, people were given 48 hours to pack up and get out. The vital parts of the powerhouse were destroyed and thrown over the side of the cliff in what is now called, "The Graveyard."

The mine has many interesting faded red buildings perched precariously in stair-step fashion on the mountainside. It includes the concentration mill, the ammonia-leaching plant, and the power plant. It is amazing that people are allowed to wander. You could easily fall through the many open areas. We couldn't go inside the buildings, but we could see in the windows. The

Kennecott Mine

mine is a National Historic Landmark, but it is all private property. The National Park Service has negotiated for years to buy it. With a tag of nearly five million dollars, it may not happen until the buildings have long gone bye-bye.

With the great piles of rocky gravel in front of the mine, people automatically assume it is tailings. Guides explain that the glacier revises the landscape in its own way, leaving a chaotic, rock, end product.

If you're feeling hardy, there are trails to the glacier, as well as between Kennicott and McCarthy.

In McCarthy, the McCarthy Lodge still offered sleeping accommodations in the Johnson Hotel or in the Bunkhouse. I didn't eat in the lodge this time but I know the food is home-cookin' good, and the atmosphere pleasant. Gary and Betty Hickling run the lodge. When I was there before, he had just bungee-jumped three times off the Kuskulana Bridge, and swore by the tremendous adrenaline rush (it sounds like Excedrin Headache #493 to me).

My adrenaline rush came from going up in a bush plane with Natalie Bay

Flight Over Kennicott Glacier

who owns Wrangell Mountain Air with her husband, Kelly. That trip over ghost towns, mines, Dall sheep, the Icefall Stairway, and the Wrangell Mountains...well, I didn't want to come down.

Rumors were rampant that a pizza place was in Beautiful Downtown McCarthy and I couldn't believe it. I thought that maybe it was something with neon signs the size of McDonald's golden arches. Jim and Jeannie Miller, long-time residents, have opened a really nice pizza parlor. You can eat inside or on the deck outside. It not only fit into McCarthy décor, it gave Ken and I a chance to discuss our day, soak in the atmosphere, and enjoy delicious pizza, all at the same time.

I noticed on the way back to the van that finishing touches were being put on the McCarthy-Kennicott Community Church, on what used to be an island between the two Kennicott River channels.

On the return to Chitina, Wen stopped and we walked across the Kuskulana Bridge. Three interesting and friendly young fellows left us to go backpacking into the mountains. My soul definitely had the adventurous desire to follow them, but I wished for more energy.

A daylong tour isn't enough to explore any of this completely. The answer to that is to stay for a while. I can't in all good conscience advise anyone to drive a RV on that road. I wasn't thrilled with the "improvements," but I'll get over it. I just hope they never go as far as paving the road, and it is being discussed. Scuttlebutt says a bridge will soon be built across the river instead of using the tram. Visit soon.

At the same time that I want everyone to experience McCarthy and Kennicott, I want them to stay away in droves. Controversy rages. If the road is improved, amenities increased, and the way cleared for anyone to get there, it will turn into a Yosemite or Denali. If improvements aren't made, a magnificent wilderness will be enjoyed by only a few. I'm selfish.

We boondocked on the banks of the Copper River, and had the opportunity to see several working fish wheels owned by Native Alaskans.

It was Ken's last full day in Alaska and he was treated to fall color at every Richardson Highway overlook, and a few moose surfaced for his benefit. We stopped to hike a couple of times and visited Worthington Glacier. This is Alaska's most accessible glacier. Park your vehicle, walk up the hill, and you are there, looking down on the glacier.

We lunched at Blueberry Lake State Recreation Area, then decided to stay. On the ocean side of the mountain pass, we had returned to summer. The picnickers who occupied the perfect campsite we coveted, not only left their campfire going, but gave us their extra wood. We had an overview of the snow-dusted Chugach Mountains, distant waterfalls, and meadow flowers blooming at our feet.

Magpies and ground squirrels entertained us as we hiked the rocky ridge. In the warm afternoon sun, we picked tiny, wild blueberries that were sweet and delicious in blueberry pancakes the next morning. It was a perfect evening for a fire, clear and cold.

Valdez is called the "Switzerland of the North." Until this trip, I wouldn't have known the Chugach Mountains surrounded it. This was my third trip through Keystone Canyon and the first time I saw it without fog. The only reason I saw Bridal Veil and Horse Tail Falls previously, was because they are in a very narrow canyon next to the road.

I have also always been there at the wrong time to go to church on the Lu-Lu Belle. From eight to nine on Sunday mornings, the Valdez First Baptist Church sponsors "A different church service," cruising the Port of Valdez. The advertising says, "Everyone Welcome," so I guess they'd let a Presbyterian aboard. Of course, there's always the chance they wouldn't let me off until I became a Baptist! *(Although I didn't get back there in 2001, I heard that the Lu-Lu Belle's regular tour is one of the best in Valdez.)*

Valdez is a good place to make arrangements to see the famous Columbia Glacier. It is also part of Klondike Gold Rush History. The Valdez Trail went over the Valdez Glacier to Eagle and then up the Yukon River to Dawson City.

The original Valdez died in the tsunami that rolled over the town in the 1964 earthquake. The townspeople rebuilt it four miles away. You can follow gold rush, Trans-Alaska Pipeline (Exxon oil spill), and earthquake history, at the Valdez Museum.

Across the bay at the Alyeska Pipeline Marine Terminal gate, is a monument to the Alaska Pipeline workers. Tours are available there and at Pump Station #9, Milepost 258. Other information and signs are at Visitor Centers, and along the Richardson and Dalton Highways.

Ken and I said our good-byes at the Valdez Airport. He was already talking about coming back to Alaska. He flew to Anchorage, then returned to California.

I turned off the Richardson Highway toward Tok and saw caribou at every curve. During the evening I wondered which direction I should take. Should I turn right at Tok and make a beeline for the lower 48? Or turn right with an immediate left, and go back across Top of the World Highway and Inuvik? The sparse fireweed petals intimidated my thinking. Only two or three blooms hung on for dear life. I called for Dempster Highway conditions. It didn't sound too bad. I decided for the right and an immediate left.

Tok to Eagle to Dawson City,

Fall, 2001

After stopping briefly at Chicken, I decided on a whim to return to Eagle. I turned at Jack Wade Junction. The drive was beautiful, steep, narrow sections overlooking canyons and streams. In some areas I could see the road winding out and around, layer after layer.

In Eagle, I went to the Eagle Trading Co. to use the telephone on the side of the building. The building had either been raised or they had dug under it and the only way to use the telephone was by standing on two cement blocks. It looked pretty unstable so I went in and asked if there was another public phone

I camped at the BLM campground for the Golden Age ½ price of $4. They have hosts now. Darlene and Bill Jones were full-timers and had been there for several summers. Bill warned me about a guy from town, "He hits on all the single women. If he knows there's one in town, he is after them. He's persistent; he won't leave you alone." I laughed and said after being a widow for 19 years, I thought I could handle any problems. When I left a week later, I still hadn't seen the guy. I didn't know whether to feel fortunate or insulted that he hadn't sought my company.

I didn't make it in time for church but the Jones' took me to the potluck in the afternoon. They no longer used the little log church as they had in 1996. Someone gave them an old building. They skidded it to its present location and fixed it up as a church. It looked great. I recognized John, the postmaster, now retired, and a couple of other people.

I went down to check my messages and heard, "Charlie." It was Judy and Terry from the Mukluk Annie campfire. I couldn't believe it. I had seen June and Vern again near Hope. We walked to the cafe for brunch and caught up on our summer travels. They were "sort of" on their way home too.

The Yukon Queen comes into Eagle every day. The passengers mill around town for a short time, climb aboard buses and go back to Dawson City by road. The bus passengers get on the Yukon Queen and go back up the Yukon River to Dawson City. Off season, the shops are only open when the riverboat is in town.

Darlene invited me to go "beading." Several community women get together weekly at Yukon Ron's Gift Shop run by Ron and Mary. They gather around long tables and with beads, colored stones, crystals, and whatever, make necklaces, earrings, and other jewelry. One lady was using porcupine quills. She had cut off the murderous tips and cut the quills to the lengths she needed. I asked how she came by the procupine quills and she said, "I shot him and very carefully laid aside each row and pulled them out. The quills from one porcupine lasts over two years." How many of you do that?

Crafting isn't my thing but I have a great appreciation for how much work and talent goes into it. In the background, Ron played one of those miraculous keyboards that does everything but wash the dishes. It had a great sound system, and he had a voice to match. Another key boardist and guitarist joined him singing sad or lively tunes we all recognized. It was a fun evening.

The Jones' dropped me off at the corner and as I went down the hill, I saw friend Bill's promised fire flickering in the night. We enjoyed trading travel stories until midnight. He was a single who came into the park for a few days. We got acquainted and hiked and had a couple of meals together at the café.

A lady who was originally from Michigan owns a small log cabin gift shop with her husband. They were about to open a small café that would be nice for the locals when the other café closes for the winter.

The library hadn't changed much except that it now has two computers for Internet access. Neither had the Eagles' trust. Bo at Telegraph Hill Service seemingly had no problem accepting a personal check when I paid for propane. At the Village Store, I paid $6.89for a gallon of milk. At the Eagle Trading Post, it was $4.95 for a half gallon.

Darlene and Bill and I had coffee at the café and watched that magnificent Yukon River and mountain scenery change second by second with rain clouds, white clouds, and sunset. They took me for a ride out to the Han Kutchin Indian Village east of town. The few Natives left were moving into new housing well away from the river because they get flooded every year when the river ice backs up. Some maintain two houses because they love it on the river and don't want to give it up.

One night we saw a flock of sandhill cranes flying in formation and headed south. That night Jones' had a campfire and invited me. I loved to hear them talk. Darlene always referred to Bill as "My Darling." He always drew out her name in that long, soft, sexy West Virginia drawl. They were such fun company and being there beside a fire in the woods, I felt very much at home. I might just have to go back.

It was decision time. I was either going to drive home or take the ferry. The ferry won out. The patient young lady at the Alaska State Ferry booked the Sprinter and me from Skagway to Bellingham, Washington, with weeklong stops at Juneau and Sitka for $1,974. I was scheduled to leave aboard the Malaspina on September 5. It is strongly recommended that you make reservations 5-6 months prior to needing them. The only reason I had no problems getting on at the last minute was the September date.

Breakfast was pleasant with Bill and Darlene at the Trading Post Café the last morning. My last two hours in Eagle were spent with Phyllis, a lady whom I met in 1996. She is a museum docent and we've kept in contact through the years. I am always fascinated with the lives of those who live in such far-removed areas.

I made brief stops throughout the day following the Taylor Highway back to Jack Wade Junction. It is a good thing I took the time to enjoy it because sometime in the night, my boondocking spot on Top of the World Highway, was catching rain and it never let up until I was well down the Klondyke Highway to Whitehorse. I was in Dawson City only long enough to drive through the streets one more time. It was too rainy and muddy to get out and walk around, and I had a schedule.

1996, Tok to Chicken to Dawson City

The thermometer registered 9° above zero somewhere on the Tok Cutoff Road. The weeds were frosted and sparkly in the first light of dawn. It was so cold the roadkill had frost on it. Steam rose from ponds and streams, all reminders that winter was coming.

Since driving from Chicken to Tok in early June, a good bit of the Taylor Highway road construction had been finished. Sooner or later all the kinks and interest will be gone from this heretofore adventurous road.

I stopped briefly again at Chicken. It was past the season's end and my friend had already gone home. I made it to the Canadian border before it closed, and proceeded along Top of the World Highway. A cow moose ran across the road in front of me.

Out of habit, I continued to check the sporadically hot ignition switch. It was cool. I parked on a gravel pull off. It was a bittersweet evening. The sunset was spectacular with clouds hovering around the sun, but I was circuitously heading "home." It was the September sixth. Autumn yellows crawled up the draws with multi-colored ground cover carpeting the mountains above the tree line, sometimes mixed with fresh snow.

I read myself to sleep. I'm not sure what awakened me but when I opened the drapes, I realized I had reached another goal. It was 12:15 a.m. and the Aurora Borealis had come to visit.

It came out of the horizon and made a long, swirling arc to the right of the Big Dipper. I watched it intently. It moved ever so slightly, taking a different shape at the curled end. The front window gave me a panoramic view. It moved to the left of the Dipper. I went to the back window, took out the screen and propped my pillow in the opening. It danced over my head. I went outdoors where I could see it all. The whole sky filled. The night was silent. The air was frigid, but even as I drew my furry robe close to my body, I knew the goosebumps were not all from the cold.

The curtain of lights rippled and became more active as time went on. Just when I thought it was fading; another arm of it brightened. I couldn't hear the crackling some have heard, but I did see very pale green color. I stood with my mouth open in complete unadulterated awe. Eventually the cold forced me inside. The lights were magnificent, startling, and completely awe-inspiring. If I hadn't already believed in God and miracles, the Aurora Borealis dancing across a frigid northern night, would have convinced me He was present.

No ice chunks huddled on the Yukon River shoreline, but frost was on the pun'kin in Dawson City. The ferry goes downstream below the landing, and looks like it will miss the dock by a mile, but it always lands perfectly. After canoeing it, I knew how hard it was to fight that current.

When I asked for the latest Dempster Highway conditions at the Northwest Territories Information Centre, Brenda referred me to a man who had just returned. He had nothing good to say. I asked if the roads were washboardy. "Yes." I asked if there were potholes. "Yes." I asked what he had driven. He drove a small car. He had an accent and I thought perhaps that he was a foreign visitor who was not used to northern roads. He was from Whitehorse, 327 miles away!

This fellow couldn't believe I wanted to drive a motorhome to Inuvik. I asked if he had driven the Denali Highway. He said he had and admitted the Dempster Highway was better. His son looked disgusted. I think the son didn't agree with Dad's assessment. He wished me a safe trip.

The ignition switch was still cool. Just for fun, I felt the wires underneath, and promptly burned myself. I stopped at Northern Superior, and Glen said he was busy and couldn't look at it until three. It was about noon and I said if I decided to wait, I would be back shortly. Prophetic. I was in denial. I wanted those wires to cool off and stay that way and somehow I talked myself into thinking if I drove on down the road, it would all go away. Pathetic.

I touched them again. They were really hot. I stopped in what I thought was a business driveway that was closed on Saturday, and got under the dash to check things out. Getting into a position to see under the dash takes a major contortionistic maneuver. I pulled out a connection. It was burned. I tried to put it back just to get me back to Northern Superior. A horn honked. Someone wanted in the driveway. I explained and apologized. She said that maybe somebody at the gold camp could help me.

The fellow who answered the door took charge and rousted his mechanic to help. He couldn't fix it but got the Sprinter started so I could return to Northern Superior. I could only thank him since he refused any money. The first fellow followed me back to Northern Superior, "In case anything happens." I cemented the appointment for 3:00.

The kind fellow asked me to go for coffee, introducing himself as "Dirty Bert." I said I wasn't sure I should go with him. He explained that he had played professional hockey for the Detroit Redwings, and one of the fans had called him Dirty Bert. The nickname stuck.

Sipping coffee at the London Grill, I learned Bert was from Manitoba. After a short stint in pro hockey, he went into management and 30 years of dam building for Canada Hydro. He had been working for the last four summers as a surveyor for a gold mining company along Six-mile Creek. The driveway where the Sprinter died, was the gold camp's winter headquarters.

Yukon Territory, Canada
Fall

Glen put a new connection on the (new in Tok) ignition and charged me only $32.58 ($23.98 U.S.) for an emergency on a Saturday afternoon. Bert invited me for a salmon dinner with his extended family. Although I was an unexpected guest, Violet, Murray, and the guys welcomed me into the fold.

I mentioned leaving, but they insisted I park in the drive until morning, and get a fresh start. We all went to Diamond Tooth Gertie's for the evening. Bert and I talked, watched the show, and he introduced me to other friends. One couple said they lived in a cabin in the middle of nowhere, and regularly had moose or bear in their yard.

Bert said the only time they came into town from the mine site was for special occasions, like the Miners Barbecue. Now they were in the process of moving the camp into Dawson for the winter. I told Bert about seeing the Northern Lights. He said it would be a good night to see them again so we drove up to The Dome. The wait was cold but they finally came out.

NW Territories Border
270 km to Inuvik, Winter

When we said goodnight, I asked him if he was into hugs. He said, "You bet," and nearly cracked my ribs. He added, "I've been with 12 guys all summer." Hmmm.

I had definitely decided to "Do the Dempster." Come on, it was another great adventure.

Doing the Dempster

1996

"Dempster Driving Tips" from the information centre.

1. Plan your trip for late June to early September (I missed that on both counts!)
2. Stock your vehicle with the basics: (much the same as I told you in the beginning) extra fluids, spare belts, basic tools (including jack and wrench), and a good full-sized spare tire.
3. Prevent accidents and flat tires -- slow down. (Didn't I tell you?) Don't overload your vehicle and don't exceed posted speeds. Drive in the worn centre of the road except when meeting or passing. Slow down, and pull over as far as possible, when meeting vehicles, especially large trucks. This will help prevent windshield rock damage. Mesh or plastic headlamp protectors are a good inexpensive investment.
4. Drive with headlights on at all times.
5. Minimize dust by closing windows, use your air conditioner or fan.
6. Protect your trailer. Rock guards and protective covers for wiring, plumbing, and front RV windows are suggested if you plan to tow a trailer or boat.
7. Insects: Take insect repellents and/or protective clothing. (With the snow, I didn't have to worry about insects a whole lot.)
8. Weather conditions can change dramatically (they aren't kidding) and even in midsummer, cold and inclement weather may sometimes be encountered. Warm layered clothing, boots, hat, and gloves are useful items to have.

Dempster Highway information panels are posted at the junction with Klondike Loop (Hwy #2). The road to Inuvik was completed in 1979, and built for supporting oil and gas exploration and development. It would be 914 gravel, round-trip miles before I returned to this spot. The Sprinter and I would drive 200 miles beyond the Arctic Circle. I was so excited I could hardly breathe.

It was one of those times I wanted to remember when I am old, sitting in my rocking chair, playing the moments of my life on the TV of my mind.

A sermon of Sunday sunlight twirled in the autumn leaves. A feast for the eyes and the soul greeted me at every curve and hill. My heart and the rushing streams sang a joyful duet. If the colors had been mixed in a carpet, I would have said it was gaudy. In nature, it was beautiful. Being in church that morning couldn't have made me any more of a believer.

My confidence grew when I saw the first of many maintenance camps where I could get help if I needed it. Fifty-one miles into the trip, depending on which publication you read, the Dempster Highway reaches its highest point at either 4,229' or 4,265', on North Fork Pass. In the higher elevations, ice coated the trees and bushes. This is "rime," a new word to me.

Hundreds of ptarmigan had already stepped into formal winter white. I came almost to a complete stop several times. They won't fly until the last second. There was no room to swerve around them. The Arctic fox and hare were halfway into their white safety camouflage as well.

Three vehicles with flat tires were abandoned along the road. A car, partially in the road, had a broken axle. Nobody was home.

Lakes were still, reflecting snowy mountains and autumn colors. Farther north, the countryside was a study in brown. Gray rock mountains were barren. Red Creek was just that, a red creek. Weakened muskeg lost its grip. Trees and land slid down the mountains, leaving great brown blemishes. A sign said, "Road closed." I nearly had a conniption fit until I realized it was temporary while an avalanche was cleared. I napped at the wheel.

The books and brochures tell of golden eagles, great gray owls, Dall sheep, grizzly bear, and caribou. They may have been in hiding because of the weather I was driving into.

I checked the campgrounds and they were very nice. At a different time of year, I would have enjoyed staying a while. The scenery is terrific. I suspect bugs would be terrific in hot weather. I was happy with being where I was, regardless of the weather.

Snowy Northwest Territories

True to what you might think in such a place, the wind howled around the Arctic Circle monument. The sun shone, but forbidding clouds gathered to howl with the wind on distant mountain peaks.

Another traveler was alone. We took pictures of each other by the monument. He had gone to Fort McPherson and turned around. He said snow was sticking to the ground a few miles beyond the Circle and "You might as well go back now. There is nothing beyond Fort McPherson. It is boring and flat." I knew I hadn't come all that distance to turn around on somebody else's opinion of what was boring. Within a couple of miles, snow covered the road. It was the only thing he was right about. I changed my watch to Mountain Time.

At the Yukon Territory and the Northwest Territories border, I drove into a totally different world. It was dark, snowy, and windy. It was more ominous looking than I wanted to admit because I didn't want to turn back. I thought hard for a few milliseconds, then I put the Sprinter in gear, and inched toward Inuvik.

The Dempster Highway is open year around. If I got into trouble, eventually someone would come along. There weren't that many places to pull off or maybe I just couldn't see them because it was blowing snow. I kept going. I was having no problems but I had to consciously relax my rigid body now and again. The Sprinter was holding the road just fine, but I also knew if it started sliding, I was in trouble. Obviously my faith was sliding, too.

The Peel River cable ferry operator said he thought I could get gasoline at Fort McPherson although it was already past 5 p.m. The station was closed. As I was looking around for a place to park, the owners returned and opened the pumps ($140.96 C $103.76 U.S.). They were on the way home but somehow they learned a customer was arriving. I was being well looked after. They asked if I was willing to take their nephew to Inuvik the next morning. I said I was willing, if I could park for the night. They discovered the nephew had found his own ride so I continued on. I stopped for the night at the Mackenzie River.

Two places along the Dempster were widened to accommodate airstrips, with appropriate warnings to watch for planes. Other signs told other stories. The North West Mounted Police chased "The Mad Trapper of Rat River," for 48 winter days. He killed one policeman and wounded another after he tampered with Native trap lines. He was killed in February of 1932.

"The Lost Patrol" is another famous story involving a four-man patrol. They froze to death on their way to Dawson City from Fort McPherson in December of 1910. Their function was to deliver mail and check on isolated trappers. Even with excellent bush skills, they made fatal errors in judgment after becoming lost in a blinding blizzard. Eating their dogs and some of the trappings and harness to survive, they traveled 620 miles in 53 days, perishing from starvation only 26 miles from the Fort. The Dempster Highway was named for Sgt. Dempster of the Royal North West Mounted Police, who found the lost patrol in March of 1911.

The ferryboat attendant said, "You're a long way from home." When I explained the Sprinter was my home and that I was living on his boat, he smiled, "Then I'll have to charge you $100." He asked if it was my first time down and I said it was my first time "up."

The ferry went first to the tiny Athabascan town of Tsiigehtchic, beyond the confluence of the Arctic Red River and the Mackenzie River, to pick up fares. It then docked at the mud dock where I drove off toward Inuvik. People who live in Tsiigehtchic call themselves, Gwycha Gwich'in, "People of the Flatlands."

The next time anyone asks you the name of the largest north-flowing river in North America, you can say the Mackenzie River in Canada's Northwest Territories. It was named after Sir Alexander Mackenzie, who in 1789, was the first non-aboriginal person to travel its entire length. That's part of the fun of RVing and traveling. You read all this great stuff which will make absolutely no difference in your life, except that you may be able to answer a trivia question at a New Year's Eve party.

It was Monday and a great adventure had begun. The sun was bright and the day beautiful. The Campbell uplift, steep cliffs on the other side of Campbell Lake, followed the road.

The road, built high above its surroundings during winter freeze, prevented vehicle damage to the tundra surface. Only the trees were cut down. All other vegetation remained in place. It was covered with thick gravel layers. The vegetation and gravel insulate the road, and keep its warmth from reaching the permafrost layer below.

At Cabin Creek Wayside, I sipped coffee and toasted my buns in front of the heater, watching the sun fade to snow flakes drifting from somber clouds. Nothing to get excited about I guess, except that September and those few flakes sticking to the cold frozen tundra, took on a whole new meaning 200 miles beyond the Arctic Circle.

The last few miles into Inuvik were paved, yellow line and all. Wow! They even have a McDonalds -- McDonald Brothers Electric.

I parked at the Western Arctic Visitors Centre and since no one seemed concerned with my presence, I stayed there the four days I was in Inuvik. I did not see the two campgrounds, but I know they are open during season.

The architecture of the Visitor Centre was impressive. Talking displays showed the Gwich'in and Dene cultures, along with the "Mad Trapper" and the "Lost RNWMP Patrol."

I overheard a fellow talking with Andrea, the attendant. He had signed up for a trip to Tuktoyaktuk for that afternoon, but there were no other takers. It was one of the places I wanted to visit. RC, an electrician and supervisor with the Ministry of Transportation and Highways near Vancouver, B.C., traveled alone too. We walked to the Arctic Nature Tours but I was only the second name on the list. Fred said tourists were pretty sparse. We needed at least three more.

We talked our way down to "To-gos" for their musk ox burgers (sometimes known as "polar beef"). The chef said, "Nobody has killed one lately." We settled for caribou burgers, a worthy substitute.

It was cold but sunny, and since both of us had been driving steadily, we hiked through the Visitre Centre fish camp and along the river path through the muskeg for exercise.

RC was an avid skier and loved the outdoors. Exchanging stories and ideas gave him an interest in learning to canoe and kayak. Though I have no interest in fishing, his being able to get close to birds and otters in a fishing float with waders, gave me a new perspective for photography.

By 3:30, we still didn't have takers for the Tuktoyaktuk trip so we talked about outfitting RC in a sandwich board to advertise. He didn't go for it. We walked around the town and into the residential area. Many houses were newly built, with as many more in progress.

Inuvik Utiladors

Aklavik was the regional administrative centre, but with constant flooding and erosion, in the mid 1950's, the centre was moved. Inuvik was built as a replacement for Aklavik. Since not everybody in Aklavik agreed, Aklavik still exists.

Inuvik is "The first community north of the Arctic Circle built to provide the normal facilities of a Canadian town. It was designed not only as a base for development and administration, but also as a centre to bring education, medical care, and new opportunity to the people of the Western Arctic."

You won't find another like it. "Utilidors," holding water and sewer pipes, snake through the town from building to building. Because of the permafrost base, everything is either on pilings or stilts above ground. Some buildings were skirted. A few yards had grass but they looked out of place. A huge log cabin I would have loved anywhere else, didn't seem to fit into that environment, although Ingamo Hall, Inuvik's Native Friendship Centre, was built with 1,000 logs rafted 850 miles down the Mackenzie River.

Inuvik means "Place of the people," and is considered a Canadian "Mosaic" of people from a variety of places, traditions and cultures. Koe Park has a triple-arched monument symbolizing the town's dominant triracial character: Inuvialuit, Gwitch'in and Caucasian.

I might have expected the same bland colors I had found in other Arctic villages if I hadn't become a friend with Tom Byrne, the fellow who played the Robert Service character in Dawson City. He lived in Inuvik for three years. He created and instituted the colorful plan for the new city. Talk about mosaic. Most of the houses and public buildings are painted bright colors. The hospital is a cheerful yellow. The apartment buildings are deep blues, greens, pinks, reds, and lavenders. Considering how cold it was, Inuvik was a cheerful place for wandering.

In the Boreal Bookstore, I succumbed, once more, to being a grandmother. I bought charming books for Rebecca about children living North of the Arctic Circle.

The lady at Northern Images told us it costs from $800 to $l,000 to rent living space. Utilities were not included and heating costs were high. She told us about missing the last Mackenzie ferry the week before, and spending the night in her vehicle without any emergency provisions. She nearly froze. It is surprising that someone from that area didn't routinely carry emergency supplies. We all make mistakes. Up there it can be fatal.

Festivals are different in the far, far North. They celebrate the May break-up of the Mackenzie River, the Midnight Madness summer solstice on June 21, and the Great Northern Arts Festival in early August. I can't imagine any of them more personally celebrated than the "Sunrise Festival" in January. The sun sets on December 6. It does not rise again until January 6. They thrill to the 59 days when the sun doesn't set at all.

RC treated me to a candlelight dinner at the Eskimo Inn, a pleasant evening with interesting conversation enjoyed over many coffee refills. We agreed it was nice to have someone with whom to share dinner. It was the next day before I realized the date was significant. It was what would have been my 40th wedding anniversary. RC was 6' 3" with brown eyes, dark hair, short beard with a touch of gray, and could have been my late husband's twin at forty something.

RC was driving a truck and camper but opted to stay at the Finto Motor Inn down from the Visitor Centre where I parked. He stopped to

Our Lady of Victory Church

walk me to town the next morning. Enough people had signed up for the tour, but it was postponed until eleven. We were ecstatic and went looking for sweatshirts.

The comical ravens didn't seem to mind the weather. Ravens are legends in Native culture, and are protected in the NWT. They live year around in the North Country, and if you understand their conversations as they raucously squawk to each other, they'll tell you all about it.

At last we were all seated in the eight-passenger plane and the props were twirling. Skies were gray but we were off to a new adventure, Tuktoyaktuk, 85 miles farther north and on the Arctic Ocean. At the end of the runway, we turned around and came back. The pilot explained we had lost the attitude indicator. Aaaagh!!. It didn't help **our** attitudes at all, but we tried to be grateful they found **any** problem while we were still on the ground. We rescheduled for two o'clock.

Our Lady of Victory Church next to the Arctic Nature Tours building, does not have regular hours. We were never able to get inside. The igloo-shaped church reflects the Arctic lifestyle, and fuses Inuvialuit and Christian cultures. Inside are paintings of the Stations of the Cross by Mona Thrasher, an Inuvialuit artist.

After lunch in a distinctly Mexican flavor cafe, we went back for the long-awaited Tuktoyaktuk flight. One man backed out because his wife wanted to leave town early. The young couple decided they didn't want the expense of staying another night in a hotel. Fred Carmichael, President of Arctic Nature Tours, felt so bad after our dogged but futile persistence, he gave us sweatshirts and Western Arctic Travel Guides.

The weather was getting more frigid by the minute. We walked back to the Visitor Centre, and picked up our certificates proclaiming we had driven across the Arctic Circle. Andrea said Brenda from the NWT office in Dawson City, had checked to make sure I got to Inuvik all right. People are good. We spent the afternoon reading in Inuvik's warm library.

That evening we went to the Aurora Research Centre for a slide show and program on "pingos." Pingo is an Eskimo word for a conical hill. It is an ice-cored hill that can only grow and persist in a permafrost environment. Roughly 1,450 pingos are in the Tuktoyaktuk Peninsula. They are hundreds of thousands of years old. (A tour is available to visit the pingos.) Professor Mackay said that with a little patience you can duplicate the natural conditions to grow a miniature pingo in a home freezer. I took the instructions for Rebecca and her science teacher father.

Summertime (although they had snow in both July and August in 1996) would be a better time for Inuvik activities. Boat rides are available on the wildlife-filled Mackenzie River Delta, one of North America largest deltas. The Keitels from St. Louis said they took a midnight trip to the Mackenzie River Delta. "Six of us sipped champagne and munched on char sandwiches while we watched the sun turn the horizons to brilliant orange. I can close my eyes and I'm there." Sounds good to me but I'd have to drive back to experience it...maybe...

Flights to various villages, including Tuktoyaktuk, are available (and more likely to happen) during season. We did have one major plus, no self-respecting bugs were out in that freezing weather. After an evening of sipping coffee while the north winds whipped fiercely around the Sprinter, RC and I said our good-byes.

The next morning I awakened to a blizzard. I settled in my cozy house, writing post cards. I planned to wait and see what the weather did. I heard a diesel pull in at 8:30. It was RC. He said he thought it would be a good idea to caravan out, since we were both alone.

My first thought was "No way, Jose." On second, third, and fourth thoughts, I decided if it didn't stop snowing, driving wasn't going to get any better. If it didn't get any warmer, the Mackenzie and Peel Rivers would freeze up and I would be living in Inuvik for the two months it takes the ice bridge to form. The road between Inuvik and the Mackenzie was quite narrow, built up high, and with lots of water on both sides. As much as I liked the adventure of being in Inuvik, my fifth thought was that I really didn't want to spend the winter there. I packed.

R.C. said I was bigger and more easily seen so I should lead. I drove in and out of whiteout conditions with no tracks to follow. The road was extremely slippery and scary. Once we started, there was no turning back. I stuck to the center except on the rare occasion of meeting a vehicle.

We arrived at the Mackenzie River in time to catch the ferry. After discussing it, we decided due to the weather and lengthy ferrying time, to skip visiting Tsiigehtchic. We both missed it on the way in. The red-roofed Catholic Church and the few white buildings on the bank of the Arctic Red River, were picturesque

McKenzie River Snowplow

The ferryman told me, "It will soon be time to take the ferry out. When the ice forms, we'll drain the fluids and dry dock it for the winter, probably in October." He did mention it was unusually cold weather for that time of year.

By the time we reached Fort McPherson, 35 miles away, we were ready for lunch and a break. The dirt streets were a real mess with the wet snow and mud. Boots are shed at the door whether it is a restaurant, store, or library. Made sense to me. People were friendly, but not quite as friendly as in Inuvik.

We parked next to the McPherson Tent and Canvas Shop. If you ever want anything made of canvas, this is the place to go. The factory was small, and clean enough to eat off the floor. They were making up teepee orders. With all the fish camps and hunting, big tents are in demand, but they also make backpacks, duffelbags, carrying cases, and other products.

We slopped through the cemetery mud and snow, looking for the grave markers of the "Lost Patrol," but we didn't find them.

At the Peel River ferry, the attendant said if we wanted to wait, they were bringing a snowplow across next, and we could follow him. We waited. The ferry ramp was so irregular, the Sprinter's hitch caught on it. The attendant found a bar to pry me off. He was matter-of-fact. I wondered how many others he had pried off of it.

Waiting for the snowplow was a mistake. He was making more of a mess, than he was cleaning it. He started up a long, steep hill. I CB'd to RC that I was going to stop and wait. The plow didn't make it. It took him forever to back down again, and when he did, I told RC I was going to make a run for it, otherwise I wouldn't make it either. I wrestled the Sprinter to the top of the hill. Piece of cake. RC had no problem.

Oophs!

The snow was deeper in the higher elevations. I had set the camera manually. All I had to do was lift it and aim through the windshield, without adjusting it. The snow was a foot deep near the summit. I was literally pushing it with the motorhome. I couldn't slow down because it would have stopped me. It was really neat; but, when I lifted the camera to get a swift shot, a semi came around a curve and full tilt up the mountain. I had no idea how far I could drive to the right without going off the mountain, but I pulled over and he shot past me. Whew!

I drove in and out of low drifts, deep snow, and areas blown bare by the wind. It took a while. I relied on the transmission because the brakes weren't working right. I figured the snow was causing problems. The "No Dust Zone" signs looked out of place.

When we hit the Northwest Territories and Yukon Border, it was again like cutting the weather with a sharp knife. The sky was clear and blue. We were also grateful for the better roads.

During the few short miles to Rock Creek Campground, the mid-afternoon weather became comfortably warm. Both rigs were a mess. RC washed his. I tried to dig the packed snow out from under the Sprinter's front end. It wouldn't budge. It was jammed up around the batteries, and down in front where the tires wore a slit through it to keep turning.

The next day we stopped again at the Arctic Circle monument for pictures, then continued to Eagle Plains. My brakes were iffy so RC added brake fluid. I filled with gas, and dug a lot of snow out from under the front end that hadn't already dropped off with the warmer weather. A wire came with it. Hmmm.

RC's time was limited by vacation days and I knew I would have to take it easy because of limited braking power. We hugged good-bye and each continued on, as we were used to doing, alone. I felt a little sad as I watched his yellow and white camper wind through the curves and hills ahead of me but I wouldn't have traded those few days of friendship for anything.

It was a long day, but that was because I pulled in beside a river and read for several hours. I took pictures of a magnificent rainbow after a rainstorm, and sunset pictures with mountains and clouds and lakes. Cars blinked their lights at me and I realized I had brights but no low beams. I got off the road for the night.

From the Dempster Corner, it was only 25 miles back into Dawson City. Once again I went to Northern Superior. They adjusted the brakes, installed a new low beam, and re-attached that low-slung wire. Because they didn't have new ones the right size, they switched the windshield wiper from the navigator's side to mine. They checked the pressure in all tires and repaired a flat dual on the back left side. I didn't even know it was flat.

I used a pressure washer to bathe the poor mud-packed Sprinter. I emptied the sewers, filled with water and gasoline, and I was ready to go again. I thought I was.

That evening Bert took me to the Jack London Restaurant for dinner. On my way to the Dome to park in my favorite spot, the newly repaired dual tire blew. The next morning I drove carefully back down the mountain to Northern Superior. This time they put on the spare.

Bert and I spent the day sightseeing around Dawson, and hiking the l-o-n-g, s-t-e-e-p mountain path to the fire lookout above The Dome. It was a sunny, but cold fall day, with great colorful views of the Yukon River as it turns at Dawson City and heads for the Bering Sea. We had coffee and cookies at Klondyke Kates. They were closing for the season.

We had dinner later and said our good-byes. He gave me three gold nuggets, one the size of the tip of my index finger for a necklace, and two the size of peas for earrings. (I still have them but only heard from him a few times after he returned to Manitoba and I returned to the States.) I talked with him on the phone after I got back to Washington. He said within a few days after I left, snow hit big time, and he had snow all the way home to Manitoba.

Between Dawson City and Whitehorse, I stopped three times. My first stop was to see the remains of Montague House, a typical log roadhouse from the turn of the century.

In 1987, when I went to Alaska with Carrs and Cushmans, we found the greatest cinnamon buns, but I despaired of ever finding them again. Braeburn Lodge advertised a cinnamon bun big enough to feed four people. It was five inches tall, and definitely as big as a plate. It was hot from the oven and served with a tub of butter. Yum! I rolled on out to the Sprinter. My last stop was in honor of Robert Service.

Winter Clouds

As I stood on the marge
Of Lake Laberge
Admirin' the snow-covered scenery
I thought -
What am I doin'
With winter storms brewin'
I shoulda gone south
With the greenery

Ralph Waldo Minshall

"Headin' Home Alone"

1996

Yukon River at Five Finger Rapids

Whitehorse was a good "filling" station. I filled with propane, gasoline, and groceries. After examining my tires thoroughly, the fellow at Canadian Tire was kind enough to tell me that I didn't need all six tires replaced, as I had intended. Four Michelin tires cost $877.40 Canadian ($646.84 US)

Happy Daze fashioned a new U-bolt to hold up the right side of my springs. Considering they gave me priority in the middle of their extremely busy afternoon schedule, I had no quarrel with the $42.44 bill ($31.28 U.S.).

It is 292 miles to the Highway #37 junction, winding in and out of Yukon Territory and British Columbia. Among other beautiful spots, were crossing the Nisutlin Bay Bridge, with views of Teslin Lake at Teslin. The bay bridge, at 1,917', is the longest water span on the Alaska Highway.

I drove until dark and stayed on the Continental Divide. If I cried, one tear would drain to the Arctic Ocean and the other to the Pacific Ocean.

The next morning began with road construction. The genial, smiling sign lady, was from Whitehorse. She and her husband lived in their RV in the construction camp. She had just heard a moose crashing about in the woods. She said sometimes there are grizzlies. I asked what she did if animals came into her "space." She said, "I get into my car. If I had to, I'd climb into a passenger car." She described working through the cold winters. She was grateful for the sunny, warm day.

After going through construction, I heard a loud pop. It sounded like a dual had blown. I thumped the tires but didn't find a problem. I continued toward the Junction, stopping several times to check tires.

"Alaska Highway's Best Coffee" was offered at the Northern Beaver Post. How could I resist, especially since I was surprised to find anything open. The lady who served coffee was restaurant sitting for the winter. It was closing in mid-October, but she was staying on to write a book about her travels and experiences teaching school in outlying Native villages. A publisher waited in the wings to look at it. That's half the battle.

I asked if she would get lonely. "Watson Lake is only 20 minutes away, and I have plenty of friends there. The Alaska Highway is open all the time, and I hope to persuade the snowplow drivers to take a swipe through the driveway once in a while so I can get out." Then she mentioned the beaver on the ponds, the token moose, and a white wolf that were hanging around. Part of me envied her.

South on the Cassiar, fall, 1996

At Junction 37, a road grader pulled up for gas while I was refueling. I asked the driver about the Cassiar Highway. He said it was pretty good. "I would drive the Cassiar any day, rather than the Alaska Highway." Personally, I would never pass up a chance to drive the Cassiar one way and the Alaska Highway the other.

I drove on and off gravel and sealcoat the first day on the Cassiar Highway. It was quite good with only occasional potholes. Sunshine and autumn reflected in the lakes and streams. Curves and scenery kept my driving to a leisurely pace.

Passing the side road to the town of Cassiar, I remembered driving the 10 miles to Cassiar with a flat dual in May of 1992, thinking I could get it fixed there. I did, but only by the skin of my teeth. Cassiar was a Cassiar Mining (Asbestos) Corporation company town, and the mine had closed. I had no way of knowing that all the townspeople had been given a really short deadline to get out, and most of them had already left. Through several people, I found the one soul who had the equipment, know-how, and kindness to fix the flat for me.

Jade City is an interesting stop, but the jade store was closed. Huge jade boulders lying around in what they call their "Jade Compound," are from the Princess Jade Mine, one of the largest jade mines in the world. This is not a big place, but they have a couple of stores, and a primitive campground. I bought an ice-cream cone next door.

The Cottonwood River rest area is off the highway on part of the old road. As I often do, I took advantage of this picturesque spot. The rushing river's peaceful sound accompanied my lunch, and a few more pages of a good book.

We talked about the biggest, bestest, tallest, and widest syndrome a while back. Dease Lake calls itself the Jade Capital of British Columbia; Jade City says they are the Jade Capital of the North. What it boils down to is this, there is a lot of green stuff along the Cassiar (not unlike the stuff in my frig, green and too hard to eat).

On previous trips along the Cassiar, I had missed much of the magnificent scenery of the Skeena and Cassiar Mountains because of foggy or blizzard conditions. I never realized how many lakes, streams, and mountains there were.

The clouds alternately covered Mt. Edziza (9,143'), part of Mount Edziza Provincial Park, and opened revealing glaciers and new snow. All around me the skies were blue again, but it looked like it was snowing at the top. I pulled into a viewpoint to feast my eyes and sip coffee.

On the other side of the road is the Spatsizi Plateau Wilderness Park. There are no roads into either of these wilderness areas, but guide services and flightseeing are available.

Many hours had passed but I had not covered all that many miles. When sleepy time finally settled in, I backed into the Eastman Kodak Wayside trees. It was a natural considering the amount of film I buy. I must own at least a small chunk, mustn't I?

In the night, I awakened and thought I heard footsteps sloshing in the mud next to the Sprinter. I froze for a few seconds, then stole quietly out of bed. I peeked outside and saw an empty parking lot. I turned on the sidelight and headlights, but didn't see anyone or anything. The noise must have been the rain coming through the leaves, or an animal. I moved the motorhome out into the parking lot and went back to sleep.

People often ask if I get frightened. No, not usually. Although I momentarily had goosebumps, I couldn't quite conceive of anyone being on that lonely road for the purpose of mayhem. I hadn't seen a vehicle for two hours prior to stopping, and the weather had turned really nasty.

About 80 miles of the Cassiar are still gravel. It wouldn't have been all that bad, but the glorious sunshine had disappeared, and it was raining. Potholes reigned, too. Driving was slow. I met two graders. One was in my lane! I did a couple of "switcheroos," and managed to avoid being sandwiched between them. Driving improved for the distance they had graded.

I saw a Mama black bear and a cub crossing the road. With his short stubby legs, Baby bear was having problems keeping up with Mama. He finally made it. He was cuddly looking, but I knew better.

At Bell Irving Bridge, I thought I had finally driven "One mile Beyond." The road was wide, the pavement new, and it actually had shoulders. It didn't last long, but then I instinctively knew it wouldn't.

It was my day for thrills. I drove around a curve and there was Mama black bear and triplet cubs. I pulled well

Here Moosey!

off the highway (on that marvelous new shoulder) and watched them for 15 minutes. They were undisturbed by the few trucks and cars. My shutting the engine off only caused Mama to stick her nose in the air and sniff. They continued munching and ambling among the bushes and trees as though I didn't exist.

The neat thing about the Cassiar is that it hasn't been completely tamed yet. A one-lane bridge still crosses 400 feet above the Nass River.

Rest areas along the rest of the Cassiar were filled with moose hunters. I finally found an empty spot by a river.

Sunbeams struggled through the fog and highlighted the fall colors lining the Skeena River as I made my early morning turn onto Yellowhead Highway. Highway #16 goes all the way from Prince Rupert to Winnipeg, Manitoba.

In 1992, I made side trips to several Indian villages. St. Paul's wooden Anglican Church is at Gitwangak, The separate, original bell tower, was built in 1893. K'san, the center of Gitksan culture, is a living museum with longhouses and an art school. Tours will take you to an archeological dig at Battle Hill in Kitwanga. Kitwancool is the home of the "Hole-in-the-ice" totem pole, "The oldest standing totem pole in the world." No one was there when I arrived so early in the season. I'm not sure what, specifically, I was looking at, but I was fascinated with the totem poles. All the villages have authentic totem poles and interesting Native crafts.

Turning onto the Yellowhead Highway, suddenly put me in a completely different world. It was a good, two-lane, paved highway with no appreciable potholes. Prosperous-looking houses settled permanently on green fertilized lawns. Horses and cattle grazed in fenced pastures on small well-kept ranches. After five months, I wasn't sure I was ready for cities, traffic, impatience, stress, and "civilization."

Bearly Enough to Eat

A big sign at a Petro Canada station, made me wonder about civilization in their terms. It said, "Worms, free coffee with fill-up." What a combo! I guess I shouldn't knock it if I haven't tried it. After all, I like Pepsi and milk.

The Sprinter's odometer turned 140,000 miles as I drove down the hill into Prince George.

I turned right on Highway #97 south.
I had come full circle.

Stopping at Cinema Second Hand, north of Quesnel, I took advantage of their free camping again. I popped in to buy a few incidentals and have a conversation.

Over coffee, Vic related the story of buying a canoe for his wife,

Theresa. "A fellow drove in with a canoe strapped to the car roof. He hung around until the other customers left. I said, 'It was nice of you to deliver Theresa's birthday canoe.' The guy looked puzzled. I told him, 'I have been wanting to buy her one.' Then the guy really looked startled. He told me he had hung around hoping I would buy it. He needed the money to get back home."

There was no doubt about it. Since I was getting close, I was like a horse heading for the barn. I was anxious to get back to Washington to see family, play grandma, and visit friends. One last new route, Highway 99, tempted me. I had heard about the "Sea to Sky Highway" from several travelers, but in my case, I would be traveling from "sky to sea."

Seven miles north of Cache Creek, I turned toward Lillooet and Vancouver. If you are into following the gold trails, the Hat Creek Heritage Ranch is just beyond the turn. It is a living museum with one of the original roadhouses. Lilliooet is the beginning of the Cariboo Trail that you will see and hear about as you travel north on Highway #97 toward Prince George.

On this route, except in the narrowest, more avalanche-prone areas, there were many pulloffs, viewpoints, and rest areas. It has lakes, streams, waterfalls, and numerous Provincial Parks, Recreation Areas, and private resorts and campgrounds, for your enjoyment. Remember that as you get closer to Vancouver, you will be sharing the highway with some of its half-million people.

Sea to Sky Highway, BC #99

It is a pretty good road, all of it paved, some of it narrow, most of it winding, but the grades are from 6 to 14%.

My brakes heated up considerably going down the mountains. I stopped at more than one view to enjoy the scenery while they cooled. I visited the Pavilion General Store and Gas Bar. They advertised they were British Columbia's Oldest Store, built in 1862. I bought a book and talked with Barry. When I said how pretty the route had been thus far, he said, "You hadn't seen anything yet." He was right. It was a neat spot. They had campsites, souvenirs, and a post office.

The first night I stopped at Seton Dam, a BC Hydro campground. It was free but only a few campsites were big enough to accommodate my 27' rig. The next morning, I stopped at Seton Lake Recreation Area overlooking the lake and stayed for a while. It was just too pretty to leave without soaking it in.

Whistler is a famous ski resort, but it offers something any time of the year. In the midst of such beauty, and within a very short driving distance of Vancouver, it is another Aspen or Vail and traffic is thick.

As I continued on, I heard a weird roaring noise, even when I wasn't on an appreciable grade. It sounded like I was in second gear all the time. I suspected it might be the clutch fan, although I didn't know that was what it was called until I had it fixed back in Leavenworth. Good guess.

Certainly the views driving through the mountains were fantastic, but starting at Squamish, I was driving along a fjord. The combination of mountains, islands, and the sun filtering through the clouds was really awesome. I think I would always prefer the "sky to sea" direction.

My last night in Canada was at Porteau Cove Provincial Park. It has water access, making it a popular park. Even though I stopped earlier than usual, since I didn't want to drive through Vancouver at rush hour, the park was packed. It was $15.50/night Canadian, with no amenities.

It was peaceful until 3:00 a.m. when the woman in the tent behind me, had a fight with her "whatever." For about 15 minutes, she raved and ranted and yelled and cursed. I thought about firing up and running over the tent, but I was nice.

The Sea to Sky Highway officially ends at the Lions Gate Bridge in the edge of Vancouver. Even after all the really spectacular scenery I had experienced over the previous five months, Highway 99 has to be one of the most beautiful 209 miles that I have traveled.

I arrived at Peace Arch Park and the Canadian/United States border, at Blaine, Washington. I thought about continuing on through and not bothering with the Canadian GST tax, but the stop was worth the $61 US refund.

As I passed through the border, the guard asked, "Did you buy anything in Canada today?"

"Today? No."

"Did you buy anything yesterday?"

"No," I told him I had been in Alaska and Canada for five months, and I still hadn't bought enough of anything to declare. That was it. Now that I had satisfied my curiosity of crossing at Blaine, I would choose a less busy route in the future.

Now that I have taken you home back along the Cassiar, let's go back to Whitehorse for a fall, 2001, excursion on the Alaska Ferry System. These were a few of the other animals I saw on my trips.

Headin' Home Alone #2

2001

It is only a short distance south from Whitehorse that you make the turn west to Skagway, following Klondike Highway #2. The Fendricks, whom I visited in Chapter #4, had lent me many wonderful books to read. I detoured a few miles off my path to return them. They were working outside but took a break. Rena, always a gracious hostess, and always prepared, served delicious tea and low-cranberry bread while we exchanged our summer stories.

This detour took me on a cut-off to the Klondike Highway that I hadn't been on before. From Jake's corners I drove #8 (Tagish Road) the 17 miles to Carcross, passing the bottom of Marsh Lake. Part of it was dirt road but in pretty good condition. I couldn't believe it, parked in the Montana Services & RV Park in Carcross, was a blue bus. Full hook-ups were only $10 and "catch up" time with June and Vern Lawton was perfect. We parted after Bobo Bakery's yummy breakfast omelets and promises to get together over the winter.

Carcross boasts the "World's smallest desert," a small deposit of sand remaining after a glacial lake disappeared. The gold rushers came through Carcross from Skagway on their way to Dawson City in 1898. In 2001, I stampeded my way down to Skagway to catch a ferry. I almost didn't make it. I stopped for road construction. When the lady motioned me on, the Sprinter started screeching and smoking. Ultimately, I discovered that the alternator had frozen up...again. The belt flew off. It was only a short distance to the top of White Pass so I decided to keep going. It was all down mountain to Skagway once I reached the top.

Driving over the pass was like driving through pea soup. The border station had moved down the mountain a ways since last time. The guard looked at the Sprinter's brag map and said, "It's out of date. The Northwest Territories have split into two."

"But I went there before they split it!"

The Garden City RV Park manager directed me to a shadetree mechanic who said, "That alternator is fried. If I can the order it and get it back by plane tonight around 6, I can put it in tomorrow morning...if it's the right part." The plane had to make it through that pea soup, too.

The time wasn't lost. I did major laundry. I would have gone to the Soapy Williams program that night but I couldn't get through on the phone. IInstead, I caught up on phone calls and read all evening. At 8 p.m., the mechanic stopped by the campground and said the part had come in and he would put it in the next morning early so I could meet my ferry schedule. After checking the batteries and putting in the new alternator, I escaped with $395 less than I started.

I packed a small suitcase and checked in for the first part of the trip to Juneau, with a late night arrival. The clerk said, "'Unofficially,' you can park the rest of the night at Carr's (Safeway) store in Juneau."

The Inland Passage, known as the "Southeast," I knew would be spectacular for someone who loves mountains, trees, and water. I briefly contemplated shipping the Sprinter to Bellingham and taking the ferry from Seward, Bed & Breakfasting and using public transportation during my stops along the way. Several shipping firms ship RVs from Anchorage and the cost seemed pretty good at around $1,100. However, given my September departure, the cost of overnights, transportation, and the fact that you had to have your RV out of the shipping company's locked Bellingham yard within two days or they charge $35/day storage fees, I opted otherwise. In September, they cut back the number of ferry boats and routes, plus the fact that there was only one date I could make the Seward departure co-incide with the Sprinter shipping date and find a way to Seward. It was more complicated than I needed.

Whenever I thought of doing the Inland Passage, I wanted to stay in several communities. Again, given the time of year and cutting back on ferry schedules, more than two stops were not an option because I would have to spend at least a week in each town and not get to Bellingham until the first part of October. And somehow, I'm not sure anyone will understand this (even me), I wanted the Sprinter with me on this major new adventure. The final cost would be about the same.

The rainy, cloudy daylight hours took us down the Lynn Canal and for a brief stop at Haines. Major and minor waterfalls plummeting down the mountain were pretty, but it was still gloomy. Approximately seven hours after leaving Skagway, I tried to find my way down the right stairway to the vehicle deck along with many others who were as confused I was. I asked the purser, "How do I get off?" He said, "Well, you could jump, but I don't recommend it." I drove into Juneau and parked at the grocery store for the night.

It rained sporadically, making it a bad day for walking the streets. I drove Veteran's Memorial Highway to the Roman Catholic Shrine of St. Therese. It is on a tiny island with only a walking causeway when the tide is in. The Stations of the Cross that surround the shrine, are fitted into tree roots and rocks with a rough path following.

The shrine is used for various activities including weddings. A gift shop off the backside was on the honor system. If you bought anything, you left your money in the box. I watched a tape of how the shrine came into being. While enjoying the view and the sun that finally came out, the beautiful shrine and the peacefulness overall, in my head twirled an article that I later wrote for RV Life entitled, "Lord, Forgive me when I Whine." This Presbyterian thoroughly appreciated St. Therese's beauty and sacredness.

I continued the 40-mile drive to the end of the road just beyond Point Bridget State Park, following the Lynn Canal. I was almost back to Haines! I returned and boondocked at an overlook above St. Therese's.

In a week, I knew my way around Juneau's few roads, a total of about 190 city and country miles. Juneau is Alaska's capital (since 1906) and only reached by sky or sea. With a population of approximately 31,000, Juneau backs up to Juneau Mountain on one side and down to the Gastineau Channel on the other. According to the Juneau Guide, the fishermen, miners, loggers, and government employees might be seen wearing a second hat at night as musicians or Native dancers.

My first stop at the Valley Public Library in the Mendenhall Center, I found 29 e-mail messages waiting. I later visited the Juneau Public Library downtown to catch up on answering and see not only the view, since it is built above the four-story parking garage, but the stained-glass window I had heard so much about.

I crossed the Douglas Bridge to the town of Douglas and to the road's end both directions. A perfect rainbow spread over Juneau just so I wouldn't mind the rain. The Gastineau Channel harbors cruise ships and floatplanes.

Driving North Douglas Highway was mostly a bust because of the fog. I finally pulled over and ate lunch, watching a bunch of newbies being instructed in kayaking on the channel below me. It was also a good place for a nap.

When I awakened it was a whole new world. Wow! So...if you sometimes think your RVing road is a total waste, take a nap. The fog had lifted. I took pictures of the colorful kayakers against the distant Mendenhall Glacier across the bay, which I couldn't even see before.

The Mendenhall Glacier is the western arm of the Juneau Icefield, North America's fifth largest icefield. The meltwater of the Icefield's eastern edge in British Columbia, forms the Yukon River. It is a "retreating glacier." In case you're wondering, as I have, **a retreating glacier melts faster at its terminus than it grows in the icefield area**. An **advancing glacier has more ice added than it loses from melting**. O.K. so you already knew that. I'm a slow learner – my retreating memory is melting faster at its terminus than it is growing in the present.

I drove to the glacier. I think they permanently painted that rainbow there because it appeared several times during that week. It was impressive even though I had seen my share of glaciers. Montana Creek USFS campground had some of the best glacier views. For the $5 a night (Golden Age Pass) and the views, it couldn't be beat.

Warnings about the lack of RV parking in downtown Juneau were valid but with fewer tourists in September, I parked in the Coast Guard parking lot for free. The Juneau Trolley Car or The Red Trolley, took me to several places I wanted to visit. With my hand stamped, I could get on and off all day and I did, hearing the same information and jokes. They picked up every 20 – 30 minutes.

Another lady by herself and a couple went around with me. Jean from Wisconsin mentioned she was hungry and I was too, so when the narrator pointed out the Red Dog Saloon (in the original redlight district) and told about the hamburger built for four, I said, "Hey, we could all go to lunch." The couple was a stitch. She hadn't gotten on by the time we were ready to leave. He said, "I always have to wait on her." When she finally came, I said, "You almost lost your husband to us."

"Well, that would give me a break after 54 years!" They continued making remarks and I said, "You should take care of him. It isn't as much fun alone."

"All the widows tell me that."

The tour driver informed us the State Office Building was locally known as the S. O. B. I didn't stop at the Governor's House but it was built originally for $40,000 and recently renovated for six million. Is that inflation or what? He pointed out a grocery store, "A bear tore the door down to get inside, ate his fill, and left without paying."

Jean and I went to the Red Dog. It was a lively place with sawdust on the floor, a balcony with tables, and later in the day, entertainment. We ordered the "for-four" hamburger. We did a pretty good job of demolishing it. Jean was married but her husband was not very well and didn't like traveling. She was on a cruise with her 31-year-old daughter. She mentioned that she wouldn't have gone into that restaurant by herself because of the "whores hanging around" and I said I thought that was back in the old days, not now. She was very pleasant and we were both pleased with having company to talk with over lunch.

The Red Trolley went up a very steep street and the guide said Juneau is often referred to as Little San Francisco because of its steep streets, used in wintertime for bobsled races. I don't know if the Sprinter could have made it or not but my legs ached from climbing the steep hill up to the 1894 octagon-shaped St. Nicholas church, southeast Alaska's oldest original Russian Orthodox Church. This tiny church with the gold onion dome wasn't open, and the priest the tour driver said was a really lively talker, wasn't there for conversation either. The gift shop wasn't open even though the cruise ships were in town. People stand up during services in these churches. That would no doubt keep people awake! It might also explain the Russian Orthodox Churches being so small.

While waiting at the trolly stop overlooking the town, the enormous cruise ships dominated the skyline. The self-tour through the Juneau-Douglas City Museum had the "Magic of 3-D photography from 1881 to the Present" plus gold mining and pioneer history.

In the Alaska State Museum, the staircase circled a two-story tree with a huge eagle's nest built on top. This beautiful building also displayed galleries of various Native cultures and history from the Russian era through the State's mining, nautical and natural history.

When they talk about "chum" in Alaska, they aren't usually referring to a close friend, but to dog salmon, so named because the Alaska Natives fed them to their dog teams. I didn't visit the salmon hatchery at DIPAC but it is a popular place.

Juneau is also a take-off point for cruises, 50 miles southeast to Tracey Arm Fjord and Endicott Arm in the Tracey Arm-Fords Terror Wilderness Area. Sounded interesting.

Back on the Merchants Wharf, I visited the famous Patsy Ann Memorial on the pier where the cruise ships dock. This dog, deaf since birth, seemed to sense when ships were coming in and was there to greet every one. She became known as Juneau's Official Greeter. Although she died in 1942, she is still a favorite character on the dock.

The Mount Roberts Tramway is owned and operated by the Alaska Native Corporation. It was a great 1,800' view from the observation point. I saw a 25 minute film, "Seeing Daylight," about the culture and heritage of the Tlingit people in the 120-seat Chilkat Theatre. The complex includes the Timberline Bar & Grill; the Raven Eagle Gift shop, which is part museum and part art gallery; nature center; and trails. They usually have Native artisans carving totems, chiseling ivory, beading handicrafts, or sewing deerskin slippers but it was too late in the day or the season. You can see Douglas and Admiralty Islands, the Gastineau Channel, Lynn Canal and the Chilkat Mountains. On the way down, a bear walked along a secondary road below us.

Morning Reflection

I woke up to glorious sunshine one morning and hiked to a Mendenhall Lake overlook. The sun was hitting the distant rugged peaks behind the glacier and a couple of icebergs in front of it with a row of fog in between the perfect reflection.

The entrance to Glacier Gardens is not RV friendly but the Sprinter's 27' wound through the tree-friendly parking lot. It would be better to take a city bus for $1.25 that stops near by.

This "Rainforest Adventure" was created from a mudslide. With major debris removed, a re-routed stream was held in place with geotextile material beneath it, plus boulders and rock. Waterfalls flowed into small ponds surrounded by magnificent flower gardens. If "rehabilitating a natural disaster" wasn't unique enough, the gardens have "flower towers."

Something I know about personally is losing your temper and really wanting to pulverize something. When the owner bulldozed some rocks, somehow a tree took a mean bite out of his bulldozer. He had had enough. He picked up the tree and slammed it down, root system up, and said, "Now you're a flower pot!" As he calmed down and looked at that shallow root system standing high in the air, an idea popped into his head. The tops (or bottoms) were first covered with fishnetting over the root system, then forest moss, then planted with flower gardens on top, thus the flower towers that were planted throughout the gardens and along the trails.

The Atrium Visitor Center features the Garden Gift Shop and Wildberry Café where I had a huge peanutbutter cookie and coffee and enjoyed the hanging baskets filled with draping petunias and other flowers.

Guide Loretta took me on a mile-long climb up steep, winding roads to the mountain top in a golf-cart type vehicle that took us to a crooked boardwalk built to accommodate the trees. It led to an overlook platform where you could see the valley spread below.

Another platform built into the trees allows you to stand and appreciate the falls cascading through the gardens. Other flower towers were planted here and there along the trail with many flowers, ponds, and gardens beside the stream as it cascaded along.

Animals do their part. Squirrels go after the bunchberry and without knowing it, become miniature gardeners spreading the seeds for more plants to grow. Bears coming out of hibernation eat the skunk cabbage blossoms to "clean out their system." In the fall, they eat the leaves to "stop up their system" for hibernation.

It reminded me a little of BC's Butchart Gardens on Vancouver Island. It was created around a limestone quarry where this is being created from a rainforest mudslide. The big difference is that Butchart is sculpted with lawn and gardens and this is more a natural setting.

I pumped gasoline and then couldn't get the Sprinter started. After trying the usual things, I gave up and called a tow truck. He found the engine battery cables loose (I had paid Skagway $32.50 for tightening them all up). He felt that was the problem and didn't charge me anything. I offered my profuse thanks and drove to the ferry dock.

A backpacking Floridian perched on a picnic table with all his gear. He had come up a month earlier with his younger brother who got a job and was staying. He told me a story about a friend who had flown up to Barrow so I told him my story about eating muktuk with the Barrow Eskimos and said I preferred pizza all the way.

Later I returned to the terminal to get my ticket. The young man tapped me on the shoulder and motioned me to follow him. He had ordered pizza and Coke. I wasn't about to turn down pizza so we ate and chatted. He was 34 and in the middle of a divorce that he obviously didn't want but couldn't seem to prevent. He adored his 10-year-old son and wanted to bring him to Alaska to experience the wilderness. I related my Yukon River wilderness canoe story and he burst out, "You are the spunkiest woman I've ever met."

This Patrick Swayze look-alike claimed to be shy but I said I hadn't noticed. He said I was just easy to talk to so we discussed how he could meet women and I had two suggestions, church and Parents without Partners. Since neither of us had cabins, and he was very restless, we alternately took lounge catnaps and stood outside in the cold talking for the rest of the night so we didn't disturb our fellow passengers.

At breakfast, our table was immediately behind the wake and looked out over a panoramic view of sun-painted sunrise clouds and snow-covered mountains. We ferried amazingly close to the lush green islands.

We never ran out of conversation. I complimented him on his shirt and he proudly admitted he picked it out himself. He hadn't done that in the 10 years he was married, a new experience. We talked until the restaurant was empty, discussing the various women who were walking the deck.

"There's one. She seems to be alone. Go talk to her."

"No."

"Why not?"

"I'm particular."

You don't even know her." I got my money out to pay for my part of the bill.

"I'll take care of it."

"No, you can't do that."

"Yes I can. You leave the tip." I love a forceful man.

Bob was so cute about taking care of me. He always opened doors and was such a gentleman. I couldn't imagine a wife letting him get away but I realize I was hearing only one side of the story.

For several hours we heard wild rumors flitting about the ferry. Shortly before we docked at 1:15 p.m. on September 11, Alaska time, the captain confirmed that terrorists had indeed attacked our land. Frankly, there in that serene setting so far removed, it was hard to believe the reality of it. Bob opted to go with me to tour Sitka rather than go with the tour group. Reality hit us when police cars and flashing lights at the Sitka Airport entrance stopped the exploring Sprinter.

After briefly investigating Sitka and hiking a USFS loop trail, we watched the salmon fighting their way upstream under Starrigavan Creek Bridge. They were almost thick enough to walk on. A few minutes later, we hugged goodbye and promised to e-mail but that never happened, as I knew it wouldn't.

My being 30 years his senior didn't matter for that 24-hour "Moment in time." As contemporaries, we discussed everything from marriage to music and childhood to dreams for the future, mine being considerably less than his.

For two days I hid out in the rainforest of Starrigavan USFS campground. The rain continued. When the lights were off at night, it was pitch black in the trees. It was a strange time of thoughts wandering to my life and motorhome problems, only to guiltily be brought back again by the realization of our national tragedy. I finally went hunting for Sitka's hometown paper. Otherwise, printed news was non-existent and they weren't sure when they would next have a major newspaper. They were isolated without air transportation for newspapers to arrive or people to leave. Public radio was my news and the telephone a connection with my kids and a saner reality.

Because of continued generator and other electrical problems, I moved to Sportman's RV Park to plug in. The caretaker and his wife had moved there in 1977. He was probably in his late 60s and had never been anywhere other than Juneau since.

Again the Sprinter wouldn't start. I called for recommendations from a parts store. A very old, very small tow truck that I wasn't sure would make it up the steep driveway, towed me to Foreign Auto who had me on my way with a new starter within a $60 hour. It's a good thing I had the starter with me because heaven only knows how long it would have taken to get one with the airport closed.

Ripe huckleberries were the snack of choice while taking the tour through Sitka National Historical Park's Native totems. Ooh, sour! The guide gave us the history of the magnificent totems. These are replicas. The deteriorating originals are stored. The area was home to the Tlingit Indians well before the Russians named it Baranov Island. The new Visitor Center was still under construction but it will document the warring history between the Russians and the Natives. A raven followed us and whenever he thought it appropriate, he added his two cents worth to the ranger's spiel.

The same loquacious tour guide, minus the raven, led us through the 1842 Russian Bishop's House, the oldest intact Russian building in Sitka. It had fallen into major disrepair and is still being restored to its original wilderness splendor.

I especially enjoyed the lively Russian Dancers at the Harrigan Centennial Hall. They are 30 local women who have learned some 38 different dances. "We are not professional. We do it for fun. Our most asked question is why there are no men in the program. Thirty years ago when we wanted to start the dance group, the men said, 'There's no way you're going to get it off the ground,' and wanted no part of it, 'No thank you.' Now that we are celebrating our 30th anniversary, they are saying maybe they would like join us and we are saying, 'No thank you.'"

In one segment four women in beautiful blue gowns seemed to glide rather than dance. A comedy routine revealed a wife looking for her husband. He lurched in with a huge stomach. The devil appeared on the scene and danced with them both. She said it was a favorite with the children.

Volta and Friend

The building where the medical and surgical work is done at the Alaska Raptor Center, also houses the offices, a gift shop, and a lecture room where we saw a short movie. A big outside deck overlooked enormous sections of caged woods that reached down to a fast-moving stream. In them were eagles, owls, ravens, and crows that had been injured and could not be released back into the wild because of their injuries. These were permanent residents and used as teaching tools. The ones being released into the wild had one or two handlers and were kept where they had little human contact.

Volta, a mature bald eagle whose fate changed when he tangled with a power line, now tours the country educating schoolchildren about wild creatures and the environment.

The Native Dances had been cancelled even though a cruise ship was in town, but St. Michael's Cathedral momentarily opened its doors. It burned in 1966 but people forming a human chain and taking them outside saved most of the artifacts. One man handed down the Chandelier to two people. When it was put back up, the 300-pound bell needed six men to lift it.

An Icon being delivered by the ship, Neva, was thought to be forever lost when the ship sank a few miles from Sitka. It later was found in a box that floated ashore. It was intact and unaffected by the saltwater.

Walking Sitka for a week took me to many historical places including Castle Hill where Russian Alaska became ours in 1867. Castle Hill held Baranov's Castle at one time and even earlier was a Tlingit village. I walked down to Totem Park and up to the Russian blockhouse replica that overlooks a deplorably maintained tiny Russian cemetery.

On Sunday I expected a rip-roaring, inspiring sermon and I was disappointed. It was luke warm at best. A special 9-11 program was held at Centennial Hall but I didn't know about it.

In my wanderings, I found the "Back-door Café" by accident. Several people played fiddles, guitars, banjos, accordions, and spoons. All ages played and sang, obviously acquainted with one another. Though there was barely enough room to move, what a fun way to spend a Sunday afternoon.

I met several fellow travelers who came in by cruise and expected to fly out. They were stranded until the next flight or ferryboat, whichever came first and suited their needs. At Victoria's Restaurant someone asked me to take a picture of his or her group. In the process, I walked out without paying. I was mortified when I realized it and went back to pay the next day. They seemed neither concerned nor interested.

On the way back to the Sprinter, I passed the Raven Radio Station, KCAW.

As we watched our departure from the Sitka dock, a fellow started talking with me. I said, "You have been here for several days; you are traveling with your son; and you use the Internet." He looked puzzled. I explained that I had seen him around town several times, once with his son, and also at a library computer. He was a barterer from Maine, trading fish, berries, mushrooms, whatever he could swap. In the fall he collects maple syrup, boils it down, and packages it in smaller amounts for Christmas gifts. He said most people never get pure maple syrup like that. We chatted several times about his life and mine the next few days.

Our days began early with this loud speaker message, "Good morning ladies and gentlemen." People-watching was definitely a major pastime, along with reading, snacking, conversing, scenery, and animal watching. Evenings offered movies like *Flying Dragon, Crouching Tiger; The Wedding Planner*, and *The Castaways*.

In the wee hours at Petersburg, a huge semi backed all the way down a curved ramp and on to the ferry. Next we went into the famous, hazardous Wrangell Narrows, the narrowness obvious by the navigational aids. I would love to have seen it in the daylight.

On the solarium deck, tents proliferated. Bodies in sleeping bags draped on reclining deck chairs and haphazardly around the floor. It didn't look comfortable. Shafts of heat came down from above but rain spray filtered through. It was eerie watching them sleeping in the night, unaware of my presence.

I'm not sure the ferry people appreciate it but all the sounds like Velcro tearing, was Velcro tearing. All back and bottom cushions were ripped from the lounge chairs and makeshift beds made for all ages and genders on the floor. Sleeping bags, blankets, backpacks, day packs, and gear were everywhere. It was all supposed to be picked up and stowed out of the way during evening movies so people could sit.

We were given 15-minute car deck calls three times a day for pet owners to tend animals but others were allowed to retrieve whatever, definitely not much time. They have perfectly nice showers aboard the big blue canoes but I really liked my own facilities and I didn't want to drag

Totem

my clothes upstairs. The water was cold but I had to move so fast that it didn't matter.

Though the rest of Alaska was colored in bright yellow and reds, with the southeast rain inches ranging from 27 to 200", I saw only deep green. I asked if autumn color would eventually come and the steward said the leaves fall rather than change colors. It was quite cold and windy most of the time, with cause for major celebration when the sun occasionally broke through.

We stopped at Wrangel for less than 20 minutes but at Ketchikan, we had three hours in port. I boarded the bus for a $10 tour. With cutting down stuff I had to carry, I had taken the wrong folder and it had no money in it. I didn't have time to return to the ferry so I asked if anyone would lend $10 to a stranger. I couldn't blame them for not responding. I stood up to leave and a young couple handed me $10. Amazing.

The narrated tour took us through Ketchikan in a double decker red bus. I think wandering its narrow steep streets would have been impossible with the Sprinter. Wooden stairways wandered drunkenly from cliff-top homes to the streets. Ketchikan leg muscles must be amazing.

At Bight Park, a fellow carved on a very long totem pole. He concentrated for a couple of minutes, then looked at us over the top of

Tribal House

his glasses to answer questions, very articulate in his speech. He reminded me of Guipetto, Pinocchio's master.

It had begun to rain quite hard outside and I stood under a tree taking pictures. A lady came over and gave me her umbrella. She had a hood she could pull up to keep the rain off of her.

The driver showed us the most picturesque part of Ketchikan, the Redlight District, built on stilts with boardwalks and salmon jumping beneath, "It might be the only place in the world where both salmon and salmon fishermen went upstream to spawn!" Hmmm.

When we came back, I took two Alaska books out of the Sprinter,

Ketchikan's Redlight District

autographed them to the young couple and the umbrella lady. They were quite delighted.

"I didn't realize there was a celebrity aboard."

"Really?" I said getting all excited. "Who?" We laughed.

Honestly, after several days aboard the ferry as a captive audience, the Coast Mountains, dense forests, countless islands, water, and rain forest, all which I dearly loved, were more than enough, even interspersed with whales, American bald eagles, porpoises, otters, birds and people. Perhaps 9-11 also prompted my need to touch the mainland again.

After giving my ID and showing my ticket, the Sprinter and I were allowed to leave the ferry at the Bellingham dock. It was September 21 and port authorities were no longer quite so cavalier about requiring identification and proof you were a legitimate passenger.

The Sprinter was the first one out. What a shocker leaving tiny Skagway, Alaska, 16 days before and suddenly being enveloped in I-5 traffic. I stopped at the rest area beyond the Cascade Mountain pass on I-2, intending to nap briefly. I woke up four hours later! Maybe next time I'll get a cabin.

It was fun sharing my love of Canada and Alaska with you.

St. Michael's Cathedral

Honest, I have only a few more comments to pass along in the last chapter. You wouldn't want to be shortchanged, would you?

Parting Thoughts

2002

Having lived a sheltered life until I was nearly 50, I now love being in an isolated place surrounded by magnificent scenery, knowing natural dangers lurk in the wilderness. It is my smidgen of "Walking on the wild side." I've contemplated flying north for a month in the wintertime, but after hearing a few, "It was so cold..." stories, I may change my mind. My friend, Doreen Woodall, whom I met in Dawson City, wrote and told me about her winter:

"When you take your first breath outside, your nose seizes up. The air splinters your throat. Your teeth turn into small white ice cubes and a dagger stabs into your chest. You feel as if you might shatter into a thousand pieces. The more shattered you feel, the colder it is."

With as dreadful as that sounds, she ended her letter this way; "The sun warmed my shoulders like a remembered blessing." Maybe I'll just go for a couple of weeks.

Everybody has their own idea of what excites them. I have given you the big picture as far as distances, activities, and accommodations, throwing in costs once in a while, so you get an idea of what they were. You might say, "Whew!" Remember that you don't **have** to go off the main roads, or spend $3,000 for a side trip, to have a perfectly exciting trip to Canada and Alaska. If you did want to do everything I've done, it might take you as many trips as I've enjoyed. I pack a lot into my travels.

Now, to some of that "packing," just in case you're looking askance, costwise, at some of my adventures. I am single; I am paying one fare. I realize the expense is doubled for couples.

If expenses make you "gulp," think it over carefully. Do you both really, truly, want to do the proposed activity above all others? Must you do it together? Are you absolutely dying for a chance to pull in a 450-pound halibut or observe Native culture in a bush community? Is it only a mediocre desire for your spouse? Maybe your spouse would rather capture iceworms on a glacial expedition. Remember the Australian lady who played with the grizzlies, sans her mate, because he was going to indulge in a guided hunting trip? Consider doing different activities at least once on your trip.

I can hear you saying (male or female), "But...but...but, I never do anything without my Snookie Wookums." Give me a break! Tours are groups of people. You won't be alone. It is easy to make new friends. Open your mouth, ask a few questions, then shut it again and listen. You'll probably make friends that you'll hear from for years. Just think how exciting it will be to share the adventure with your mate later. Yes, I know, you haven't done anything separately for 40 years. Maybe it's about time -- you might just appreciate each other and the activity more.

Okay. Supposing you absolutely must do everything together, and whitewater rafting or taking a terrific cruise to the Aleutian Islands is just plain too expensive. I'm well aware that the expense is on top of gasoline, campgrounds, etcetera, etcetera, etcetera.

Look at it this way. A trip to Alaska is expensive, but it is also the trip of a lifetime. Allow extra money for an activity that you may not even know about when you leave your driveway back in wherever. The desire may surface as you travel or read.

If you spend $1,000 above and beyond what is already in the pot for "known expenses and possible problems," will its absence make a significant difference in your life over the next year? If it will, would it be worth it? Are we talking the actual loss of food from your mouths or eliminating season tickets to whatever?

My side trips any given year were very expensive, but notice I mentioned house-sitting in Washington State over the 1997 winter. And this winter I'm stationary at North Ranch in Arizona. In 1997, I needed the time to write two books. In 2002, I needed to revise this book. During those times, my investment income was accumulating, or more truthfully, recuperating. I would rather live a few quiet winter months, than give up the adventure of a lifetime (or several lifetimes!) that I have had in Alaska and Canada.

Don't be afraid to treat yourself once in a while, and this is one of those times, even if you are a young family with children. Have a family meeting and decide a year (or two) in advance, who can contribute what? Who can give up what? How can you gather the kind of money it takes for a trip of this magnitude?

There are a great variety of tours. Interests range from diving, cruising, boating, fishing, hiking, biking, golfing, flightseeing, horseback riding, mountain climbing, tennis, shopping, restaurants, nightlife, bird watching, bear watching, whale watching, and llama trek trips.

Maybe you'd be satisfied with activities I indulge in during the majority of my days. I watch the tide go in and out, eagles soaring, fish struggling upstream, storm clouds settling over mountain tops, and bear families playing. I pan for gold, hike in high mountain meadows, and walk through the mud puddles of historical sites. I listen to rushing streams and flowers growing. I smell the fragrance of spring and the dust of summer. I crunch through the broken leaves of autumn and thrill to the Aurora Borealis of winter. I observe people. That is all free. You only have to be there.

If none of this floats your boat, study the human migration from Siberia across the land bridge of Beringia, to North America 40,000 years ago. If that doesn't go back far enough, dig into (so to speak) the mammoths and mastodons. The trip will be whatever you make it.

And you know what, as much as I have traveled and experienced Canada and Alaska in four trips, I still haven't been on the Alaska Railroad, cruised through the Aleutians, hiked the Chilkoot Trail, or driven to Yellowknife. According to a BLM brochure, "If you could see one million acres of Alaska every day, it would take you the entire year to see the whole state." You may never get to do it all so relax and enjoy.

What is the Land of the Midnight Sun? You didn't know there would be a quiz, did you? The correct answer is? It is a lot more than salmon and moose poop jewelry. It is isolated villages, wild animals, wild rivers, and wild-erness. It is glaciers, bald eagles, and northern lights. It is gravel roads with no shoulders and paved roads with the heaves. It is pleasantly warm in summer, and frigid enough in winter, to shatter your spit when it hits the ground. (You never know what cultured activities you'll read about in my books.)

The challenge of driving has pretty much been eliminated, except for the distances involved, providing, of course, that you use your head about slowing down when the roads are flagged.

Alaska, northern British Columbia, the Yukon Territory, and the Northwest Territories are excitement, romance, intrigue, and incredible beauty. I hope you'll be as fascinated with them as I continue to be.

For those who are alone and wonder if I get lonely traveling solo. No, I like stopping at my whim to take photographs, sipping a cup of coffee, absorbing the scenery, and thanking God I'm alive. I like meeting people. If I'm fortunate enough to run into a local character, my trip is enhanced. If an adventure hits me head on, I'm all for it. If it's snowing, I pray it doesn't get too deep before a thaw. If it's raining or foggy, I curl up with a book. If I'm lazy, I just curl up. If it's sunny, ah, it's time to enjoy the glories of RVing.

It's time to say good-bye (Have you notice I do that a lot?). Again, I'm not an expert about Alaska and Canada because I haven't done it all (yet!). My intention was to give you a taste of the North Country through my experiences, with enough details to give you approximate costs, guidance, and I hope, a little inspiration. My personal adventures won't parallel yours; but perhaps they will serve as a catalyst for planning your trip. If you want to go to Alaska, find a way to make it happen.

I guess what I want to leave you with most is this. Don't rush it. Spend an extra day or two in Eagle or Hope or Ninilchik or Dawson City. Walk that trail into town. I know you can fix your own food in your RV but have breakfast or lunch where the locals eat. Take part in some local activity. Talk with people. Find out what their lives are like. Before you know it, three months will have passed, four, maybe even five.

Having read Michener's, *Alaska*, on this trip, I highly recommend reading it if you have the least bit of interest in Alaska's history. The docent in Sitka disagreed with some of the book but it gives you a great feel for where it all began and progresses through the years. I wouldn't have had nearly the interest before or after my first trip, however. My interest was sparked more after seeing a great deal of it and learning to love it. I wish you enough returns to Alaska to love it like I do.

Maybe you'll never go back, but what terrific stories you can tell or at least remember…

When you are old,
Sitting in your rocking chair,
Playing the moments of your life
On the TV of your mind.

Go for it!

Send me a post card!

God Bless

"Charlie"

Glossary

AK State bird, tree, mineral, flower, sport, gem, and fish.	Willow ptarmigan, Sitka spruce, Gold, Forget-me-not, Dog mushing, Jade, and King salmon.
Arctic Circle	Line of latitude approximately 66 degrees 33 feet north of the equator, circumscribing northern frigid zone.
Aurora Borealis or "Dawn of the North"	The aurora is essentially a solar-powered light show that results from interactions between the solar wind and our magnetic planet.
Bear Bells	Small bells that attach to your clothing or backpack to warn bears you are coming (Alaskans refer to them as "dinner bells")
Big Blue Canoes	Alaska State Ferries
Black water	Sewage from toilet (Or "toilette" depending on cost of your rig)
BLM	Bureau of Land Management
Boondock	Parking without amenities other than in a campground
Bore Tide	Steep-fronted tide crests caused by tides flowing into constricted inlets at speeds up to 12 MPH
Burger Burps	Glaciers calve and little ice burgers burp like popping champagne.
Calving	Tidewater glacier shedding icebergs off its face into the sea.
Cariboo, Caribou	Route 97 follows the old"Cariboo" trail to the old Cariboo gold fields. Caribou – North American reindeer
Cheechako	New to the North Country (Greenhorn)
Chip-seal	Oil and rock put on the surface of road to "seal" against wear and weather, usually redone every couple of years
Crevasses	Cracks made when nunataks disrupt the glacier's flow
CRS	Can't Remember Sugar
Denali National Park Annual Pass	$20 covers entry into park for all immediate family traveling with permit holder
Doghouse	Cover over the engine inside motorhome
Dry camp	Without amenities
Fjord	As tidewater glaciers retreat, the steep-sided valleys carved by the glacial action fill in with sea water, creating a fjord
Fresh water	Hopefully, your drinking water
Glacier	When more snow falls in the winter than melts in the summer, a glacier begins. Over tens of thousands of years, this snow builds up and recrystallizes into a solid mass of ice. When the accumulation of ice becomes so great that the force of gravity causes it to move, a glacier is born.
Glacier blue ice	Highly compressed ice crystals. Dense crystals absorb all colors of the light spectrum except blue. What you see is reflected blue light.
Golden Access Pass	This is a free lifetime entrance pass for persons who are blind or permanently disabled. It is available to citizens or permanent residents of the United States, regardless of age.
Golden Age Pass	This is a lifetime entrance pass for those 62 years or older. The Golden Age Passport has a one time processing charge of $10. You must purchase a Golden Age Passport in person.
Golden Eagle Pass	An entrance pass to national parks, monuments, historic sites, recreation areas, and national wildlife refuges that charge an entrance fee. It costs $50 and is valid for one year
GPS	Global Positioning System
Gray water	Used dish/bath/cleaning water

Halibut Facts	It is not uncommon for halibut to weigh over 200 pounds.
Hanging Glacier	(valley glacier). Glaciers that flow down out of mountain valleys. The terminus is above sea level.
Ice field or Nunatak	Large interconnecting glaciers separated by mountain peaks and ridges, called nunataks, projecting through the ice.
Iceworms	Thread sized Iceworms living between ice crystals near surface of glaciers.
Kittiwake	Member of the gull family
Lining	Pulling the canoe along the shore by rope
Marge	Margin
Muskeg	Sphagnum moss
N.W.T.	Northwest Territories (Canada)
NPS	National Park Service
Permafrost	Ground remaining frozen for two or more years.
Pingo	An ice-covered hill that can only grow and persist in a permafrost environment
Placer gold flour	Finer than dust
Qiviut (Key-vee-ute)	Soft underwool of the musk ox
RCMP	Royal Canadian Mountain Police
Rime	"An accumulation of granular ice tufts on the windward sides of exposed objects that is formed from supercooled fog or cloud and built out directly against the wind."
RNWMP	Royal North West Mounted Police
RV, rig	Recreational Vehicle
Salmon Facts	Salmon hatch in fresh water, spend a portion of life in the ocean; return to fresh water where they change size, shape, and color prior to spawning. King salmon is the largest of Pacific salmon and can weigh in at more than 100 pounds.
Seracs	Frozen spires of ice
SKPs	Escapees, Inc. (National RVing Group)
Slough	An inlet on a river
Sourdough	Seasoned survivor, Old timer
Subsistence	Rights to minimum food and shelter necessary to support life
Tag or Tow	Vehicle being towed behind RV
Taiga	"Land of little sticks," a Russian interpretation
The Outside	Northern Canadian and Alaskan reference to "Lower 48."
Tidewater glacier	(Fjord glacier) This is a valley glacier that occupies a fjord. The terminus lies below sea level and generally has an almost vertical face that sheds huge chunks of glacial ice.
TLC	Tender Loving Care
Tsunami	A great sea wave produced by submarine earth movement or volcanic eruption, tidal wave
Tundra	Dwarfed shrubs and miniaturized wildflowers adapted to a short growing season.
USFS	United States Forest Service
Utilidors	Hold water and sewer pipes

Resources

Alaska Alcohol, Tobacco, and Firearms
907-271-5701

Alaska Department of Transportation
Road Conditions Hotline
1-907-456-7623

Alaska Ferry System Information Reservations & Ticketing
1-800-382-9229
www.akmhs.com

Alaska Public Lands Info Center
Anchorage: 907-271-2737
Fairbanks: 907-456-0527
nps.gov/akplic

Alaska Railroad
1-800-544-0552
reservations@akrr.com
www.alaskarailroad.com

British Columbia Ferries
1-250-386-3431
www.bcferries.com

British Columbia Information
1-800-435-5622
www.HelloBC.com

Bureau of Land Management
1-907-474-2200
http://aurora.ak.blm.gov

Canadian Customs Information
Western Canada: 204-983-3500

Computer Problems Enroute?
Custom Computers
44750 Funny River Rd.
Soldotna, AK 99669
1-907-262-1200

Denali National Park and Preserve
Denali reservations:
1-800-622-7275
www.nps.gov/dena

GST Rebate Centres/Duty Free Shops
Sumas, WA border – Hwy #11
Osoyoos, BC – Hwy #97
Kingsgate, BC – Hwy #95

GST Tax Information
1-800-668-4748 (Canada)
1-902-432-5608 in the US.

N.W.T. Tourism "Hot line"
1-800-661-0788
Road and Ferry Report:
1-800-661-0752
www.nwttravel.nt.ca

Other Alaska Books
RVing by Land and Sea
Bill and Jan Moeller
Amazon.com

Traveler's Guide to Alaskan Camping
Mike & Terri Church
1-888-265-6555
www.rollinghomes.com

The Milepost
1-800-726-4707
www.themilepost.com

Tourism Yukon
1-867-667-5340
www.touryukon.com

Volunteer in Parks program
www.nps.gov/personnel

Non-Fiction Titles
Sharlene "Charlie" Minshall

RVing Adventures with the Silver Gypsy

This book takes readers through "every day" RVing days that fit between extraordinary moments of pure pleasure. Combining RVing with motorcycling; kayaking with dolphins; and exploring national parks and polar bears; this sixty-something full-time solo RVer takes you through her experiences.

Review Gypsy Journal 2002: ...experiences from the magnificent to the mundane, including spending the day on a commercial lobster boat, meeting old friends on the road, fighting off invading mice, and kayaking Mexico's Sea of Cortez. Some of us look at life as a glass half full, others look at is as half empty. Charlie just wants to finish the glass and get a refill so she can see what new adventures it holds.

Excerpt: A frigid November wind swirled around the solitary building, blowing snow between the steel bars. It clung tenaciously to the windowpanes, bringing the Arctic winter up close and personal. Shivering with the knowledge that I couldn't leave this building without armed guards, I quietly descended the ladder...

Full-Time RVing: How to Make it Happen (Completely Revised)

A "How-to" book that lets you in on the mobile lifestyle that millions are enjoying! How do I get started? What should I keep? What should I take? How do I keep relationships with family and friends intact? How do I cross borders into Canada or Mexico? What happens if I break down? How can I prevent breaking down? What is the daily life of a full-time RVer really like? It has two full-time budget comparisons, ways to cut costs, info on personal safety, getting mail, establishing residency, and the nitty-gritty details you need to know to become full-time or extended-time RVers. Basic and non-technical.

In Pursuit of a Dream

"Charlie," widowed at 45, inspires you with a positive and personal story of "How and Why" she quit her 9 – 5 job to become a full-time RVer, writer-photographer, and public speaker. Laugh and shake your head as you read her tales of Alaska, new romance, and living on a beach in Baja, Mexico, among other adventures.

Freedom Unlimited: The Fun and Facts of Fulltime RVing
(Co-author: Tech writer and columnist Bill Farlow)

A view from all sides of the full-time spectrum by two long-time, full-timing RV columnists. Learn the "Nuts and bolts" of full-time RVing from such chapters as "Is the Impossible Dream Possible?" (Finances and Costs), and "Cutting Your Apron Strings" (Roots to Enroute) about maintaining contact with your family, friends, mail, phone and church. From the technical to the "fluff stuff," the authors cover questions about the full-time or extended-time RV lifestyle in a personal and humorous style.

RVing North America, Silver, Single, and Solo (To be reprinted in 2003)
Follow the Silver Gypsy in her adventures into Mexico, Alaska, Canada, and all around the "lower 48." This is the daily life of a full-time RVer.

ORDER FORM

For AUTOGRAPHED copies, complete form and send a check or money order (US Funds) to:

Sharlene Minshall
% Gypsy Press
150 Rainbow Drive PMB #5024
Livingston, TX 77399-1050

RVING ADVENTURES with the SILVER GYPSY...$14.95

RVING ALASKA and CANADA (Revised Edition)..$16.95

*FULL-TIME RVING How to Make it Happen (*Revised Edition) $14.95

FREEDOM UNLIMITED The Fun and Facts of Fulltime RVing
(Co-author Bill Farlow)...$ 8.00

IN PURSUIT OF A DREAM ....$ 8.00

RVING NORTH AMERICA Silver, Single & Solo   (Available again 2003)..............$14.95

Name _____

Address _____

City, State, Zip _____

	Price	Qty	Total
RVING ADVENTURES with the SILVER GYPSY	$14.95	_____	_____
RVING ALASKA AND CANADA	$16.95	_____	_____
FULL-TIME RVING: HOW TO MAKE IT HAPPEN	$14.95	_____	_____
IN PURSUIT OF A DREAM	$ 8.00	_____	_____
FREEDOM UNLIMITED	$ 8.00	_____	_____
RVING NORTH AMERICA: Silver/Single/Solo	$14.95	_____	_____

$2 DISCOUNT on combo of three books   **Subtotal** _____ _____

$3 DISCOUNT on combo of five books   **Discount** -_____

Postage & Handling   Subtotal _____

$3.50 for one book   **P&H** +_____

$1.00 for each additional book   **Total** _____

Canadian orders: Add $1.50 to above shipping costs for each book.

Please allow six weeks for delivery.

For quicker response: Internet: Amazon or Barnes & Noble

ORDER FORM

For AUTOGRAPHED copies, complete form and send a check or money order (US Funds) to:

Sharlene Minshall
% Gypsy Press
150 Rainbow Drive PMB #5024
Livingston, TX 77399-1050

RVING ADVENTURES with the SILVER GYPSY $14.95

RVING ALASKA and CANADA (Revised Edition) $16.95

FULL-TIME RVING How to Make it Happen (Revised Edition) $14.95

FREEDOM UNLIMITED The Fun and Facts of Fulltime RVing
(Co-author Bill Farlow) ....$ 8.00

IN PURSUIT OF A DREAM ....$ 8.00

RVING NORTH AMERICA Silver, Single & Solo   (Available again 2003) $14.95

Name _____

Address _____

City, State, Zip _____

	Price	Qty	Total
RVING ADVENTURES with the SILVER GYPSY	$14.95	_____	_____
RVING ALASKA AND CANADA	$16.95	_____	_____
FULL-TIME RVING: HOW TO MAKE IT HAPPEN	$14.95	_____	_____
IN PURSUIT OF A DREAM	$ 8.00	_____	_____
FREEDOM UNLIMITED	$ 8.00	_____	_____
RVING NORTH AMERICA: Silver/Single/Solo	$14.95	_____	_____

$2 **DISCOUNT** on combo of three books	**Subtotal** _____	_____
$3 **DISCOUNT** on combo of five books	**Discount**	-_____
Postage & Handling	Subtotal	_____
$3.50 for one book	**P&H**	+_____
$1.00 for each additional book	**Total**	_____

Canadian orders: Add $1.50 to above shipping costs for each book.

Please allow six weeks for delivery.

For quicker response: Internet: Amazon or Barnes & Noble

Breinigsville, PA USA
02 May 2010
237192BV00001B/52/A